D0863200

THE HISTORY OF
THE STANDARD OIL COMPANY

IDA M. TARBELL

THE HISTORY OF
THE STANDARD OIL COMPANY

BRIEFER VERSION
edited by
DAVID M. CHALMERS

"An Institution is the lengthened shadow of one man."—
EMERSON, IN ESSAY ON "SELF-RELIANCE"

*"The American Beauty Rose can be produced in its splendor
and fragrance only by sacrificing the early buds which grow
up around it."*—J. D. ROCKEFELLER, JR., IN AN ADDRESS ON
TRUSTS, TO THE STUDENTS OF BROWN UNIVERSITY

W · W · NORTON & COMPANY
New York · London

Books That Live

The Norton imprint on a book means that in the publisher's
estimation it is a book not for a single season but for the years.
W. W. Norton & Company, Inc.

ISBN 0-393-00496-1

W. W. Norton & Company, Inc., 500 Fifth Avenue, New York, N.Y. 10110
W. W. Norton & Company Ltd., 37 Great Russell Street, London WC1B 3NU

CONTENTS

1. THE BIRTH OF AN INDUSTRY

Petroleum first a curiosity and then a medicine—Discovery of its real value—The story of how it came to be produced in large quantities—Great flow of oil—Swarm of problems to solve—Storage and transportation—Refining and marketing—Rapid extension of the field of operation—Workers in great numbers with plenty of capital—Costly blunders frequently made—But every difficulty being met and overcome —The normal unfolding of a new and wonderful opportunity for individual endeavour.

2. THE RISE OF THE STANDARD OIL COMPANY

John D. Rockefeller's first connection with the oil business— Stories of his early life in Cleveland—His first partners— Organisation of the Standard Oil Company in June, 1870 —Rockefeller's able associates—First evidence of railway discriminations in the oil business—Rebates found to be generally given to large shippers—First plan for a secret combination—The South Improvement Company—Secret contracts made with the railroads providing rebates and drawbacks—Rockefeller and associates force Cleveland refiners to join the new combination or sell—Rumour of the plan reaches the oil regions.

8. THE COMPROMISE OF 1880

The producers' suit against Rockefeller and his associates used by the Standard to protect itself—Suits against the transportation companies are delayed—Trial of Rockefeller and his associates for conspiracy postponed—All of the suits withdrawn in return for agreements of the Standard and the Pennsylvania to cease their practices against the producers—with this compromise the Second Petroleum Producers' Union comes to an end—Producers themselves to blame for not standing behind their leaders—Standard again enforces orders objectionable to producers—More outbreaks in the oil regions—Rockefeller having silenced organised opposition proceeds to silence individual complaint.

9. THE FIGHT FOR THE SEABOARD PIPE-LINE

Project for Seaboard Pipe-line pushed by independents—Tidewater Pipe Company formed—Oil pumped over mountains for the first time—Independent refiners ready to unite with Tidewater because it promises to free them from railroads—The Standard face to face with a new problem—Day of the railroads over as long distance transporters of oil—National Transit Company formed—War on the Tidewater begun—Plan to wreck its credit and buy it in—Rockefeller buys a third of the Tidewater's stock—The Standard and Tidewater become allies—National Transit Company now controls all pipe-lines—Agreement entered into with Pennsylvania Railroad to divide the business of transporting oil.

10. CUTTING TO KILL

Rockefeller now plans to organise oil marketing as he had already organised oil transporting and refining—Wonderfully efficient and economical system installed—Curious practices introduced—Reports of competitors' business secured from railway agents—Competitors' clerks sometimes secured as allies—In many instances full records of all oil shipped are given Standard by railway and steamship companies—This information is used by Standard to fight competitors—Competitors driven out by underselling—Evidence

14. THE BREAKING UP OF THE TRUST

15. A MODERN WAR FOR INDEPENDENCE

16. THE PRICE OF OIL

17. THE LEGITIMATE GREATNESS OF THE STANDARD OIL COMPANY

18. CONCLUSION

Introduction
to the paperback edition

BY

DAVID M. CHALMERS

DURING the post-Civil War industrialization of the United States, the great monopolists gained power because they were even greater competitors. John D. Rockefeller and his associates did not build the Standard Oil Company in the board rooms of Wall Street banks and investment houses, water their stock and rig the market. They fought their way to control by rebate and drawback, bribe and blackmail, espionage and price cutting, and perhaps even more important, by ruthless, never slothful efficiency of organization and production.

The Standard Oil Company was the first major industrial monopoly in the United States. Until 1901, when J. P. Morgan floated his giant United States Steel Corporation, Standard Oil was the largest corporation in the nation. At its peak, it controlled as much as eighty-five per cent of oil refining in America. During the early years of its success, Standard Oil seldom recorded less than a twenty per cent return on its aggregating investment. Even after its dissolution in 1911, its primary fragment, the Standard Oil Company of New Jersey, remained among the nation's top corporate powers. By the 1960's, Standard Oil of New Jersey had reached net annual earnings of over a billion dollars a year and ranked in the top three in corporate assets and profits.

But clouding this success was one important failure. John D. Rockefeller's great wealth and power did not protect him from defeat at the hands of the magazine journalist Ida Minerva Tarbell. The forceful muckraker historian of the Standard Oil Company did more than single out Rockefeller as the architect and the driving force behind the trust. She offered the oil man as the symbol and the cause of all that she felt was wrong in the national life.

Growing up in the oil city of Titusville, where her family

moved from the Erie County, Pennsylvania, farm on which she was born in 1857, Ida Minerva Tarbell absorbed the feminist ideas of her mother's friends that were to keep her unhappily single all her life and to set her on the path of a career. She attended Allegheny College, earned a B. A. and M. A., taught at a seminary in Ohio, and worked for eight years as an editor on the *Chautauquan*.

Seeking to combine her career and her interest in women's rights, Ida Tarbell went off to Paris to learn her craft as a biographer and write about the role of women in the French Revolution. S. S. McClure, the flamboyant magazine impresario, found her there and brought her back to furnish *McClure's* contribution to the then popular interest in Napoleon. When her articles were collected as a book, it sold a hundred thousand copies. After the publication of her *Life of Madam Roland* in 1896, she began what was to be a thirty-year study of the life of Abraham Lincoln. Eventually she wrote nine books on Lincoln, ghosted Charles A. Dana's *Recollections of the Civil War*, and talked Carl Schurz into writing his *Reminiscences*. Although primarily a popularizer, she has been credited with being the first of the modern scholars who attempted to present the man rather than the myth of Lincoln.[1]

Despite her oil-country childhood, there is no evidence that Ida Tarbell had cherished a desire to strike out at John D. Rockefeller and the Standard Oil Company, nor was she initially particularly interested in industrial and social conditions. S. S. McClure was. While other popular journals ignored the impact of the trusts, McClure recognized that they had created the most important issue of the day, one which ought to be covered in *McClure's*. Ida Tarbell was, at this time, acting as editor, and so he pressed her to select one of the great monopolies and write about it for the magazine. They discussed the possibility of using either the Steel or the Sugar Trust, but somehow neither he nor Ida Tarbell could get beyond the initial stage of enthusiasm and work out a proper approach. Then a letter came into the office from Ray Stannard Baker in which he talked about the discovery of oil in California. Their topic, they decided happily, would be the Oil Trust, and Ida Tarbell tried unsuccessfully to get Baker interested in doing it. Finally, with S. S. McClure off in Europe, the daughter of the oil fields came to accept her fate:

[1] Benjamin P. Thomas, *Portrait For Prosperity* (New Brunswick, 1947), Chapter 7.

she would become the historian of the Standard Oil Company and prepare *McClure's* big series for 1902. She started collecting her material in the fall of 1901, and a year later her series had begun to appear.[2]

In *The History of the Standard Oil Company*, Ida Tarbell described John D. Rockefeller's relentless march toward control of the industry, and in subsequent articles for *McClure's* she proceeded to sum up the man and his legacy. Rockefeller himself, was, she wrote, "the victim of a money-passion which blinds him to every other consideration in life," including any sense of justice or humanity. His example, she went on, had led to the "threatened saturation" of American life with "commercial Machiavellism." To get ahead by any means possible had become the highest moral goal of American business society, and this, she argued, was directly the fault of John D. Rockefeller.[3]

There can be little doubt that the ethics of American business life were far from admirable. Even though neither business nor the businessmen ever achieved the unity or acted with the degree of uniformity that the muckrakers and other critics have claimed, American ideals and practical behavior had become increasingly commercialized. It was perhaps Ida Tarbell's lasting accomplishment that she placed the blame for this development at the door of John D. Rockefeller. Blending together descriptions of his business operations, his personal characteristics, and even his physical appearance, she fashioned an image of a cunning, ruthless Shylock, with a crabbed and miserly visage and soul.[4] It is a picture which not even a subsequent half-century of Rockefeller philanthropy has successfully dispelled. Little wonder, therefore, that when at the time an associate reportedly tried to get Rockefeller to counter her charges, the oilman burst forth in exasperation: "Not a word. Not a word about that mis-

[2] Peter Lyon, *Success Story, The Life and Times of S. S. McClure* (New York, 1963), pages 175-181, 190-215. For further biographical information, see Ida Tarbell's autobiography, *All in the Day's Work* (New York, 1939), the Tarbell papers, the bulk of which are carefully organized in the Reis Library of Allegheny College, Meadville, Pennsylvania, and David M. Chalmers, "Ida M. Tarbell," *Notable American Women, 1607-1950*, Edward T. James, editor (Cambridge, forthcoming, 1967).

[3] Ida M. Tarbell, "John D. Rockefeller, A Character Study," *McClure's*, XXV (1905), 227-249, 386-398; "Commercial Machiavellianism," *McClure's*, XXVI (1905), 453-463.

[4] For later contributions to the Rockefeller "legend" and image, see John T. Flynn, *God's Gold: John D. Rockefeller and His Times* (New York, 1932); Matthew Josephson, *The Robber Barons* (New York, 1934).

guided woman."[5] And so, although the Standard Oil Company won the battle of organization and control, Ida Tarbell helped produce a widespread critical attitude toward the oilman.

The result, Rockefeller's classic biographer Allan Nevins has maintained, was of dubious accuracy and fairness. John D. Rockefeller, Nevins explained, was but the leading member of an exceedingly well-integrated team of extremely strong-willed men. By the 1890's, Rockefeller himself was in practical retirement, although this information was not generally known. Much of the blame placed upon him, particularly for the trust's expansion, belonged more correctly to others. H. H. Rogers and William Rockefeller, rather than John D., were primarily responsible for the spreading speculative empire of the Standard Oil group, but Rogers did not hesitate to focus Ida Tarbell's attention on Rockefeller.[6]

John D. Rockefeller himself was the exemplar of the defects of an overly diligent application to an earthly calling, but the flaw of *The History of the Standard Oil Company* was that Ida Tarbell was as strongly committed to a competitive society as Rockefeller was to a monopolistic one. Free competition was her Eden, and life outside of it could not help but be sinful. The location of the Garden was in the oil fields of Western Pennsylvania where she had grown up. Her picture of the oil region in its early days was one of triumphant individualism exuberantly developing a vast natural wealth and at the same time creating a forward-looking society. "Life ran swift and ruddy and joyous in these men. . . . they looked forward with all the eagerness of the young who have just learned their powers, to the years of struggle and development. They would solve all these perplexing problems of overproduction, of railroad discrimination, of speculation. They would meet their own needs. . . . There was nothing too good for them, nothing they did not hope and dare."[7]

The men of the region had been producing oil and creating a

[5] Ida M. Tarbell, *All in the Day's Work*, page 239.

[6] Allan Nevins, *Study in Power, John D. Rockefeller, Industrialist and Philanthropist* (New York, 1953), Volume II, Chapters XXIII, XXXIII, XXXIX.

[7] Ida M. Tarbell, *The History of the Standard Oil Company* (New York: Harper Torchbook, 1966), pages 20-21; also see David M. Chalmers, *The Social and Political Ideas of the Muckrakers* (New York, 1964), Chapter 5.

satisfying life for themselves. John D. Rockefeller spoiled all this, leaving in his wake personal tragedy as well as economic ruin. Since Ida Tarbell believed that the early individualism of the oil fields was healthy, she had to maintain that Standard had triumphed by the use of unfair tactics. Much of her history, therefore, consisted of a description of the dishonest methods by which Standard took over control of oil in America, and she carefully argued that the misbehavior she chronicled was not necessary either for Standard's own protection or to solve the problems of the industry. Nevertheless, the trust ground inexorably onward, individual enterprise was stamped out, and the public ended up paying monopoly prices.

Many years later in her autobiography Ida Tarbell wrote that she had objected only to the illegitimate practices rather than the size and wealth of the monopoly itself,[8] but this was not the message of her *History*. Experience taught the lesson, she had claimed earlier, that autocratic power had always been used to defraud the public, whether that power lay in the hands of kings, emperors, or the Standard Oil Company.[9]

The trust's power, she explained, was based on railroad favoritism which penalized and often destroyed the competitive potential of smaller producers and refiners. Across the pages of her history, she pursued the conspiracy between Standard and the railroads through mountains of affidavits, records, court cases, and governmental investigations. It was a telling piece of research and one which has remained free of the questions raised about Miss Tarbell's classic stories of the cheating of the Widow Backus and the harassment of the competing Buffalo Lubricating Company.

However, the major defect in *The History of the Standard Oil Company* was not in its research and documentation. Nor did it lie in Ida Tarbell's distaste for the oil trust, despite the feeling of H. H. Rogers and of later historians that she should, as she wrote in her autobiography, "submerge my contempt for their illegitimate practices in my admiration for their genius in organization and the boldness of their imagination and execution."[10] The

[8] *All in the Day's Work*, page 230.

[9] *The History of the Standard Oil Company*, pages 194-195.

[10] *All in the Day's Work*, page 230; David M. Chalmers, "From Robber Barons to Industrial Statesmen: Standard Oil and the Business Historians," *The American Journal of Economics and Sociology*, 20 (1960), pages 47-58.

problem lay in a paradox. Throughout the book ran the implicit theme of what historians were to call the "organizational revolution."[11] Repeatedly, the muckraker-journalist showed the inability of the free enterprisers to stick together and organize effective opposition to Standard Oil and the railroads. If the independent producers and refiners were overcome by a Standard Oil conspiracy, it was because they were not resolute and perceptive enough to battle the would-be monopoly effectively. In order to do so, they would have had to give up their individualism for combination. The underlying and unaccepted message of Ida Tarbell's study was that the only solution to the problem of Standard Oil power was a similar but opposing concentration.

Although her strong feelings about John D. Rockefeller and the Standard Oil Company remained unchanged, Ida Tarbell did work her way around to accepting the need for an organizational revolution. That she had done so was apparent in the volume which she wrote for Arthur Schlesinger and Dixon Ryan Fox's famous "History of American Life" series. The title she gave her analysis of the period 1878-1898 was *The Nationalizing of Business*. Writing in the mid-1930's, she presented a well-balanced survey which accepted nation-wide organization and economic consolidation. Nevertheless, while reconciled to bigness and power, she had not come to like Rockefeller any better. She was willing to credit him with an unparalleled genius for organization and a sincere desire to end the disorders and uncertainties which he believed that free competition caused. "Yet," she wrote, "considering the remarkable abilities of John D. Rockefeller . . . it may well be asked whether the company had needed to resort to the unfair methods of competition to gain preëminence in the field."[12] Nor did she feel more kindly about the railroad favoritism which had contributed so much to make this possible.

Ida Tarbell's acceptance of the organizational revolution had taken place over a period of some three decades. Despite her belief in the truth of her Standard Oil and later tariff exposés,[13] she was worried about the charge of destructive criticism which President Theodore Roosevelt and others had levied at the muckrakers. Although continuing in her role as critic and re-

[11] Samuel P. Hays, *The Response to Industrialism, 1885-1914* (Chicago, 1957), Chapter III; also see Richard Hofstadter, *The Age of Reform* (New York, 1955), Chapter VI.

[12] Ida M. Tarbell, *The Nationalizing of Business, 1878-1898* (New York, 1936), page 74.

[13] Ida M. Tarbell, *The Tariff in Our Times* (New York, 1911).

former, she increasingly sought signs of the social regeneration of business. She found hopeful indications of changing attitudes in the scientific management theories of Frederick W. Taylor and later in "enlightened" businessmen such as U. S. Steel boss Elbert Gary and General Electric Chairman Owen D. Young, about whom she wrote undistinguished biographies; this seems to have satisfied her.[14]

The pattern she found increasingly attractive was cooperation between labor and management. She praised the early labor policies of Henry Ford and was a member of the Woman's Committee of the official Council of National Defense, one of the branches of the American corporate state during the First World War. After the war, she served on President Wilson's Industrial Conference and, in 1921 on his successor's Unemployment Conference. During the 1920's she found further examples of cooperation and conciliation in the League of Nations and the Washington Disarmament Conference. Enforced national prohibition, on the other hand, did not satisfy her notion of voluntarism.

Although advocating collective bargaining, Ida Tarbell was alarmed over the persistent disharmony and violence of labor-management relations. Perhaps because of this she was impressed with Mussolini's corporate state in Italy, on which she wrote a series of articles for *McCall's* in 1926. However, her enthusiasm was restrained by the absence of political liberty and the degree to which the Italian regime was based on violence. Seeking compulsionless cooperation in the place of conflict, she also failed to find the answer in Soviet Russia. For a while it looked as though Franklin Roosevelt was coming closer. However, by the mid-thirties, as the New Deal swung from corporate code-making to trust-busting and an enhanced combative power for labor, her doubts grew. The National Labor Relations Act of 1935 and the growing wave of strikes were dramatically unlike the labor-management conciliation which she praised in *The Nationalizing of Business*. In 1940, she supported the Republican candidate, Wendell Wilkie, for the presidency.

Her death in 1944 ended a career of more than half a century

[14] Ida M. Tarbell, "Golden Rule in Business," *American*, LXXVIII (October, 1914), pages 16-17; (November, 1914), pages 11-17; (December, 1914), pages 24-29; *New Ideals in Business* (New York, 1916); *The Life of Elbert H. Gary* (New York, 1925); *Owen D. Young, A New Type of Industrial Leader* (New York, 1932).

during which this daughter of the Pennsylvania oil fields had been one of the nation's prime popular educators on social and economic topics. As muckraker, historian, journalist, lecturer, and long-time regular on the Chautauqua and Lyceum lecture circuits, she offered her views to a wide public, but nothing she later wrote on industrial and labor problems or on the status of women matched her famous early work.

With *The History of the Standard Oil Company,* which helped inaugurate the muckraker movement, Ida Tarbell's life path and her permanent place in American history were set. As Allan Nevins wrote in his *Study in Power: John D. Rockefeller, Industrialist and Philanthropist* (New York, 1953), "The time, the magazine, and the writer combined to make this serialized book the most spectacular success of the muckraking school of journalism, and its most enduring achievement."[15]

University of Florida
Gainesville, Florida
March, 1966

---

[15] Volume II, page 339.

A Note about the Paperback Edition

The History of the Standard Oil Company began its run in *McClure's* for November 1902, and continued for seventeen more monthly installments. When it was subsequently published in book form in 1904, its two volumes totaled 554 pages of text. There were also 242 pages of 64 appendices containing the copies of tables, contracts, charters, and testimony before investigating bodies, from which she footnoted her text and documented its statements. In addition there were maps, charts, tables, and reproductions of letters and records included in the text, as well as 32 pages of illustrations.

In this shortened paperback edition the text has been cut approximately in half. No chapters have been eliminated in their entirety, and, with the exception of one bracketed insert, the words and the order are Ida Tarbell's. It is the hope of the editor that there has been no substantial loss of style, continuity, thesis, or information. The primary distortion, other than in length and in forceful annotated bulk, may well be that of unduly sharpening the presentation of her thesis by paring away some of the narrative detail.

The cutting has chiefly eliminated repetition, and the names and incidents which do not have a significant or continuing role in the story. The more famous incidents such as those of the Widow Backus, the missing barrel bungs, and the sabotage of the Buffalo refinery remain. The primary effort was to make the work more quickly and easily readable, hopefully without loss of flavor or substance.

PREFACE

THIS work is the outgrowth of an effort on the part of the editors of McClure's Magazine to deal concretely in their pages with the trust question. In order that their readers might have a clear and succinct notion of the processes by which a particular industry passes from the control of the many to that of the few, they decided a few years ago to publish a detailed narrative of the history of the growth of a particular trust. The Standard Oil Trust was chosen for obvious reasons. It was the first in the field, and it has furnished the methods, the charter, and the traditions for its followers. It is the most perfectly developed trust in existence; that is, it satisfies most nearly the trust ideal of entire control of the commodity in which it deals. Its vast profits have led its officers into various allied interests, such as railroads, shipping, gas, copper, iron, steel, as well as into banks and trust companies, and to the acquiring and solidifying of these interests it has applied the methods used in building up the Oil Trust. It has led in the struggle against legislation directed against combinations. Its power in state and Federal government, in the press, in the college, in the pulpit, is generally recognised. The perfection of the organisation of the Standard, the ability and daring with which it has carried out its projects, make it the pre-eminent trust of the world—the one whose story is best fitted to illuminate the subject of combinations of capital.

Another important consideration with the editors in deciding that the Standard Oil Trust was the best adapted to illustrate their meaning, was the fact that it is one of the very few business organisations of the country whose growth could be traced in trustworthy documents. . . . This has come about largely from the fact that almost constantly since its organisation in 1870 the Standard Oil Company has been under investigation by the Congress of the United States and by the Legislatures of various states in which it has operated, on the suspicion that it was receiving rebates from the railroads and was practising methods in restraint of free trade. In 1872 and again in 1876 it was before Congressional committees, in 1879 it was

before examiners of the Commonwealth of Pennsylvania and before committees appointed by the Legislatures of New York and
of Ohio for investigating railroads. Its operations figured constantly in the debate which led up to the creation of the Interstate Commerce Commission in 1887, and again and again since
that time the Commission has been called upon to examine directly or indirectly into its relation with the railroads.

In 1888, in the Investigation of Trusts conducted by Congress
and by the state of New York, the Standard Oil Company was
the chief subject for examination. In the state of Ohio, between
1882 and 1892, a constant warfare was waged against the Standard in the courts and Legislature, resulting in several volumes of
testimony. The Legislatures of many other states concerned
themselves with it. This hostile legislation compelled the trust
to separate into its component parts in 1892, but investigation
did not cease; indeed, in the last great industrial inquiry, conducted by the Commission appointed by President McKinley, the
Standard Oil Company was constantly under discussion, and
hundreds of pages of testimony on it appear in the nineteen volumes of reports which the Commission has submitted.

This mass of testimony, all of it submitted under oath it should
be remembered, contains the different charters and agreements
under which the Standard Oil Trust has operated, many contracts and agreements with railroads, with refineries, with pipe-
lines, and it contains the experiences in business from 1872 up to
1900 of multitudes of individuals. These experiences have exactly the quality of the personal reminiscences of actors in great
events, with the additional value that they were given on the witness stand, and it is fair, therefore, to suppose that they are more
cautious and exact in statements than many writers of memoirs
are. These investigations, covering as they do all of the important steps in the development of the trust, include full accounts
of the point of view of its officers in regard to that development,
as well as their explanations of many of the operations over
which controversy has arisen. Hundreds of pages of sworn testimony are found in these volumes from John D. Rockefeller,
William Rockefeller, Henry M. Flagler, H. H. Rogers, John D.
Archbold, Daniel O'Day and other members of the concern.

Aside from the great mass of sworn testimony accessible to the
student there is a large pamphlet literature dealing with different
phases of the subject, and there are files of the numerous
daily newspapers and monthly reviews, supported by the Oil Re-

gions, in the columns of which are to be found not only statistics but full reports of all controversies between oil men. . . .

But the documentary sources of this work are by no means all printed. The Standard Oil Trust and its constituent companies have figured in many civil suits, the testimony of which is still in manuscript in the files of the courts where the suits were tried. These manuscripts have been examined on the ground, and in numerous instances full copies of affidavits and of important testimony have been made for permanent reference and study. I have also had access to many files of private correspondence and papers, the most important being that of the officers and counsel of the Petroleum Producers' Union from 1878 to 1880, that covering the organisation from 1887 to 1895 of the various independent companies which resulted in the Pure Oil Company, and that containing the material prepared by Roger Sherman for the suit brought in 1897 by the United States Pipe Line against certain of the Standard companies under the Sherman anti-trust law.

As many of the persons who have been active in the development of the oil industry are still living, their help has been freely sought. Scores of persons in each of the great oil centres have been interviewed, and the comprehension and interpretation of the documents on which the work is based have been materially aided by the explanations which the actors in the events under consideration were able to give.

When the work was first announced in the fall of 1901, the Standard Oil Company, or perhaps I should say officers of the company, courteously offered to give me all the assistance in their power, an offer of which I have freely taken advantage. In accepting assistance from Standard men as from independents I distinctly stated that I wanted facts, and that I reserved the right to use them according to my own judgment of their meaning, that my object was to learn more perfectly what was actually done—not to learn what my informants thought of what had been done. It is perhaps not too much to say that there is not a single important episode in the history of the Standard Oil Company, so far as I know it, or a notable step in its growth, which I have not discussed more or less fully with officers of the company.

It is needless to add that the conclusions expressed in this work are my own.

I. M. T.

1   THE BIRTH OF AN INDUSTRY

Petroleum first a curiosity and then a medicine—Discovery of its real value—The story of how it came to be produced in large quantities—Great flow of oil—Swarm of problems to solve—Storage and transportation—Refining and marketing—Rapid extension of the field of operation —Workers in great numbers with plenty of capital—Costly blunders frequently made—But every difficulty being met and overcome—The normal unfolding of a new and wonderful opportunity for individual endeavour.

ONE of the busiest corners of the globe at the opening of the year 1872 was a strip of Northwestern Pennsylvania, not over fifty miles long, known the world over as the Oil Regions. Twelve years before this strip of land had been but little better than a wilderness; its chief inhabitants the lumbermen, who every season cut great swaths of primeval pine and hemlock from its hills, and in the spring floated them down the Allegheny River to Pittsburg. The great tides of Western emigration had shunned the spot for years as too rugged and unfriendly for settlement, and yet in twelve years this region avoided by men had been transformed into a bustling trade centre, where towns elbowed each other for place, into which three great trunk railroads had built branches, and every foot of whose soil was fought for by capitalists. It was the discovery and development of a new raw product, petroleum, which had made this change from wilderness to market-place. This product in twelve years had not only peopled a waste place on the earth, it had revolutionised the world's methods of illumination and added millions upon millions of dollars to the wealth of the United States.

Petroleum as a curiosity, and indeed in a small way as an article of commerce, was no new thing when its discovery in quantities called the attention of the world to this corner of Northwestern Pennsylvania. The journals of many an early explorer of the valleys of the Allegheny and its tributaries tell of springs and streams the surfaces of which were found covered with a thick oily substance which burned fiercely when ignited and which the Indians believed to have curative

1

properties. As the country was opened, more and more was heard of these oil springs. Certain streams came to be named from the quantities of the substance found on the surface of the water, as "Oil Creek" in Northwestern Pennsylvania, "Old Greasy" or Kanawha in West Virginia. The belief in the substance as a cure-all increased as time went on and in various parts of the country it was regularly skimmed from the surface of the water as cream from a pan, or soaked up by woollen blankets, bottled, and peddled as a medicine for man and beast.

Up to the beginning of the 19th century no oil seems to have been obtained except from the surfaces of springs and streams. That it was to be found far below the surface of the earth was discovered independently at various points in Kentucky, West Virginia, Ohio and Pennsylvania by persons drilling for salt-water to be used in manufacturing salt. Not infrequently the water they found was mixed with a dark-green, evil-smelling substance which was recognised as identical with the well-known "rockoil." It was necessary to rid the water of this before it could be used for salt, and in many places cisterns were devised in which the brine was allowed to stand until the oil had risen to the surface. It was then run into the streams or on the ground. This practice was soon discovered to be dangerous, so easily did the oil ignite. In several places, particularly in Kentucky, so much oil was obtained with the salt-water that the wells had to be abandoned. Certain of these deserted salt wells were opened years after, when it was found that the troublesome substance which had made them useless was far more valuable than the brine the original drillers sought.

Naturally the first use made of the oil obtained in quantities from the salt wells was medicinal. By the middle of the century it was without doubt the great American medicine. "Seneca Oil" seems to have been the earliest name under which petroleum appeared in the East. It was followed by a large output of Kentucky petroleum sold under the name "American Medicinal Oil." Several hundred thousand bottles of this oil are said to have been put up in Burkesville, Kentucky, and to have been shipped to the East and to Europe. The point at which the business of bottling petroleum for medicine was carried on most systematically and extensively was Pittsburg. Near that town, at Tarentum in Alleghany County, were located salt wells owned and operated in the forties by Samuel M. Kier. The oil which came up with the salt-water was sufficient to be a nuisance, and Mr. Kier sought a way to use it. Believing it had curative qualities he began to bottle it. By 1850 he had worked up this business until "Kier's Petroleum, or Rock-Oil" was sold all over the United States. The crude petroleum was put up in eight-ounce bottles wrapped in a circular setting forth in good patent-medicine style its virtues as a cure-all, and giving directions about its use. While it was admitted to be chiefly a liniment it was recommended for cholera morbus, liver complaint, bronchitis and consumption, and the dose prescribed was three teaspoonfuls three times a day! . . . . Although his trade in this oil was so extensive he was not satisfied that petroleum was useful only as a medicine. He was interested in it as a lubricator and a luminant. That petroleum had the qualities of both had been discovered at more than one point before 1850. More than one mill-owner in the districts where petroleum had been found was using it in a crude way for oiling his machines or lighting his works, but though the qualities of both lubricator and luminant were present, the impurities of the natural oil were too great to make its use general. Mr. Kier seems to have been the first man to have attempted to secure an expert opinion as to the possibility of refining it. In 1849 he sent a bottle of oil to a chemist in Philadelphia, who advised him to try distilling it and burning it in a lamp. Mr. Kier followed the advice, and a five-barrel still which he used in the fifties for refining petroleum is still to be seen in Pittsburg. . . .

Although Mr. Kier seems to have done a good business in rock-oil, neither he nor any one else up to this point had thought it worth while to seek petroleum for its own sake. They had all simply sought to utilise what rose before their eyes on springs and streams or came to them mixed with the salt-water for which they drilled. In 1854, however, a man was found who took rock-oil more seriously. This man was George H. Bissell, a graduate of Dartmouth College, who, worn out by an experience of ten years in the South as a journalist and teacher, had come North for a change. At his old college the latest curiosity of the laboratory was shown him—the bottle of rock-oil—and the professor contended that it was as good, or better, than coal for making illuminating oil. Bissell inquired into its origin, and was told that it came from oil springs located in Northwestern Pennsylvania. . . .

Bissell seems to have been impressed with the commercial possibilities of the oil, for he at once organized a company, the Pennsylvania Rock-Oil Company, the first in the United States, and leased the lands on which these oil springs were located. He then sent a quantity of the oil to Professor Silliman of Yale College, and paid him for analysing it. The professor's report was published and received general attention. From the rock-oil might be made as good an illuminant as any the world knew. It also yielded gas, paraffine, lubricating oil. "In short," declared Professor Silliman, "your company have in their possession a raw material from which, by simple and not expensive process, they may manufacture very valuable products. It is worthy of note that my experiments prove that nearly the whole of the raw product may be manufactured without waste, and this solely by a well-directed process which is in practice in one of the most simple of all chemical processes."

The oil was valuable, but could it be obtained in quantities great enough to make the development of so remote a locality worth while? The only method of obtaining it known to Mr. Bissell and his associates in the new company was from the surface of oil springs. Could it be obtained in any other way? There has long been a story current in the Oil Regions that the Pennsylvania Rock-Oil Company received its first notion of drilling for oil from one of those trivial incidents which so often turn the course of human affairs. As the story goes, Mr. Bissell was one day walking down Broadway when he halted to rest in the shade of an awning before a drug store. In the window he saw on a bottle a curious label, "Kier's Petroleum, or Rock-Oil," it read, "Celebrated for its wonderful curative powers. A natural Remedy; Produced from a well in Allegheny Co., Pa., four hundred feet below the earth's surface," etc. On the label was the picture of an artesian well. It was from this well that Mr. Kier got his "Natural Remedy." Hundreds of men had seen the label before, for it went out on every one of Mr. Kier's circulars, but this was the first to look at it with a "seeing eye." As quickly as the bottle of rock-oil in the Dartmouth laboratory had awakened in Mr. Bissell's mind the determination to find out the real value of the strange substance, the label gave him the solution of the problem of getting oil in quantities—it was to bore down into the earth where it was stored, and pump it up.

Professor Silliman made his report to the Pennsylvania Rock-

Oil Company in 1855, but it was not until the spring of 1858 that a representative of the organisation, which by this time had changed hands and was known as the Seneca Oil Company, was on the ground with orders to find oil. The man sent out was a small stockholder in the company, Edwin L. Drake, "Colonel" Drake as he was called. Drake had had no experience to fit him for his task. A man forty years of age, he had spent his life as a clerk, an express agent, and a railway conductor. His only qualifications were a dash of pioneer blood and a great persistency in undertakings which interested him. . . .

The task before Drake was no light one. The spot to which he had been sent was Titusville, a lumberman's hamlet on Oil Creek, fourteen miles from where that stream joins the Allegheny River. Its chief connection with the outside world was by a stage to Erie, forty miles away. This remoteness from civilisation and Drake's own ignorance of artesian wells, added to the general scepticism of the community concerning the enterprise, caused great difficulty and long delays. It was months before Drake succeeded in getting together the tools, engine and rigging necessary to bore his well, and before he could get a driller who knew how to manipulate them, winter had come, and he had to suspend operations. People called him crazy for sticking to the enterprise, but that had no effect on him. As soon as spring opened he borrowed a horse and wagon and drove over a hundred miles to Tarentum, where Mr. Kier was still pumping his salt wells, and was either bottling or refining the oil which came up with the brine. Here Drake hoped to find a driller. He brought back a man, and after a few months more of experiments and accidents the drill was started. One day late in August, 1859, Titusville was electrified by the news that Drake's Folly, as many of the onlookers had come to consider it, had justified itself. The well was full of oil. The next day a pump was started, and twenty-five barrels of oil were gathered.

There was no doubt of the meaning of the Drake well in the minds of the people of the vicinity. They had long ago accepted all Professor Silliman had said of the possibilities of petroleum, and now that they knew how it could be obtained in quanity, the whole country-side rushed out to obtain leases. . . .

On every rocky farm, in every poor settlement of the region, was some man whose ear was attuned to Fortune's call, and who had the daring and the energy to risk everything he possessed in an oil lease. It was well that he acted at once; for, as the news of the discovery of oil reached the open, the farms and towns of Ohio, New York, and Pennsylvania poured out a stream of ambitious and vigorous youths, eager to seize what might be there for them, while from the East came men with money and business experience, who formed great stock companies, took up lands in parcels of thousands of acres, and put down wells along every rocky run and creek, as well as over the steep hills. In answer to their drill, oil poured forth in floods. In many places pumping was out of the question; the wells flowed 2,000, 3,000, 4,000 barrels a day—such quantities of it that at the close of 1861 oil which in January of 1860 was twenty dollars a barrel had fallen to ten cents.

Here was the oil, and in unheard-of quantities, and with it came all the swarm of problems which a discovery brings. The methods Drake had used were crude and must be improved. The processes of refining were those of the laboratory and must be developed. Communication with the outside world must be secured. Markets must be built up. Indeed, a whole new commercial machine had to be created to meet the discovery. These problems were not realised before the region teemed with men to wrestle with them—men "alive to the instant need of things." They had to begin with so simple and elementary a matter as devising something to hold the oil. There were not barrels enough to be bought in America, although turpentine barrels, molasses barrels, whiskey barrels—every sort of barrel and cask —were added to new ones made especially for oil. Reservoirs excavated in the earth and faced with logs and cement, and box-like structures of planks or logs were tried at first but were not satisfactory. A young Iowa school teacher and farmer,[1] visiting at his home in Erie County, went to the region. Immediately he saw his chance. It was to invent a receptacle which would hold oil in quantities. Certain large producers listened to his scheme and furnished money to make a trial tank. It was a success, and before many months the school-teacher was buying thousands of feet of lumber, employing scores of men, and working them and himself—day and night. For nearly ten years he built these wooden tanks. Then seeing that iron tanks—huge

[1] The young schoolteacher was Ida Tarbell's father, Franklin S. Tarbell. [Ed.]

receptacles holding thousands of barrels where his held hundreds—were bound to supersede him, he turned, with the ready adaptability which characterised the men of the region, to producing oil for others to tank.

After the storing problem came that of transportation. There was one waterway leading out—Oil Creek, as it had been called for more than a hundred years,—an uncertain stream running the length of the narrow valley in which the oil was found, and uniting with the Allegheny River at what is now known as Oil City. From this junction it was 132 miles to Pittsburg and a railroad. Besides this waterway were rough country roads leading to the railroads at Union City, Corry, Erie and Meadville. There was but one way to get the oil to the bank of Oil Creek or to the railroads, and that was by putting it into barrels and hauling it. Teamsters equipped for this service seemed to fall from the sky. The farms for a hundred miles around gave up their boys and horses and wagons to supply the need. It paid. There were times when three and even four dollars a barrel were paid for hauling five or ten miles. It was not too much for the work. The best roads over which they travelled were narrow, rough, unmade highways, mere openings to the outer world, while the roads to the wells they themselves had to break across fields and through forests. These roads were made almost impassable by the great number of heavily freighted wagons travelling over them. From the big wells a constant procession of teams ran, and it was no uncommon thing for a visitor to the Oil Regions to meet oil caravans of a hundred or more wagons. Often these caravans were held up for hours by a dangerous mud-hole into which a wheel had sunk or a horse fallen. If there was a possible way to be made around the obstruction it was taken, even if it led through a farmer's field. Indeed, a sort of guerilla warfare went on constantly between the farmers and the teamsters. Often the roads became impassable, so that new ones had to be broken, and not even a shot-gun could keep the driver from going where the passage was least difficult. . . .

With the wages paid him the teamster could easily become a kind of plutocrat. . . . Indispensable to the business they became the tyrants of the region—working and brawling as suited them, a genius not unlike the flatboat-men who once gave colour to life on the Mississippi, or the cowboys who make the plains picturesque to-day. Bad as their reputation was, many a man

7

found in their ranks the start which led later to wealth and influence in the oil business. . . .

In this problem of transportation the most important element after the team was Oil Creek and the flatboat. A more uncertain stream never ran in a bed. In the summer it was low, in the winter frozen; now it was gorged with ice, now running mad over the flats. The best service was gotten out of it in time of low water through artificial freshets. Milldams, controlled by private parties, were frequent along the creek and its tributaries. By arrangement these dams were cut on a certain day or days of the week, usually Friday, and on the flood or freshet the flatboats loaded with barrels of oil were floated down stream. The freshet was always exciting and perilous and frequently disastrous. From the points where they were tied up the boatmen watched the coming flood and cut themselves loose the moment after its head had passed them. As one fleet after another swung into the roaring flood the danger of collision and jams increased. Rare indeed was the freshet when a few wrecks did not lie somewhere along the creek, and often scores lay piled high on the bank—a hopeless jam of broken boats and barrels, the whole soaked in petroleum and reeking with gas and profanity. If the boats rode safely through to the river, there was little further danger.

The Allegheny River traffic grew to great proportions—fully 1,000 boats and some thirty steamers were in the fleet, and at least 4,000 men. This traffic was developed by men who saw here their opportunity of fortune, as others had seen it in drilling or teaming. The foremost of these men was an Ohio River captain, driven northward by the war, one J. J. Vandergrift. Captain Vandergrift had run the full gamut of river experiences from cabin-boy to owner and commander of his own steamers. . . . He towed 4,000 empty casks up the river, saw at once the need of some kind of bulk transportation, took his hint from a bulk-boat which an ingenious experimenter was trying, ordered a dozen of them built, towed his fleet to the creek, bought oil to fill them, and then returned to Pittsburg to sell his cargo. On one alone he made $70,000.

But the railroad soon pressed the river hard. At the time of the discovery of oil three lines, the Philadelphia and Erie, the Buffalo and Erie (now the Lake Shore), connecting with the Central, and the Atlantic and Great Western, connecting with the Erie, were within teaming distance of the region. . . . The amount of freight the railroads carried the first year of the business was enormous. . . . Connecting lines were built as rapidly a men could work. . . .

The railroads built, the vexatious, time-taking, and costly problem of getting the oil from the well to the shipping point still remained. The teamster was still the tyrant of the business. His day was almost over. He was to fall before the pipe-line, The feasibility of carrying oil in pipes was discussed almost from the beginning of the oil business. Very soon after the Drake well was struck oil men began to say that the natural way to get this oil from the wells to the railroads was through pipes. In many places gravity would carry it; where it could not, pumps would force it. . . . In 1863 at least three short pipe-lines were put into operation. . . . The one which attracted the most attention was a line two and one-half miles in length carrying crude oil from the Tarr farm to the Humboldt refinery at Plumer. Various other experiments were made, both gravity and pumps being trusted for propelling the oil, but there was always something wrong; the pipes leaked or burst, the pumps were too weak; shifting oil centres interrupted experiments which might have been successful. Then suddenly the man for the need appeared, Samuel Van Syckel. He came to the creek in 1864 with some money, hoping to make more. He handled quantities of oil produced at Pithole, several miles from a shipping point, and saw his profits eaten up by teamsters. Their tyranny aroused his ire and his wits and he determined to build a pipe-line from the wells to the railroad. He was greeted with jeers, but he went doggedly ahead, laid an two-inch pipe, put in three relay pumps, and turned in his oil. From the start the line was a success, carrying eighty barrels of oil an hour. The day that the Van Syckel pipe-line began to run oil a revolution began in the business. After the Drake well it is the most important event in the history of the Oil Regions.

The teamsters saw its meaning first and turned out in fury, dragging the pipe, which was for the most part buried, to the surface, and cutting it so that the oil would be lost. It was only by stationing an armed guard that they were held in check. A second line . . . suffered even more. . . . The teamsters . . . burned the tanks in which oil was stored, laid in wait for employees, threatened with destruction the wells which furnished the oil, and so generally terrorised the country that the governor of the state was called upon in April, 1866, to protect the property and men of the lines. The day of the teamster was over, however, and the more philosophical of them accepted the situation; scores disappeared from the region, and scores more took to drilling. They died hard, and the cutting and plugging of pipe-lines was for years a pastime of the remnant of their race.

If the uses to which oil might be put and the methods for manufacturing it had not been well understood when the Drake well was struck, there would have been no such imperious demand as came for the immediate opening of new territory and developing methods of handling and carrying it on a large scale. But men knew already what the oil was good for, and, in a crude way, how to distill it. The process of distillation also was free to all. The essential apparatus was very simple—a cast-iron still, usually surrounded by brick-work, a copper worm, and two tin- or zinc-lined tanks. The still was filled with crude oil, which was subjected to a high enough heat to vapourise it. The vapour passed through a cast-iron goose-neck fitted to the top of the still into the copper worm, which was immersed in water. Here the vapour was condensed and passed into the zinc-lined tank. This product, called a distillate, was treated with chemicals, washed with water, and run off into the tin-lined tank, where it was allowed to settle. Anybody who could get the apparatus could "make oil," and many men did—badly, of course, to begin with, and with an alarming proportion of waste and explosions and fires, but with experience they learned, and some of the great refineries of the country grew out of these rude beginnings.

Luckily not all the men who undertook the manufacturing of petroleum in these first days were inexperienced. The chemists to whom are due chiefly the processes now used—Atwood, Gessner, and Merrill—had for years been busy making oils from coal. They knew something of petroleum, and when it came in quantities began at once to adapt their processes to it. Merrill at the time was connected with Samuel Downer, of Boston, in manufacturing oil from Trinidad pitch and from coal bought in Newfoundland. The year oil was discovered Mr. Downer distilled 7,500 tons of this coal, clearing on it at least $100,000. As soon as petroleum appeared he and Mr. Merrill saw that here was a product which was bound to displace their coal, and with courage and promptness they prepared to adapt their works.

In order to be near the supply they came to Corry, fourteen miles from the Drake well, and in 1862 put up a refinery which cost $250,000. Here were refined thousands of barrels of oil, most of which was sent to New York for export. To the Boston works the firm sent crude, which was manufactured for the home trade and for shipping to California and Australia. The processes used in the Downer works at this early day were in all essentials the same as are used to-day. . . .

As men and means were found to put down wells, to devise and build tanks and boats and pipes and railroads for handling the oil, to adapt and improve processes for manufacturing, so men were found from the beginning of the oil business to wrestle with every problem raised. They came in shoals, young, vigorous, resourceful, indifferent to difficulties, greedy for a chance, and with each year they forced more light and wealth from the new product. By the opening of 1872 they had produced nearly 40,000,000 barrels of oil, and had raised their product to the fourth place among the exports of the United States, over 152,000,000 gallons going abroad in 1871. . . . As for the market, they had developed it until it included almost every country of the earth—China, the East and West Indies, South America and Africa. Over forty different European ports received refined oil from the United States in 1871. Nearly a million gallons were sent to Syria, about a half million to Egypt, about as much to the British West Indies, and a quarter of a million to the Dutch East Indies. Not only were illuminating oils being exported. In 1871 nearly seven million gallons of naphtha, benzine, and gasoline were sent aboard, and it became evident now for the first time that a valuable trade in lubricants made from petroleum was possible. A discovery by Joshua Merrill of the Downer works opened this new source of wealth to the industry. Until 1869 the impossibility of deodorising petroleum had prevented its use largely as a lubricant, but in that year Mr. Merrill discovered a process by which a deodorised lubricating oil could be made. He had both the apparatus for producing the oil and the oil itself patented. The oil was so favourably received that the market sale by the Downer works was several hundred per cent. greater in a single year than the firm had ever sold before.

The oil field had been extended from the valley of Oil Creek and its tributaries down the Allegheny River for fifty miles and probably covered 2,000 square miles. The early theory that oil followed the streams had been exploded, and wells were now drilled on the hills. It was known, too, that if oil was found in the first sand struck in the drilling, it might be found still lower in a second or third sand. The Drake well had struck oil at 69½ feet, but wells were now drilled as deep as 1,600 feet. The extension of the field, the discovery that oil was under the hills as well as under streams, and to be found in various sands, had cost enormously. It had been done by "wild-catting," as putting down experimental wells was called, by following superstitions in locating wells, such as the witch-hazel stick, or the spiritualistic medium, quite as much as by studying the position of wells in existence and calculating how oil belts probably ran. As the cost of a well was from $3,000 to $8,000, according to its location, and as 4,374 of the 5,560 wells drilled in the first ten years of the business (1859 to 1869) were "dry-holes," or were abandoned as unprofitable, something of the daring it took to operate on small means, as most producers did in the beginning, is evident. But they loved the game, and every man of them would stake his last dollar on the chance of striking oil.

With the extension of the field rapid strides had been made in tools, in rigs, in all of the various essentials of drilling a well. They had learned to use torpedoes to open up hard rocks, naphtha to cut the paraffine which coated the sand and stopped the flow of oil, seed bags to stop the inrush of a stream of water. They lost their tools less often, and knew better how to fish for them when they did. In short, they had learned how to put down and care for oil wells.

Equal advances had been made in other departments. . . . The wooden tank holding 200 to 1,200 barrels had been rapidly replaced by the great iron tank holding 20,000 or 30,000 barrels. The pipe-lines had begun to go directly to the wells instead of pumping from a general receiving station, or "dump," as it was called, thus saving the tedious and expensive operation of hauling. From beginning to end the business had been developed, systematised, simplified.

Most important was the simplification of the transportation problem by the development of pipe-lines. By 1872 they were the one oil gatherer. Several companies were carrying on the pipe-line business, and two of them had acquired great power in the Oil Regions because of their connection with trunk lines.

These were the Empire Transportation Company and the Pennsylvania Transportation Company. . . . The Empire Transportation Company had been organised in 1865 to build up an east and west freight traffic *via* the Philadelphia and Erie Railroad, a new line which had just been leased by the Pennsylvania. Some ten railroads connected in one way or another with the Philadelphia and Erie, forming direct routes east and west. In spite of their evident community of interest these various roads were kept apart by their jealous fears of one another. Each insisted on its own time-table, its own rates, its own way of doing things. The shipper *via* this route must make a separate bargain with each road and often submit to having his freight changed at terminals from one car to another because of the difference of gauge. The Empire Transportation Company undertook to act as a mediator between the roads and the shipper, to make the route cheap, fast, and reliable. It proposed to solicit freight, furnish its own cars and terminal facilities, and collect money due. It did not make rates, however; it only harmonised those made by the various branches in the system. It was to receive a commission on the business secured, and a rental for the cars and other facilities it furnished.

It was a difficult task the new company undertook, but it had at its head a remarkable man to cope with difficulties. This man, Joseph D. Potts, was in 1865 thirty-six years old. He had come of a long and honourable line of iron-masters of the Schuylkill region of Pennsylvania, but had left the great forge towns with which his ancestors had been associated—Pottstown, Glasgow Forge, Valley Forge—to become a civil engineer. His profession led him to the service of the Pennsylvania Railroad, where he had held important positions in connection with which he now undertook the organisation of the Empire Transportation Company. Colonel Potts . . . possessed a clear and vigorous mind; he was far-seeing, forceful in execution, fair in his dealings. To marked ability and integrity he joined a gentle and courteous nature. . . .

Now the Empire agency had hardly been established when the Van Syckel pipe-line began to carry oil . . . to the railroad. Lines began to multiply. The railroads saw at once that they were destined speedily to do all the gathering and hastened to secure control of them. . . .

One of the cleverest of the pipe-line devices of the Empire

13

Company was its assessment for waste and fire. In running oil through pipes there is more or less lost by leaking and evaporation. In September, 1868, Mr. Hatch announced that thereafter he would deduct two per cent. from oil runs for wastage. The assessment raised almost a riot in the region, meetings were held, the Empire Transportation Company was denounced as a highway robber, and threats of violence were made if the order was enforced. While this excitement was in progress there came a big fire on the line. Now the company's officials had been studying the question of fire insurance from the start. Fires in the Oil Regions were as regular a feature of the business as explosions used to be on the Mississippi steamboats, and no regular fire insurance company would take the risk. It had been decided that at the first fire there should be announced what was called a "general average assessment," that is, a fire tax, and to be ready, blanks had been prepared. Now in the thick of the resistance to the wastage assessment came a fire and the line announced that the producers having oil in the line must pay the insurance. The controversy at once waxed hotter than ever, but was finally compromised by the withdrawal in this case of the fire insurance if the producers would consent to the tax for waste. They did consent, and later when fires occurred the general average assessment was applied without serious opposition. Both of these practices prevail to-day. By the end of 1871 the Empire Transportation Company was one of the most efficient and respected business organisations in the oil country.

Its chief rival was the Pennsylvania Transportation Company, an organisation which had its origin in the second pipe-line laid in the Oil Regions. This line was built by Henry Harley, a man who for fully ten years was one of the most brilliant figures in the oil country. Harley was a civil engineer by profession, a graduate of the Troy Polytechnic Institute, and had held a responsible position for some time as an assistant of General Herman Haupt in the Hoosac Tunnel. He became interested in the oil business in 1862, first as a buyer of petroleum, then as an operator in West Virginia. In 1865 he laid a pipe-line from one of the rich oil farms of the creek to the railroad. It was a success, and from this venture Harley and his partner, W. H. Abbott, one of the wealthiest and most active men in the country, developed an important transportation system. In 1868 Jay Gould, who as president of the Erie road was eager to increase his oil freight, bought a controlling interest in the Abbott and Harley lines, and made Harley "General Oil Agent" of the Erie system. Harley now became closely associated with Fisk and Gould, and the three carried on a series of bold and piratical speculations in oil which greatly enraged the oil country. They built a refinery near Jersey City, extended their pipe-line system, and in 1871, when they reorganised under the name of the Pennsylvania Transportation Company, they controlled probably the greatest number of miles of pipe of any company in the region, and then were fighting the Empire bitterly for freight.

There is no part of this rapid development of the business more interesting than the commercial machine the oil men had devised by 1872 for marketing oil. A man with a thousand-barrel well on his hands in 1862 was in a plight. He had got to sell his oil at once for lack of storage room or let it run on the ground, and there was no exchange, no market, no telegraph, not even a post-office within his reach where he could arrange a sale. He had to depend on buyers who came to him. These buyers were the agents of the refineries in different cities, or of the exporters of crude in New York. They went from well to well on horseback, if the roads were not too bad, on foot if they were, and at each place made a special bargain varying with the quantity bought and the difficulty in getting it away, for the buyer was the transporter, and, as a rule, furnished the barrels or boats in which he carried off his oil. It was not long before the speculative character of the oil trade due to the great fluctuations in quantity added a crowd of brokers to the regular buyers who tramped up and down the creek. When the railroads came in the trains became the headquarters for both buyers and sellers. This was the more easily managed as the trains on the creek stopped at almost every oil farm. These trains became, in fact, a sort of travelling oil exchange, and on them a large percentage of all the bargaining of the business was done.

The brokers and buyers first organised and established headquarters in Oil City in 1869, but there was an oil exchange in New York City as early as 1866. Titusville did not have an exchange until 1871. By this time the pipe-lines had begun to issue certificates for the oil they received, and the trading was done to a degree in these. The method was simple, and much more convenient than the old one. The producer ran his oil into a pipe-line, and for it received a certificate showing that the line held so much to his credit; this certificate was transferred when the sale was made and presented when the oil was wanted.

One achievement of which the oil men were particularly proud was increasing the refining capacity of the region. At the start the difficulty of getting the apparatus for a refinery to the creek had been so enormous that the bulk of the crude had been driven to the nearest manufacturing cities—Erie, Pittsburg, Cleveland. Much had gone to the seaboard, too, and Boston, New York, Philadelphia and Baltimore were all doing considerable refining. There was always a strong feeling in the Oil Regions that the refining should be done at home. Before the railroads came the most heroic efforts were made again and again to get in the necessary machinery. Brought from Pittsburg by water, as a rule, the apparatus had to be hauled from Oil City, where it had been dumped on the muddy bank of the river—there were no wharfs—over the indescribable roads to the site chosen. It took weeks—months sometimes—to get in the apparatus. The chemicals used in the making of the oil, the barrels in which to store it—all had to be brought from outside. The wonder is that under these conditions anybody tried to refine on the creek. But refineries persisted in coming, and after the railroads came, increased; by 1872 the daily capacity had grown to nearly 10,000 barrels, and there were no more complete or profitable plants in existence than two or three of those on the creek. The only points having larger daily capacity were Cleveland and New York City. Several of the refineries had added barrel works. Acids were made on the ground. Iron works at Oil City and Titusville promised soon to supply the needs of both drillers and refiners. The exultation was great, and the press and people boasted that the day would soon come when they would refine for the world. There in their own narrow valleys should be made everything which petroleum would yield. Cleveland, Pittsburg—the seaboard—must give up refining. The business belonged to the Oil Regions, and the oil men meant to take it. . . .

The odds against the oil men in developing the business had not been merely physical ones. There had been more than the wilderness to conquer, more than the possibilities of a new product to learn. Over all the early years of their struggle and hardships hovered the dark cloud of the Civil War. They were so cut off from men that they did not hear of the fall of Sumter for four days after it happened, and the news for the time blotted out interest even in flowing wells. Twice at least when Lee invaded Pennsylvania the whole business came to a stand-still, men abandoning the drill, the pump, the refinery to make ready to repel the invader. They were taxed for the war—taxes rising to ten dollars per barrel in 1865—one dollar on crude and twenty cents a gallon on refined (the oil barrel is usually estimated at forty-two gallons). They gave up their quota of men again and again at the call for recruits, and when the end came and a million men were cast on the country, this little corner of Pennsylvania absorbed a larger portion of men probably than any other spot in the United States. The soldier was given the first chance everywhere at work, he was welcomed into oil companies, stock being given him for the value of his war record. There were lieutenants and captains and majors—even generals—scattered all over the field, and the field felt itself honoured, and bragged, as it did of all things, of the number of privates and officers who immediately on disbandment had turned to it for employment.

It was not only the Civil War from which the Oil Regions had suffered; in 1870 the Franco-Prussian War broke the foreign market to pieces and caused great loss to the whole industry. And there had been other troubles. From the first, oil men had to contend with wild fluctuations in the price of oil. In 1859 it was twenty dollars a barrel, and in 1861 it had averaged fifty-two cents. Two years later, in 1863, it averaged $8.15, and in 1867 but $2.40. In all these first twelve years nothing like a steady price could be depended on, for just as the supply seemed to have approached a fixed amount, a "wildcat" well would come in and "knock the bottom out of the market." Such fluctuations were the natural element of the speculator, and he came early, buying in quantities and holding in storage tanks for higher prices. If enough oil was held, or if the production fell off, up went the price, only to be knocked down by the throwing of great quantities of stocks on the market. . . . To develop a business in face of such fluctuations and speculation in the raw product took not only courage—it took a dash of the gambler. It never could have been done, of course, had it not been for the streams of money which flowed unceasingly and apparently from choice into the regions. In 1865 Mr. Wright calculated that the oil country was using a capital of $100,000,000. In

1872 the oil men claimed the capital in operation was $200,000,000. It has been estimated that in the first decade of the industry nearly $350,000,000 was put into it.

Speculation in oil stock companies was another great evil. It reached its height in 1864 and 1865—the "flush times" of the business. Stocks in companies whose holdings were hardly worth the stamps on the certificates were sold all over the land. In March, 1865, the aggregate capital of the oil companies whose charters were on file in Albany, New York, was $350,000,000, an in Philadelphia alone in 1864 and 1865 1,000 oil companies, mostly bogus, are said to have been formed. These swindles were dignified by the names of officers of distinction in the United States army, for the war was coming to an end and the name of a general was the most popular and persuasive argument in the country. Of course there came a collapse. The "oil bubble" burst in 1866, and it was nothing but the irrepressible energy of the region which kept the business going in the panic which followed.

Then there was the disturbing effect of foreign competition. What would become of them if oil was found in quantities in other countries? A decided depression of the market occurred in 1866 when the government sent out reports of developments of foreign oil fields. If there was oil in Japan, China, Burma, Persia, Russia, Bavaria, in the quantities the government reports said, why, there was trouble in store for Pennsylvania, the oil men argued, and for a day the market fell—it was only for a day. Men forgot easily in the Oil Regions in the sixties.

An evil in their business which they were only beginning to grasp fully in 1871 was the unholy system of freight discrimination which the railroads were practising. Three trunk lines competed for the business by 1872—the Pennsylvania, which had leased the Philadelphia and Erie, the Erie and the Central. . . . The Pennsylvania claimed the oil traffic as a natural right; for the Oil Regions were in Pennsylvania, and did not Tom Scott own that state? The Erie road for about five years had been in the hands of those splendid pirates, Jay Gould and "Jim" Fisk. Naturally they took all they could get of the oil traffic and took it by freebooting methods. "Corners" and "rings" were their favourite devices for securing trade, and more than once their aid had carried through daring and unscrupulous speculations in oil. The Central in this period was waging its famous desperate war on the Erie, Commodore Vanderbilt having marked that highway for his own along with most other things in New York State. All three of the roads began as early as 1868 to use secret rebates on the published freight rates in oil as a means of securing traffic. This practice had gone on until 1871 any big producer, refiner, or buyer could bully a freight agent into a special rate. Those "on the inside," those who had "pulls," also secured special rates. The result was that the open rate was enforced only on the innocent and the weak.

Serious as all these problems were, there was no discouragement or shrinking from them. The oil men had rid themselves of bunco men and burst the "oil bubbles." They had harnessed the brokers in exchanges and made strict rules to govern them. They had learned not to fear the foreigners, and to take with equal *sang froid* the "dry-hole" which made them poor, or the "gusher" which made them rich. For every evil they had a remedy. They were not afraid even of the railroads, and loudly declared that if the discriminations were not stopped they would build a railroad of their own. Indeed, the evils in the oil business in 1871, far from being a discouragement, rather added to the interest. They had never known anything but struggle—with conquest—and twelve years of it was far from cooling their ardour for a fair fight.

More had been done in the Oil Regions in the first .dozen years than the development of a new industry. From the first there had gone with the oil men's ambition to make oil to light the whole earth a desire to bring civilisation to the wilderness from which they were drawing wealth, to create an orderly society from the mass of humanity which poured pell-mell into the region. A hatred of indecency first drew together the better element of each of the rough communities which sprang up. Whiskey-sellers and women flocked to the region at the breaking out of the excitement. Their first shelters were shanties built on flatboats which were towed from place to place. They came to Rouseville—a collection of pine shanties and oil derricks built on a muddy flat—as forlorn and disreputable a town in appearance as the earth ever saw. They tied up for trade, and the next morning woke up from their brawl to find themselves twenty miles away, floating down the Allegheny River. Rouseville meant to be decent. She had cut them loose, and by such summary vigilance she kept herself decent. Other towns adopted the same policy. By common consent vice was corralled largely in one town. Here a whole street was given up to dance-houses and saloons, and those who must have a "spree" were expected to go to Petroleum Centre to take it.

. . . Vice cut adrift, they looked for a school teacher. . . . It was not long, too, before there was a church, a union church. To worship God was their primal instinct; to defend a creed a later development. In the beginning every social contrivance was wanting. There were no policemen, and each individual looked after evil-doers. There were no firemen, and every man turned out with a bucket at a fire. There were no bankers, and each man had to put his wealth away as best he could until a per-ipatetic banker from Pittsburg relieved him. . . . There were no hospitals, and in 1861, when the horrible possibilities of the oil fire were first demonstrated by the burning of the Rouse well, a fire at which nineteen persons lost their lives, the many in-jured found welcome and care for long weeks in the little shan-ties of women already overburdened by the difficulties of caring for families in the rough community.

Out of this poverty and disorder they had developed in ten years a social organisation as good as their commercial. Titus-ville, the hamlet on whose outskirts Drake had drilled his well, was now a city of 10,000 inhabitants. It had an opera house, where in 1871 Clara Louise Kellogg and Christine Nilsson sang, Joe Jefferson and Janauschek played, and Wendell Phillips and Bishop Simpson spoke. It had two prosperous and fearless news-papers. Its schools prepared for college. Oil City was not behind, and between them was a string of lively towns. . . .

Indeed, by the opening of 1872, life in the Oil Regions had ceased to be a mere make-shift. Comforts and orderliness and decency, even opportunities for education and for social life, were within reach. It was a conquest to be proud of, quite as proud of as they were of the fact that their business had been developed until it had never before, on the whole, been in so satisfactory a condition.

Nobody realised more fully what had been accomplished in the Oil Regions than the oil men themselves. . . .

But what had been done was, in their judgment, only a be-ginning. Life ran swift and ruddy and joyous in these men. They were still young, most of them under forty, and they looked for-ward with all the eagerness of the young who have just learned their powers, to years of struggle and development. They would solve all these perplexing problems of over-production, of railroad discrimination, of speculation. They would meet their own needs. They would bring the oil refining to the region where it belonged. They would make their towns the most beautiful in the world. There was nothing too good for them, nothing they did not hope and dare. But suddenly, at the very heyday of this confidence, a big hand reached out from nobody knew where, to steal their conquest and throttle their future. The suddenness and the blackness of the assault on their business stirred to the bottom their manhood and their sense of fair play, and the whole region arose in a revolt which is scarcely paralleled in the commercial history of the United States.

2   THE RISE OF THE STANDARD OIL COMPANY

John D. Rockefeller's first connection with the oil business—Stories of his early life in Cleveland—His first partners—Organisation of the Standard Oil Company in June, 1870—Rockefeller's able associates—First evidence of railway discriminations in the oil business—Rebates found to be generally given to large shippers—First plan for a secret combination—The South Improvement Company—Secret contracts made with the railroads providing rebates and drawbacks—Rockefeller and associates force Cleveland refiners to join the new combination or sell—Rumour of the plan reaches the oil regions.

THE chief refining competitor of Oil Creek in 1872 was Cleveland, Ohio. Since 1869 that city had done annually more refining than any other place in the country. Strung along the banks of Walworth and Kingsbury Runs, the creeks to which the city frequently banishes her heavy and evil-smelling burdens, there had been since the early sixties from twenty to thirty oil refineries. . . . By rail and water Cleveland commanded the entire Western Market. It had two trunk lines running to New York, both eager for oil traffic, and by Lake Erie and the canal it had for a large part of the year a splendid cheap waterway. Thus, at the opening of the oil business, Cleveland was destined by geographical position to be a refining center.

Men saw it, and hastened to take advantage of the opportunity. There was grave risk. The oil supply might not hold out. As yet there was no certain market for refined oil. But a sure result was not what drew people into the oil business in the early sixties. Fortune was running fleet-footed across the country, and at her garment men clutched. They loved the chase almost as they did success, and so many a man in Cleveland tried his luck in an oil refinery, as hundreds on Oil Creek were trying it in an oil lease. . . .

Among the many young men of Cleveland who, from the start, had an eye on the oil-refining business and had begun to take an active part in its development as soon as it was demonstrated that there was a reasonable hope of its being permanent was. . . . John D. Rockefeller. He was but twenty-three years old when he first went into the oil business, but he had already got his feet firmly on the business ladder, and had got them there by his own efforts. The habit of driving good bargains and of saving money had started him. . . .

"Among the early experiences that were helpful to me that I recollect with pleasure was one in working a few days for a neighbour in digging potatoes—a very enterprising, thrifty farmer, who could dig a great many potatoes. I was a boy of perhaps thirteen or fourteen years of age, and it kept me very busy from morning until night. It was a ten-hour day. And as I was saving these little sums I soon learned that I could get as much interest for fifty dollars loaned at seven per cent.—the legal rate in the state of New York at that time for a year—as I could earn by digging potatoes for 100 days. The impression was gaining ground with me that it was a good thing to let the money be my slave and not make myself a slave to money." Here we have the foundation principles of a great financial career.

When young Rockefeller was thirteen years old, his father moved from the farm in Central New York, where the boy had been born (July 8, 1839), to a farm near Cleveland, Ohio. He went to school in Cleveland for three years. In 1855 it became necessary for him to earn his own living. It was a hard year in the West and the boy walked the streets for days looking for work. . . . "As good fortune would have it I went down to the dock and made one more application, and I was told that if I would come in after dinner—our noon-day meal was dinner in those days—they would see if I could come to work for them. I went down after dinner and I got the position, and I was permitted to remain in the city." The position, that of a clerk and bookkeeper, was not lucrative. According to a small ledger which has figured frequently in Mr. Rockefeller's religious instructions, he earned from September 26, 1855, to January, 1856, fifty dollars. "Out of that," Mr. Rockefeller told the young men of his Sunday-school class, "I paid my washerwoman and the lady I boarded with, and I saved a little money to put away."

He proved an admirable accountant—one of the early-and-late sort, who saw everything, forgot nothing and never talked. In 1856 his salary was raised to twenty-five dollars a month, and he went on always "saving a little money to put away." In 1858 came a chance to invest his savings. Among his acquaintances was a young Englishman, M. B. Clark. Older by twelve years than Rockefeller he had left a hard life in England when he was twenty to seek fortune in America. . . . They were two of a kind, Clark and Rockefeller, and in 1858 they pooled their earnings and started a produce commission business on the Cleveland docks. The venture succeeded. Local historians credit Clark and Rockefeller with doing a business of $450,000 the first year. The war came on, and as neither partner went to the front, they had full chance to take advantage of the opportunity for produce business a great army gives. A greater chance than furnishing army supplies . . . was in the oil business . . . and in 1862, when an Englishman of ability and energy, one Samuel Andrews, asked them to back him in starting a refinery, they put in $4,000 and promised to give more if necessary. Now Andrews was a mechanical genius. He devised new processes, made a better and better quality of oil, got larger and larger percentages of refined from his crude. The little refinery grew big, and Clark and Rockefeller soon had $100,000 or more in it. In the meantime Cleveland was growing as a refining centre. The business which in 1860 had been a gamble was by 1865 one of the most promising industries of the town. It was but the beginning—so Mr. Rockefeller thought—and in that year he sold out his share of the commission business and put his money into the oil firm of Rockefeller and Andrews.

In the new firm Andrews attended to the manufacturing. The pushing of the business, the buying and the selling, fell to Rockefeller. From the start his effect was tremendous. He had the frugal man's hatred of waste and disorder, of middlemen and unnecessary manipulation, and he began a vigorous elimination of these from his business. The residuum that other refineries let run into the ground, he sold. Old iron found its way to the junk shop. He bought his oil directly from the wells. He made his own barrels. He watched and saved and contrived. The ability with which he made the smallest bargain furnishes topics to Cleveland story-tellers to-day. Low-voiced, soft-footed, humble, knowing every point in every man's business, he never tired until he got his wares at the lowest possible figure. . . . To drive a good bargain was the joy of his life. "The only time I ever saw John Rockefeller enthusiastic," a man told the writer once, "was when a report came in from the creek that his buyer had secured a cargo of oil at a figure much below the market price. He bounded from his chair with a shout of joy, danced up and down, hugged me, threw up his hat, acted so like a madman that I have never forgotten it." . . .

These qualities told. The firm grew as rapidly as the oil business of the town, and started a second refinery—William A. Rockefeller and Company. They took in a partner, H. M. Flagler, and opened a house in New York for selling oil. Of all these concerns John D. Rockefeller was the head. Finally, in June, 1870, five years after he became an active partner in the refining business, Mr. Rockefeller combined all his companies into one—the Standard Oil Company. The capital of the new concern was $1,000,000. The parties interested in it were John D. Rockefeller, Henry M. Flagler, Samuel Andrews, Stephen V. Harkness, and William Rockefeller.

The strides the firm of Rockefeller and Andrews made . . . were attributed for three or four years mainly to his extraordinary capacity for bargaining and borrowing. Then its chief competitors began to suspect something. . . . They believed they bought, on the whole, almost as cheaply as he, and they knew they made as good oil and with as great, or nearly as great, economy. He could sell at no better price than they. Where was his advantage? There was but one place where it could be, and that was in transportation. He must be getting better rates from the railroads than they were. In 1868 or 1869 a member of a rival firm long in the business, which had been prosperous from the start, and which prided itself on its methods, its economy and its energy, Alexander, Scofield and Company, went to the Atlantic and Great Western road, then under the Erie management, and complained. "You are giving others better rates than you are us," said Mr. Alexander, the representative of the firm. "We cannot compete if you do that." The railroad agent did not attempt to deny it—he simply agreed to give Mr. Alexander a rebate also. The arrangement was interesting. Mr. Alexander was to pay the open, or regular, rate on oil from the Oil Regions to Cleveland, which was then forty cents a barrel. At the end of each month he was to send to the railroad vouchers for the amount of oil shipped and paid for at forty cents, and was to get back from the railroad, in money, fifteen cents on each barrel. . . . Mr. Alexander claims he was never able to get his rate lowered on his Eastern shipments. The railroad took the position with him that if he could ship as much oil as the Standard he could have as low a rate, but not otherwise. Now in 1870 the Standard Oil Company had a daily capacity of about 1,500 barrels of crude. The refinery was the largest in the town, though it had some close competitors. Nevertheless on the strength of its large capacity it received the special favour. It was a plausible way to get around the theory generally held then, as now, though not so definitely crystallised into law, that the railroad being a common carrier had no right to discriminate between its patrons. . . .

It would seem from the above as if the one man in the Cleveland oil trade in 1870 who ought to have been satisfied was Mr. Rockefeller. . . . Not only did Mr. Rockefeller control the largest firm in this most prosperous centre of a prosperous business, he controlled one of amazing efficiency. The combination, in 1870, of the various companies with which he was connected had brought together a group of remarkable men. Samuel Andrews, by all accounts, was the ablest mechanical superintendent in Cleveland. William Rockefeller, the brother of John D. Rockefeller, was not only an energetic and intelligent business man, he was a man whom people liked. He was open-hearted, jolly, a good story-teller, a man who knew and liked a good horse— not too pious, as some of John's business associates thought him, not a man to suspect or fear, as many a man did John. Old oil men will tell you on the creek to-day how much they liked him in the days when he used to come to Oil City buying oil for the Cleveland firm. The personal quality of William Rockefeller was, and always has been, a strong asset of the Standard Oil Company. Probably the strongest man in the firm after John D. Rockefeller was Henry M. Flagler. He was, like the others, a young man, and one who, like the head of the firm, had the passion for money, and in a hard self-supporting experience . . . had learned . . . some of the principles of making it. He was untiring in his efforts to increase the business, quick to see an advantage, as quick to take it. . . . He was not a secretive man, like John D. Rockefeller, not a dreamer, but he could keep his mouth shut when necessary and he knew the worth of a financial dream when it was laid before him. It must have been evident to every business man who came in contact with the young Standard Oil Company that it would go far. The firm itself must have known it would go far. . . .

With such a set of associates, with his organisation complete from his buyers on the creek to his exporting agent in New York, with the transportation advantages which none of his competitors had had the daring or the persuasive power to get, certainly Mr. Rockefeller should have been satisfied in 1870. But Mr. Rockefeller was far from satisfied. He was a brooding, cautious, secretive man, seeing all the possible dangers as well as all the possible opportunities in things, and he studied, as a player at chess, all the possible combinations which might imperil his supremacy. These twenty-five Cleveland rivals of his —how could he at once and forever put them out of the game? He and his partners had somehow conceived a great idea—the advantages of combination. What might they not do if they could buy out and absorb the big refineries now competing with them in Cleveland? The possibilities of the idea grew as they discussed it. Finally they began tentatively to sound some of their rivals. But there were other rivals than these at home. There were the creek refiners! They were there at the mouth of the wells. What might not this geographical advantage do in time? Refining was going on there on an increasing scale; the capacity of the Oil Regions had indeed risen to nearly 10,000 barrels a day—equal to that of New York, exceeding that of Pittsburg by nearly 4,000 barrels, and almost equalling that of Cleveland. The men of the oil country loudly declared that they meant to refine for the world. They boasted of an oil kingdom which eventually should handle the entire business and compel Cleveland and Pittsburg either to abandon their works or bring them to the oil country. In this boastful ambition they were encouraged particularly by the Pennsylvania Railroad, which naturally handled the largest percentage of the oil. How long could the Standard Oil Company stand against this competition?

There was another interest as deeply concerned as Mr. Rockefeller in preserving Cleveland's supremacy as a refining centre, and this was the Lake Shore and New York Central Railroads. Let the bulk of refining be done in the Oil Regions and these roads were in danger of losing a profitable branch of business. . . .

As competition grew between the roads, they grew more reckless in granting rebates, the refiners more insistent in demanding them. . . .

Under these conditions of competition it was certain that the New York Central system must work if it was to keep its great oil freight, and the general freight agent of the Lake Shore road began to give the question special attention. This man was Peter H. Watson. Mr. Watson was an able patent lawyer who served under the strenuous Stanton as an Assistant-Secretary of War, and served well. After the war he had been made general freight agent of the Lake Shore and Michigan Southern Railroad, and later president of the branch of that road which ran into the Oil Regions. He had oil interests principally at Franklin, Pennsylvania, and was well known to all oil men. . . . As the Standard Oil Company was the largest shipper in Cleveland and had already received the special favour from the Lake Shore which General Devereux describes, it was natural that Mr. Watson should consult frequently with Mr. Rockefeller on the question of holding and increasing his oil freight. . . . But while the menace in their geographical positions was the first ground of sympathy between these gentlemen, something more than local troubles occupied them. This was the condition of the refining business as a whole. . . . First, it was overdone. The great profits on refined oil and the growing demand for it had naturally caused a great number to rush into its manufacture. . . . The result was that the price of refined oil was steadily falling. Where Mr. Rockefeller had received on an average 58¾ cents a gallon for the oil he exported in 1865, the year he went into business, in 1870 he received but 26⅜ cents. In 1865 he had a margin of forty-three cents, out of which to pay for transportation, manufacturing, barrelling and marketing and to make his profits. In 1870 he had but 17⅛ cents with which to do all this. To be sure his expenses had fallen enormously between 1865 and 1870 but so had his profits. The multiplication of refiners with the intense competition threatened to cut them down still lower. Naturally Mr. Rockefeller and his friends looked with dismay on this lowering of profits through gaining competition.

Another anxiety of the American refiners was the condition of the export trade. Oil had risen to fourth place in the exports of the United States in the twelve years since its discovery, and every year larger quantities were consumed abroad, but it was crude oil, not refined, which the foreigners were beginning to demand; that is, they had found they could import crude, refine it at home, and sell it cheaper than they could buy American refined. France, to encourage her home refineries, had even put a tax on American refined.

In the fall of 1871, while Mr. Rockefeller and his friends were occupied with all these questions, certain Pennsylvania refiners, it is not too certain who, brought to them a remarkable scheme, the gist of which was to bring together secretly a large enough body of refiners and shippers to persuade all the railroads handling oil to give the company formed special rebates on its oil, and drawbacks on that of other people. If they could get such rates it was evident that those outside of their combination could not compete with them long and that they would become eventually the only refiners. They could then limit their output to actual demand, and so keep up prices. This done, they could easily persuade the railroads to transport no crude for exportation, so that the foreigners would be forced to buy American refined. They believed that the price of oil thus exported could easily be advanced fifty per cent. The control of the refining interests would also enable them to fix their own price on crude. As they would be the only buyers and sellers, the speculative character of the business would be done away with. In short, the scheme they worked out put the entire oil business in their hands. . . .

The first thing was to get a charter—quietly. At a meeting held in Philadelphia late in the fall of 1871 a friend of one of the gentlemen interested mentioned to him that a certain estate then in liquidation had a charter for sale which gave its owners the right to carry on any kind of business in any country and in any way; that it could be bought for what it would cost to get a charter under the general laws of the state, and that it would be a favour to the heirs to buy it. The opportunity was promptly taken. The name of the charter bought was the "South (often written Southern) Improvement Company." For a beginning it was as good a name as another, since it said nothing. . . .

Mr. Watson was elected president and W. G. Warden of Philadelphia secretary of the new association. . . . The company most heavily interested in the South Improvement Company was the Standard Oil of Cleveland. . . .

It has frequently been stated that the South Improvement Company represented the bulk of the oil-refining interests in the country. The incorporators of the company in approaching the railroads assured them that this was so. As a matter of fact . . . the thirteen gentlemen . . . who were the only ones ever holding stock in the concern, did not control over one-tenth of the refining business of the United States in 1872. That business in the aggregate amounted to a daily capacity of about 45,000 barrels . . . and the stockholders of the South Improvement Company owned a combined capacity of not over 4,600 barrels. In assuring the railroads that they controlled the business, they were dealing with their hopes rather than with facts.

The organisation complete, there remained contracts to be made with the railroads. Three systems were to be interested: The Central, which, by its connection with the Lake Shore and Michigan Southern, ran directly into the Oil Regions; the Erie, allied with the Atlantic and Great Western, with a short line likewise tapping the heart of the region; and the Pennsylvania, with the connections known as the Allegheny Valley and Oil Creek Railroad. The persons to be won over were: W. H. Vanderbilt, of the Central; H. F. Clark, president of the Lake Shore and Michigan Southern; Jay Gould, of the Erie; General G. B. McClellan, president of the Atlantic and Great Western; and Tom Scott, of the Pennsylvania. There seems to have been little difficulty in persuading any of these persons to go into the scheme after they had been assured by the leaders that all of the refiners were to be taken in. This was a verbal condition, however; not found in the contracts they signed. . . .

A second objection to making a contract with the company came from Mr. Scott of the Pennsylvania road and Mr. Potts of the Empire Transportation Company. The substance of this objection was that the plan took no account of the oil producer —the man to whom the world owed the business. Mr. Scott was strong in his assertion that they could never succeed unless they took care of the producers. . . . So strongly did Mr. Scott argue . . . that finally the members of the South Improvement Company yielded, and a draft of an agreement, to be proposed to the producers, was drawn up in lead-pencil; it was never presented. It seems to have been used principally to quiet Mr. Scott.

The work of persuasion went on swiftly. By the 18th of January the president of the Pennsylvania road, J. Edgar Thompson, had put his signature to the contract, and soon after Mr. Vanderbilt and Mr. Clark signed for the Central system, and Jay Gould and General McClellan for the Erie. The contracts to which these gentlemen put their names fixed gross rates of freight from all *common points*, as the leading shipping points within the Oil Regions were called, to all the great refining and shipping centres—New York, Philadelphia, Baltimore, Pittsburg and Cleveland. For example, the open rate on crude to New York was put at $2.56. On this price the South Improvement Company was allowed a rebate of $1.06 for its shipments; but it got not only this rebate, it was given in cash a like amount on each barrel of crude shipped by parties outside the combination.

The open rate from Cleveland to New York was two dollars, and fifty cents of this was turned over to the South Improvement Company, which at the same time received a rebate enabling it to ship for $1.50. Again, an independent refiner in Cleveland paid eighty cents a barrel to get his crude from the Oil Regions to his works, and the railroad sent forty cents of this money to the South Improvement Company. At the same time it cost the Cleveland refiner in the combination but forty cents to get his crude oil. Like drawbacks and rebates were given for all points—Pittsburg, Philadelphia, Boston and Baltimore.

An interesting provision in the contracts was that full waybills of all petroleum shipped over the roads should each day be sent to the South Improvement Company. This, of course, gave them knowledge of just who was doing business outside of their company—of how much business he was doing, and with whom he was doing it. Not only were they to have full knowledge of the business of all shippers—they were to have access to all books of the railroads.

The parties to the contracts agreed that if anybody appeared in the business offering an equal amount of transportation, and having equal facilities for doing business with the South Improvement Company, the railroads might give them equal advantages in drawbacks and rebates, but to make such a miscarriage of the scheme doubly improbable each railroad was bound to co-operate as "far as it legally might to maintain the business of the South Improvement Company against injury by competition, and lower or raise the gross rates of transportation for such times and to such extent as might be necessary to overcome the competition. The rebates and drawbacks to be varied *pari passu* with the gross rates."

The reason given by the railroads in the contract for granting these extraordinary privileges was that the "magnitude and extent of the business and operations" purposed to be carried on by the South Improvement Company would greatly promote the interest of the railroads and make it desirable for them to encourage their undertaking. The evident advantages received by the railroad were a regular amount of freight,—the Pennsylvania was to have forty-five per cent. of the East-bound shipments, the Erie and Central each 27½ per cent., while West-bound freight was to be divided equally between them—fixed rates, and freedom from the system of cutting which they had all found so harassing and disastrous. That is, the South Improvement Company, which was to include the entire refining capacity of the company, was to act as the evener of the oil business.

It was on the second of January, 1872, that the organisation of the South Improvement Company was completed. . . . There were at that time some twenty-six refineries in the town—some of them very large plants. All of them were feeling more or less the discouraging effects of the last three or four years of railroad discriminations in favour of the Standard Oil Company. To the owners of these refineries Mr. Rockefeller now went one by one, and explained the South Improvement Company. "You see," he told them, "this scheme is bound to work. It means an absolute control by us of the oil business. There is no chance for anyone outside. But we are going to give everybody a chance to come in. You are to turn over your refinery to my appraisers, and I will give you Standard Oil Company stock or cash, as you prefer, for the value we put upon it. I advise you to take the stock. It will be for your good." Certain refiners objected. They did not want to sell. They did want to keep and manage their business. Mr. Rockefeller was regretful, but firm. It was useless to resist, he told the hesitating; they would certainly be crushed if they did not accept his offer, and he pointed out in detail, and with gentleness, how beneficent the scheme really was—preventing the creek refiners from destroying Cleveland, ending competition, keeping up the price of refined oil, and eliminating speculation. Really a wonderful contrivance for the good of the oil business. . . .

A few of the refiners contested before surrendering. Among these was Robert Hanna, an uncle of Mark Hanna, of the firm of Hanna, Baslington and Company. Mr. Hanna had been refining since July, 1869. According to his own sworn statement he had made money, fully sixty per cent. on his investment the first year, and after that thirty per cent. Some time in February, 1872, the Standard Oil Company asked an interview with him and his associates. They wanted to buy his works, they said. "But we don't want to sell," objected Mr. Hanna. "You can never make any more money, in my judgment," said Mr. Rockefeller. "You can't compete with the Standard. We have all the large refineries now. If you refuse to sell, it will end in your being crushed." Hanna and Baslington were not satisfied. They went to see Mr. Watson, president of the South Improvement Company and an officer of the Lake Shore, and General Devereux, manager of the Lake Shore road. They were told that the Standard had special rates; that it was useless to try to compete with them. General Devereux explained to the gentlemen that the privileges granted the Standard were the legitimate and necessary advantage of the larger shipper over the smaller, and that if Hanna, Baslington and Company could give the road as large a quantity of oil as the Standard did, with the same regularity, they could have the same rate. General Devereux says they "recognised the propriety" of his excuse. They certainly recognised its authority. They say that they were satisfied they could no longer get rates to and from Cleveland which would enable them to live, and "reluctantly" sold out. It must have been reluctantly, for they had paid $75,000 for their works, and had made thirty per cent. a year on an average on their investment, and the Standard appraiser allowed them $45,000. "Truly and really less than one-half of what they were absolutely worth, with a fair and honest competition in the lines of transportation," said Mr. Hanna, eight years later, in an affidavit.

Under the combined threat and persuasion of the Standard, armed with the South Improvement Company scheme, almost the entire independent oil interest of Cleveland, collapsed in three months' time. Of the twenty-six refineries, at least twenty-one sold out. From a capacity of probably not over 1,500 barrels of crude a day, the Standard Oil Company rose in three months' time to one of 10,000 barrels. By this manœuvre it became master of over one-fifth of the refining capacity of the United States. . . .

3   THE OIL WAR OF 1872

Rising in the oil regions against the South Improvement Company—
Petroleum Producers' Union organised—Oil blockade against members of
South Improvement Company and against railroads implicated—Congressional investigation of 1872 and the documents it revealed—Public
discussion and general condemnation of the South Improvement Company—Railroad officials confer with committee from Petroleum Producers'
Union—Watson and Rockefeller refused admittance to conference—Railroads revoke contracts with South Improvement Company and make
contract with Petroleum Producers' Union—Blockade against South Improvement Company lifted—Oil War officially ended—Rockefeller con-
tinues to get rebates—His great plan still a living purpose.

IT WAS not until after the middle of February, 1872
that the people of the Oil Regions heard anything of the plan
which was being worked out for their "good." Then an uneasy
rumour began running up and down the creek. Freight rates
were going up. Now an advance in a man's freight bill may ruin
his business; more, it may mean the ruin of a region. Rumour
said that the new rate meant just this; that is, that it more than
covered the margin of profit in any branch of the oil business.
The railroads were not going to apply the proposed tariffs to
everybody. They had agreed to give to a company unheard of
until now—the South Improvement Company—a special rate
considerably lower than the new open rate. . . .

On the morning of February 26, 1872, the oil men read in their
morning papers that the rise which had been threatening had
come; moreover, that all members of the South Improvement
Company were exempt from the advance. . . .

In twenty-four hours after the announcement of the increase
in freight rates a mass-meeting of 3,000 excited, gesticulating
oil men was gathered in the opera house at Titusville. Producers,
brokers, refiners, drillers, pumpers were in the crowd. Their
temper was shown by the mottoes on the banners which they
carried: "Down with the conspirators"—"No compromise"—
"Don't give up the ship!" Three days later as large a meeting
was held at Oil City, its temper more warlike if possible; and so
it went. They organised a Petroleum Producers' Union, pledged

themselves to reduce their production by starting no new wells for sixty days and by shutting down on Sundays, to sell no oil to any person known to be in the South Improvement Company, but to support the creek refiners and those elsewhere who had refused to go into the combination, to boycott the offending railroads, and to build lines which they would own and control themselves. They sent a committee to the Legislature asking that the charter of the South Improvement Company be repealed, and another to Congress demanding an investigation of the whole business on the ground that it was an interference with trade. They ordered that a history of the conspiracy, giving the names of the conspirators and the designs of the company, should be prepared, and 30,000 copies sent to "judges of all courts, senators of the United States, members of Congress and of State Legislatures, and to all railroad men and prominent business men of the country, *to the end that enemies of the freedom of trade may be known and shunned by all honest men."*

They prepared a petition ninety-three feet long praying for a free pipe-line bill, something which they had long wanted, but which, so far, the Pennsylvania Railroad had prevented their getting, and sent it by a committee to the Legislature; and for days they kept 1,000 men ready to march on Harrisburg at a moment's notice if the Legislature showed signs of refusing their demands. In short, for weeks the whole body of oil men abandoned regular business and surged from town to town intent on destroying the "Monster," the "Forty Thieves," the "Great Anaconda," as they called the mysterious South Improvement Company. Curiously enough, it was chiefly against the combination which had secured the discrimination from the railroads—not the railroads which had granted it—that their fury was directed. They expected nothing but robbery from the railroads, they said. They were used to that; but they would not endure it from men in their own business. . . .

Naturally the burning question throughout the Oil Regions . . . was, Who are the conspirators? Whether the gentlemen concerned regarded themselves in the light of "conspirators" or not, they seem from the first to have realised that it would be discreet not to be identified publicly with the scheme, and to have allowed one name alone to appear in all signed negotiations. This was the name of the president, Peter H. Watson. However anxious the members of the South Improvement Company were that Mr. Watson should combine the honours of president with the trials of the scapegoat, it was impossible to keep their names concealed. The Oil City Derrick, at that time one of the most vigorous, witty, and daring newspapers in the country, began a black list at the head of its editorial columns the day after the raise in freight was announced, and it kept it there until it was believed complete.

All of these refineries had their buyers on the creek, and all though several of them were young men generally liked for their personal and business qualities, no mercy was shown them. They were refused oil by everybody, though they offered from seventy-five cents to a dollar more than the market price. . . .

The stopping of the oil supply finally forced the South Improvement Company to recognise the Producers' Union officially by asking that a committee of the body be appointed to confer with them on a compromise. The producers sent back a pertinent answer. They believed the South Improvement Company meant to monopolise the oil business. If that was so they could not consider a compromise with it. If they were wrong, they would be glad to be enlightened, and they asked for information. First: the charter under which the South Improvement Company was organised. Second: the articles of association. Third: the officers' names. Fourth: the contracts with the railroads which signed them. Fifth: the general plan of management. Until we know these things, the oil men declared, we can no more negotiate with you than we could sit down to negotiate with a burglar as to his privileges in our house.

The Producers' Union did not get the information they asked from the company at that time, but it was not long before they had it, and much more. The committee which they had appointed to write a history of the South Improvement Company reported on March 20, and in April the Congressional Committee appointed at the insistence of the oil men made its investigation. . . .

When the course of this charter through the Pennsylvania Legislature came to be traced, it was found to be devious and uncertain. The company had been incorporated in 1871, and vested with all the "powers, privileges, duties and obligations" of an earlier company—incorporated in April, 1870—the Pennsylvania Company; both of them were children of that interesting body known as the "Tom Scott Legislature." The act incorporating the company was not published until after the oil war; its sponsor was never known, and no votes on it are recorded. The origin of the South Improvement Company has always remained in darkness. It was one of several "improvement" companies chartered in Pennsylvania at about the same time, and enjoying the same commercial *carte blanche*.

Bad as the charter was in appearance, the oil men found that the contracts which the new company had made with the railroads were worse. These contracts advanced the rates of freight from the Oil Regions over 100 per cent.—an advance which more than covered the margin of profit on their business—but it was not the railroad that got the greater part of this advance; it was the South Improvement Company. Not only did it ship its own oil at fully a dollar a barrel cheaper on an average than anybody else could, but it received fully a dollar a barrel "rake-off" on every barrel its competitors shipped. It was computed and admitted by the members of the company who appeared before the investigating committee of Congress that this discrimination would have turned over to them fully $6,000,000 annually on the carrying trade. The railroads expected to receive about one and a half millions more than from the existing rates. That is, an additional cost of about $1.25 a barrel was added to crude oil, and it was computed that this would enable the refiners to advance their wholesale price at least four cents a gallon. It is hardly to be wondered at that when the oil men had before them the full text of these contracts they refused absolutely to accept the repeated assertions of the members of the South Improvement Company that their scheme was intended only for "the good of the oil business." The committee of Congress could not be persuaded to believe it either. "Your success meant the destruction of every refiner who refused for any reason to join your company, or whom you did not care to have in, and it put the producers entirely in your power. It would make a monopoly such as no set of men are fit to handle," the chairman of the committee declared. . . .

No part of the testimony before the committee made a worse impression than that showing that the chief object of the combination was to put up the price of refined oil to the consumer, though nobody had denied from the first that this was the purpose. . . .

Mr. Watson contended that the price could be put up with

benefit to the consumer. And when he was asked how, he replied: "By steadying the trade. You will notice what all those familiar with this trade know, that there are very rapid and excessive fluctuations in the oil market; that when these fluctuations take place the retail dealers are always quick to note a rise in price, but very slow to note a fall. Even if two dollars a barrel had been added to the price of oil under a steady trade, I think the price of the retail purchaser would not have been increased. That increased price would only amount to one cent a quart (four cents a gallon), and I think the price would not have been increased to the retail dealer because the fluctuations would have been avoided. That was one object to be accomplished."

The committee were not convinced, however, that a scheme which began by adding four cents to the price of a gallon of oil could be to the good of the consumer. Nor did anything appear in the contracts which showed how the fluctuations in the price of oil were to be avoided. These fluctuations were due to the rise and fall in the crude market, and that depended on the amount of crude coming from the ground. The South Improvement Company might assert that they meant to bring the producers into their scheme and persuade them to keep down the amount of production in the same way they meant to keep down refined, so that the price could be kept steadily high, but they had nothing to prove that they were sincere in the intention, nothing to prove that they had thought of the producer seriously until the trouble in the Oil Regions began. . . . It was robbery, cried the newspapers all over the land. "Under the thin guise of assisting in the development of oil-refining in Pittsburg and Cleveland," said the New York Tribune, "this corporation has simply laid its hand upon the throat of the oil traffic with a demand to 'stand and deliver.'" And if this could be done in the oil business, what was to prevent its being done in any other industry? Why should not a company be formed to control wheat or beef or iron or steel, as well as oil? If the railroads would do this for one company, why not for another? The South Improvement Company, men agreed, was a menace to the free trade of the country. If the oil men yielded now, all industries must suffer from their weakness. The railroads must be taught a lesson as well as would-be monopolists.

The oil men had no thought of yielding. With every day of the war their backbone grew stiffer. The men were calmer, too, for their resistance had found a ground which seemed impregnable to them, and arguments against the South Improvement Company now took the place of denunciations. On all sides men said, This is a transportation question, and now is the time to put an end once and forever to the rebates. . . . The Petroleum Producers' Union which had been formed to grapple with the "Monster" actually demanded interstate regulation, for in a circular sent out to newspapers and boards of trade asking their aid against the conspiracy they included this paragraph: "We urge you to exert all your influence with your representatives in Congress to support such measures offered there as will prohibit for all future time any monopoly of railroads or other transportation companies from laying embargoes upon the trade between states by a system of excessive freights or unjust discrimination against buyers or shippers in any trade by the allowance of rebates or drawbacks to any persons whatever. This is a matter of national importance, and only the most decided action can protect you and us from the scheming strength of these monopolies." . . .

The railroads tried in various ways to appease the oil men. They did not enforce the new rates. They had signed the contracts, they declared, only after the South Improvement Company had assured them that all the refineries and producers were to be taken in. Indeed, they seem to have realised within a fortnight that the scheme was doomed, and to have been quite ready to meet cordially a committee of oil men which went East to demand that the railroads revoke their contracts with the South Improvement Company. . . .

The final all-important conference with the railroad men was held on March 25, at the Erie offices. Horace Clark, president of the Lake Shore and Michigan Southern Railroad, was chairman of this meeting, and, according to H. H. Rogers' testimony before the Hepburn Committee, in 1879, there were present, besides the oil men, Colonel Scott, General McClellan, Director Diven, William H. Vanderbilt, Mr. Stebbins, and George Hall. The meeting had not been long in session before Mr. Watson, president of the South Improvement Company, and John D. Rockefeller presented themselves for admission. Up to this time Mr. Rockefeller had kept well out of sight in the affair. He had given no interviews, offered no explanations. He had allowed the president of the company to wrestle with the excitement in his own way, but things were now in such critical shape that he came forward in a last attempt to save the organisation by which he had been able to concentrate in his own hands the refining interests of Cleveland. With Mr. Watson he knocked for admission to the council going on in the Erie offices. The oil men flatly refused to let them in. A dramatic scene followed, Mr. Clark, the chairman, protesting in agitated tones against shutting out his "life-long friend, Watson." The oil men were obdurate. They would have nothing to do with anybody concerned with the South Improvement Company. So determined were they that although Mr. Watson came in he was obliged at once to withdraw. A Times reporter who witnessed the little scene between the two supporters of the tottering company after its president was turned out of the meeting remarked sympathetically that Mr. Rockefeller soon went away, "looking pretty blue." . . . So well did the committee fight its battle and so strongly were they supported by the New York refiners that the railroads were finally obliged to consent to revoke the contracts and to make a new one embodying the views of the Oil Regions. The contract finally signed at this meeting . . . agreed that all shipping of oil should be made on "a basis of perfect equality to all shippers, producers, and refiners, and that no rebates, drawbacks, or other arrangements of any character shall be made or allowed that will give any party the slightest difference in rates or discriminations of any character whatever." It was also agreed that the rates should not be liable to change either for increase or decrease without first giving William Hasson, president of the Producers' Union, at least ninety days' notice.

The same rate was put on refined oil from Cleveland, Pittsburg and the creek, to Eastern shipping points; that is, Mr. Rockefeller could send his oil from Cleveland to New York at $1.50 per barrel; so could his associates in Pittsburg; and this was what it cost the refiner on the creek; but the latter had this advantage: he was at the wells. Mr. Rockefeller and his Pittsburg allies were miles away, and it cost them, by the new contract, fifty cents to get a barrel of crude to their works. The Oil Regions meant that geographical position should count, that the advantages Mr. Rockefeller had by his command of the Western market and by his access to a cheap Eastward waterway should be considered as well as their own position beside the raw product.

This contract was the first effective thrust into the great bubble. Others followed in quick succession. On the 28th the railroads officially annulled their contracts with the company. About the same time the Pennsylvania Legislature repealed the charter. On March 30 the committee of oil men sent to Washington to be present during the Congressional Investigation, now about to begin, spent an hour with President Grant. They wired home that on their departure he said: "Gentlemen, I have noticed the progress of monopolies, and have long been convinced that the national government would have to interfere and protect the people against them." The President and the members of Congress of both parties continued to show interest in the investigation, and there was little or no dissent from the final judgment of the committee, given early in May, that the South Improvement Company was the "most gigantic and daring conspiracy" a free country had ever seen. This decision finished the work. The "Monster" was slain, the Oil Regions proclaimed exultantly. . . . No triumph could stifle the suspicion and the bitterness which had been sown broadcast through the region. Every particle of independent manhood in these men whose very life was independent action had been outraged. Their sense of fair play, the saving force of the region in the days before law and order had been established, had been violated. These were things which could not be forgotten. There henceforth could be no trust in those who had devised a scheme which, the producers believed, was intended to rob them of their property.

It was inevitable that under the pressure of their indignation and resentment some person or persons should be fixed upon as responsible, and should be hated accordingly. Before the lifting of the embargo this responsibility had been fixed. It was the Standard Oil Company of Cleveland, so the Oil Regions decided, which was at the bottom of the business, and the "Mephistopheles of the Cleveland company," as they put it, was John D. Rockefeller. . . . But what did more than anything else to fix the conviction was what they had learned of the career of the Standard Oil Company in Cleveland. Before the Oil War the company had been known simply as one of several successful firms in that city. It drove close bargains, but it paid promptly, and was considered a desirable customer. Now the Oil Regions learned for the first time of the sudden and phenomenal expansion of the company. Where there had been at the beginning of

1872 twenty-six refining firms in Cleveland, there were but six left. In three months before and during the Oil War the Standard had absorbed twenty plants. . . . "Why," cried the oil men, "the Standard Oil Company has done already in Cleveland what the South Improvement Company set out to do for the whole country, and it has done it by the same means."

By the time the blockade was raised, another unhappy conviction was fixed on the Oil Regions—the Standard Oil Company meant to carry out the plans of the exploded South Improvement Company. The promoters of the scheme were partly responsible for the report. Under the smart of their defeat they talked rather more freely than their policy of silence justified, and their remarks were quoted widely. Mr. Rockefeller was reported in the Derrick to have said to a prominent oil man of Oil City that the South Improvement Company could work under the charter of the Standard Oil Company, and to have predicted that in less than two months the gentlemen would be glad to join him. . . . The effect of these reports in the Oil Regions was most disastrous. Their open war became a kind of guerilla opposition. Those who sold oil to the Standard were ostracised, and its president was openly scored.

If Mr. Rockefeller had been an ordinary man the outburst of popular contempt and suspicion which suddenly poured on his head would have thwarted and crushed him. But he was no ordinary man. He had the powerful imagination to see what might be done with the oil business if it could be centered in his hands —the intelligence to analyse the problem into its elements and to find the key to control. He had the essential element of all great achievement, a steadfastness to a purpose once conceived which nothing can crush. The Oil Regions might rage, call him a conspirator, and all those who sold him oil, traitors; the railroads might withdraw their contracts and the Legislature annul his charter; undisturbed and unresting he kept at his great purpose. Even if his nature had not been such as to forbid him to abandon an enterprise in which he saw promise of vast profits, even if he had not had a mind which, stopped by a wall, burrows under or creeps around, he would nevertheless have been forced to desperate efforts to keep up his business. He had increased his refining capacity in Cleveland to 10,000 barrels on the strength of the South Improvement Company contracts. These contracts were annulled, and in their place was one signed by officials of all the oil-shipping roads refusing rebates to every-body. His geographical position was such that it cost him under these new contracts fifty cents more to get oil from the wells to New York than it did his rivals on the creek. True, he had many counterbalancing advantages—a growing Western market almost entirely in his hands, lake traffic, close proximity to all sorts of accessories to his manufacturing, but this contract put him on a level with his rivals. By his size he should have better terms than they. What did he do?

He got a rebate. Seven years later Mr. Rockefeller's partner, H. M. Flagler, was called before a commission of the Ohio State Legislature appointed to investigate railroads. He was asked for the former contracts between his company and the railroads, and among others he presented one showing that from "the first of April until the middle of November, 1872," their East-bound rate was $1.25, twenty-five cents less than that set by the agreement of March 25th, between the oil men and the railroads. . . . How had Mr. Rockefeller been able to get this rebate? Simply as he had always done—by virtue of the quantity he shipped. He was able to say to Mr. Vanderbilt, I can make a contract to ship sixty carloads of oil a day over your road—nearly 4,800 barrels: I cannot give this to you regularly unless you will make me a concession; and Mr. Vanderbilt made the concession while he was signing the contract with the oil men. Of course the rate was secret, and Mr. Rockefeller probably understood now, as he had not two months before, how essential it was that he keep it secret. His task was more difficult now, for he had an enemy active, clamorous, contemptuous, whose suspicions had reached that acute point where they could believe nothing but evil of him—the producers and independent refiners of the Oil Regions. . . .

They believed in independent effort—every man for himself and fair play for all. They wanted competition, loved open fight. They considered that all business should be done openly; that the railways were bound as public carriers to give equal rates; that any combination which favoured one firm or one locality at the expense of another was unjust and illegal. This belief long held by many of the oil men had been crystallised by the uprising into a common sentiment. It had become the moral code of the region.

Mr. Rockefeller's point of view was different. He believed that the "good of all" was in a combination which would control the business as the South Improvement Company proposed to control it. Such a combination would end at once all the abuses the business suffered. As rebates and special rates were essential to this control, he favoured them. Of course Mr. Rockefeller must have known that the railroad was a common carrier, and that the common law forbade discrimination. But he knew that the railroads had not obeyed the laws governing them, that they had regularly granted special rates and rebates to those who had large amounts of freight. . . . Moreover, Mr. Rockefeller probably believed that, in spite of the agreements, if he did not get rebates somebody else would; that they were for the wariest, the shrewdest, the most persistent. If somebody was to get rebates, why not he? This point of view was no uncommon one. Many men held it and felt a sort of scorn, as practical men always do for theorists, when it was contended that the shipper was as wrong in taking rates as the railroads in granting them. . . .

This lack of comprehension by many men of what seems to other men to be the most obvious principles of justice is not rare. Many men who are widely known as good, share it. Mr. Rockefeller was "good." There was no more faithful Baptist in Cleveland than he. Every enterprise of that church he had supported liberally from his youth. He gave to its poor. He visited its sick. He wept with its suffering. Moreover, he gave unostentatiously to many outside charities of whose worthiness he was satisfied. He was simple and frugal in his habits. He never went to the theatre, never drank wine. He gave much time to the training of his children, seeking to develop in them his own habits of economy and of charity. Yet he was willing to strain every nerve to obtain for himself special and unjust privileges from the railroads which were bound to ruin every man in the oil business not sharing them with him. He was willing to array himself against the combined better sentiment of a whole industry, to oppose a popular movement aimed at righting an injustice, so revolting to one's sense of fair play as that of railroad discriminations. Religious emotion and sentiments of charity, propriety and self-denial seem to have taken the place in him of notions of justice and regard for the rights of others.

Unhampered, then, by any ethical consideration, undismayed by the clamour of the Oil Regions, believing firmly as ever that relief for the disorders in the oil business lay in combining and controlling the entire refining interest, this man of vast patience and foresight took up his work. That work now was to carry out some kind of a scheme which would limit the output of refined oil. He had put his competitors in Cleveland out of the way. He had secured special privileges in transportation, but there were still too many refineries at work to make it possible to put up the price of oil four cents a gallon. It was certain, too, that no scheme could be worked to do that unless the Oil Regions could be mollified. That now was Mr. Rockefeller's most important business. . . .

4   "AN UNHOLY ALLIANCE"

Rockefeller and his party now propose an open instead of a secret combination—"The Pittsburg Plan"—The scheme is not approved by the oil regions because its chief strength is the rebate—Rockefeller not discouraged—Three months later becomes President of National Refiners' Association—Four-fifths of refining interest of United States with him—Oil regions aroused—Producers' Union order drilling stopped and a thirty day shut-down to counteract falling price of crude—Petroleum Producers' Agency formed to enable producers to control their own oil—Rockefeller outgenerals his opponents and forces a combination of refiners and producers—Producers' Association and Producers' Agency snuffed out—National Refiners' Association disbands—Rockefeller steadily gaining ground.

THE FEELING of outrage and resentment against the Standard Oil Company, general in the Oil Regions at the close of the Oil War . . . was intensified . . . by the knowledge that Mr. Rockefeller had been so enormously benefited. . . . Here he was shipping Eastward over one road between 4,000 and 5,000 barrels of refined oil a day—oil wrung from his neighbours by an outrageous conspiracy, men said bitterly. This feeling was still keen when Mr. Rockefeller and several of his colleagues in the South Improvement scheme suddenly, in May, 1873, appeared on the streets of Titusville. . . .

For several days the visiting gentlemen slipped around, bland and smiling, from street corner to street corner, from office to office, explaining, expostulating, mollifying. "You misunderstand our intention," they told the refiners. "It is to save the business, not to destroy it, that we are come. You see the disorders competition has wrought in the oil industry. Let us see what combination will do. Let us make an experiment—that is all. If it does not work, then we can go back to the old method."

Although Mr. Rockefeller was everywhere, and heard everything in these days, he rarely talked. "I remember well how little he said," one of the most aggressively independent of the Titusville refiners told the writer. "One day several of us met at the office of one of the refiners, who, I felt pretty sure, was being persuaded to go into the scheme which they were talking up.

Everybody talked except Mr. Rockefeller. He sat in a rocking-chair, softly swinging back and forth his hands over his face. I got pretty excited when I saw how those South Improvement men were pulling the wool over our men's eyes, and making them believe we were all going to the dogs if there wasn't an immediate combination to put up the price of refined and prevent new people coming into the business, and I made a speech which I guess, was pretty warlike. Well, right in the middle of it John Rockefeller stopped rocking and took down his hands and looked at me. You never saw such eyes. He took me all in, saw just how much fight he could expect from me, and I knew it, and then up went his hands and back and forth went his chair." . . .

The knowledge that a considerable body of the creek refiners had gone over to Mr. Rockefeller awakened a general bitterness among those who remained independent. "Deserters," "ringsters," "monopolists," were the terms applied to them, and the temper of the public meetings, as is evident from the full reports the newspapers of the Oil Region published, became at once uncertain. . . .

The upshot of the negotiations was that again the advocates of combination had to retire from the Oil Regions defeated. *"Sic semper tyrannis, sic transit gloria* South Improvement Company," sneered the Oil City Derrick, which was given to sprinkling Latin phrases into its forceful and picturesque English. But the Derrick underrated both the man and the principle at which it sneered. A great idea was at work in the commercial world. It had come to them saddled with crime. They now saw nothing in it but the crime. The man who had brought it to them was not only endowed with far vision, he was endowed with an indomitable purpose. He meant to control the oil business. By one manœuvre, and that a discredited one, he had obtained control of one-fifth of the entire refining outputs of the United States. He meant to secure the other four-fifths. He might retire now, but the Oil Region would hear of him again. It did. Three months later, in August, 1872, it was learned that the scheme of consolidation which had been presented in vain at Titusville in May had been quietly carried out, that four-fifths of the refining interest of the United States, including many of the creek refiners, had gone into a National Refiners' Association, of which Mr. Rockefeller was president, and one of their own men, J. J. Vandergrift, was vice-president. . . .

47

The news that the refiners had actually consolidated aroused something more than resentment. The producers generally were alarmed. If the aggregation succeeded they would have one buyer only for their product, and there was not a man of them who believed that this buyer would ever pay them a cent more than necessary for their oil. Their alarm aroused them to energy. The association which had scattered the South Improvement Company was revived, and began at once to consider what it could do to prevent the consolidated refiners getting the upper hand in the business. . . .

The president of the association was Captain William Hasson, a young man both by his knowledge of the Oil Regions and the oil business well fitted for the position. Captain Hasson was one of the few men in the association who had been in the country before the discovery of oil. His father had bought, in the fifties, part of the grant of land at the mouth of Oil Creek, made in 1796 to the Indian chief Cornplanter, and had moved on it with his family. Four years after the discovery of oil he and his partner disposed of 300 acres of the tract they owned for $750,000. Young Hasson had seen Cornplanter, as the site of his father's farm was called, become Oil City; he had seen the mill, blacksmith shop and country tavern give way to a thriving town of several thousand inhabitants. All of his interests and his pride were wrapped up in the industry which had grown up about him. Independent in spirit, vigorous in speech, generous and just in character, William Hasson had been thoroughly aroused by the assault of the South Improvement Company, and under his presidency the producers had conducted their successful campaign. The knowledge that the same man who had been active in that scheme had now organised a national association had convinced Captain Hasson of the necessity of a counter move, and he threw himself energetically into an effort to persaude the oil producers to devise an intelligent and practical plan for controlling their end of the business, and then stand by what they decided on.

Captain Hasson and those who were working with him would have had a much more difficult task in arousing the producers to action if it had not been for the general dissatisfaction over the price of oil. . . . The oil men as a class had been brought up to enormous profits, and held an entirely false standard of values. As the Derrick told them once in a sensible editorial, "their business was born in a balloon going up, and spent all its early years in the sky." They had seen nothing but the extreme of fortune. One hundred per cent. per annum on an investment was in their judgment only a fair profit. If their oil property had not paid for itself entirely in six months, and begun to yield a good percentage, they were inclined to think it a failure. Now nothing but five-dollar oil would do this, so great were the risks in business; and so it was for five-dollar oil, regardless of the laws of supply and demand, that they struggled. . . . As a matter of fact the oil-producing business was going through a stage in its natural development similar to oil refining. Both, under the stimulus of the enormous profits in the years immediately following the discovery of oil, had been pushed until they had outstripped consumption. The competition resulting from the inrush of producers and refiners and the economies which had been worked out were bringing down profits. The combinations attempted by both refiners and producers in these years were really efforts to keep up prices to the extravagant point of the early speculative years. . . .

Under the direction of the Producers' Association an agitation at once began in favour of stopping the drill for six months. It was a drastic measure. There was hardly an oil operator in the entire region who had not on hand some piece of territory on which he was planning to drill, or on which he had not wells under way. Stopping the drill meant that all of the aggressive work of his business should cease for six months. It meant that his production, unreplenished, would gradually fall off, until at the end of the period he would have probably not over half of what he had now; that then he must begin over again to build up. It meant, too, that he was at the mercy of neighbours who might refuse to join the movement, and who by continuing to drill would drain his territory. It seemed to him the only way of obtaining a manageable output of crude, however, and accordingly, when late in the month of August the . . . pledge to stop the drill was circulated, the great majority of the producers signed it. . . .

There was nothing but public opinion to hold the producers to their pledge. But public opinion in those days in the Oil Regions was fearless and active and asserted itself in the daily newspapers and in every meeting of the association. The whole body of oil men became a vigilance committee intent on keeping one another loyal to the pledge. Men who appeared at church on Sunday in silk hats, carrying gold-headed canes—there were such in the Oil Region in 1872—now stole out at night to remote localities to hunt down rumours of drilling wells. If they found them true, their dignity did not prevent their cutting the tools loose or carrying off a band wheel.

Stopping the drill afforded no immediate relief to the producers. It was for the future. And as soon as the Petroleum Producers' Association had the movement well under way, it proposed another drastic measure—a thirty days' shut-down—by which it was meant that all wells should cease pumping for a month. Nothing shows better the compact organisation and the determination of the oil producers at this time than the immediate response they gave to this suggestion. In ten days scarcely a barrel of oil was being pumped from end to end of the Oil Regions. . . . While the producers were inaugurating these movements, Captain Hasson and a committee were busy making out the plan of the permanent association which was to control the business of oil-producing and prevent its becoming the slave of the refining interest. The knowledge that such an organisation was being worked out kept the oil country in a ferment. In every district suggestions, practical and impractical, wise and foolish, occupied every producers' meeting and kept the idle oil men discussing from morning until night. . . .

Toward the end of October Captain Hasson presented the scheme which he and the committee had prepared. It proposed that there should be established what was called a Petroleum Producers' Agency. This agency was really an incorporated company with a capital of one million dollars, the stock of which was to be subscribed to only by the producers or their friends. This agency was to purchase all the oil of the members of the association at at least five dollars a barrel. If stocks could be kept down so that the market took all of the oil at once, the full price was to be paid at once in cash; if not, the agency was to store the oil in tanks it was to build, and a portion of the price was to be paid in tank certificates. By thus controlling all the oil, the agency expected to protect the weakest as well as the strongest producer, to equalise the interest of different localities, to prevent refiners and exporters from accumulating stocks, and to prevent gambling in oil. . . . For the first time in the history of the oil business the producers were united in an organisation, which, if carried out, would regulate the production of oil to something like the demand for it, would prevent stocks from falling into the hands of speculators, and would provide a strong front to any combination with monopolistic tendencies. Only one thing was necessary now to make the producer a fitting opponent to his natural enemy, the refiner. That thing was loyalty to the agency he had established. The future of the producer at that moment was in his own hand. Would he stick? . . .

The formation of the Producers' Agency brought the refiners back to the Oil Regions in greater earnest than ever. The success of that organisation gave them an active antagonist, one which, as it held the raw material, could at any time actually shut up their refineries by withholding oil. The vigour, the ability, the determination the new organisation had displayed made it a serious threat to the domination Mr. Rockefeller and his associates had dreamed. It must be placated. On November 8, immediately after it was announced that the entire million dollars' worth of stock was taken, an agent of the Standard Oil Company in Oil City was ordered to buy oil from the agency—6,000 barrels of oil at $4.75 a barrel. . . .

A more adroit move could not have been made at this moment. This purchase was a demonstration that the Refiners' Association could and would pay the price the producers asked; that they asked nothing better, in fact, than to ally themselves with the agency. The events of the next three weeks, on the contrary, showed the agency that it would be some time before anybody else would pay them any such price as that Mr. Rockefeller promised. The reason was evident enough. In spite of the stopping of the drill, in spite of the thirty days' shut-down, production was increasing. . . . A large number of wells under way when the drill was stopped had "come in big." New territory had been opened up by unexpected wildcats. The shut-down had done less than was expected to decrease stocks. It was evident that the Producers' Association had a long and severe task before it to bring the crude output down to anything like the demand. Could the great body of producers be depended upon to take still further measures to lesson their production. . . . Their tanks were overflowing. Many of them were in debt and depending on their sales to meet their obligations—even to meet their daily personal expenses. It was little wonder that they grew restive. . . . With every day they became more impatient . . . and the leaders soon realised that some immediate tangible results must be given the mass of oil men, or there was danger of a stampede.

A strong feature of the genius of John D. Rockefeller has always been his recognition of the critical moment for action in complicated situations. He saw it now, and his representatives again came to the creek seeking an alliance. . . .

Overwhelmed by the length and severity of the struggle before them if they insisted on independence, fearful lest the scattered and restless producers could not be held much longer, convinced by their confident arguments that the refiners could keep their promise, the council finally agreed to a plan of union. . . .

On December 12 the proposed treaty was laid before the producers at Oil City. It aroused a debate so acrimonious that even the Derrick suppressed it. Captain Hasson led the opposition. In his judgment there was but one course for the producers—to keep themselves free from all entanglements and give themselves time to build up solidly the structure they had planned. If they had followed his advice the whole history of the Oil Regions would have been different. But they did not follow it. The treaty was ratified by a vote of twenty-seven to seven. The excitement and the personalities the association indulged in at their meeting augured ill for its future, but when a week later a committee sent to see the refiners came back from New York with a contract signed by Mr. Rockefeller, the president, and bearing with them an order for 200,000 barrels of oil at $3.25, there was a general feeling that, after all, an alliance might not be so bad a thing. 200,000 barrels was a big order and would do much to relieve their distress. Their formal sense was quieted, too, by the assurance that the producers before signing the contract had insisted that the Refiners' Combination enter into an agreement to take no rebates as long as the alliance lasted. The main points of the agreement decided upon were that the Refiners' Association should admit all *existing* refiners to its society, and the Producers' Association *all* producers present and to come—that the former company should buy only of the latter, the latter sell only to the former, and that the agency should bind all producers enjoying its privileges to handle their oil through it. The refiners were to buy such daily quantities as the markets of the world would take and at a price governed by the price of refined, five dollars per barrel when refined was selling at twenty-six cents a gallon. Either association could discontinue the agreement on ten days' notice. The producers, before signing the contract, insisted that the Refiners' Combination sign an agreement to take no rebates as long as the alliance lasted. . . . As we now know, Mr. Rockefeller himself was receiving rebates when he signed this agreement.

And now, at last, after five months of incessant work, the agency was ready to begin disposing of oil. They set to work diligently at once to apportion the 200,000 barrels the refiners had bought among the different districts. It was a slow and irritating task, for a method of apportionment and of gathering had to be devised, and, as was to be expected, it aroused more or less dissatisfaction and many charges of favouritism. The agency had the work well under way, however, and had shipped about 50,000 barrels when, on January 14, it was suddenly announced that the refiners had *refused to take any more of the contract oil!*

There was a hurried call of the Producers' Council and a demand for an explanation. A plausible one was ready from Mr. Rockefeller. "You have not kept your part of the contract—you have not limited the supply of oil—there is more being pumped to-day than ever before in the history of the region. We can buy all we want at $2.50, and oil has sold within the week at two dollars. If you will not, or cannot, stop over-production, can you expect us to pay your price? . . . The breaking of the alliance proved the death of the agency and the association. The leaders who had disapproved of the treaty withdrew from active work; the supporters of the alliance, demoralised by its failure, were glad to keep quiet. A few spasmodic efforts to stop the drill, to inaugurate another shut-down, were made, but failed. . . . The Producers' Association, after ten months of as exciting and strenuous effort as an organisation has ever put in, was snuffed out almost in a day. It was to be five years before the oil men recovered sufficiently from the shock of this collapse to make another united effort. If Mr. Rockefeller felt in the fall of 1872 that the "good of the oil business" required the disollution of the Producers' Agency, he could not have acted with more acumen than he did in leading them into an alliance, and at the psychological moment throwing up his contract.

Humiliated as the producers were by their failure, they soon found consolation in the knowledge that the Refiners' Association was in trouble. . . . the exports of refined oil had fallen off for the first time in the history of the business. In 1871, 132,178,-843 gallons had been exported. In 1872, only 118,259,832 were exported. Just as alarming was the proof that the shale and coal oil refineries of Europe had taken a fresh start—that they were selling their products more cheaply than kerosene could be imported and sold. There was a general outcry from all over the country that Mr. Rockefeller and his associates were running the oil business by keeping up the price of refined oil beyond what the price of crude justified. . . . In the meantime the Refiners' Association was having troubles of its own. The members were not limiting their output as they had agreed. . . . Again, what was more fatal to the success of the association, members sometimes sold at a lower price than that set by Mr. Rockefeller. These restrictions were fundamental to the success of the combination, and the members were called together at Saratoga in June, 1873, and after a long session the association was dissolved.

There was loud exultation in the unthinking part of the Oil Regions over the dissolution of the refiners. The "Junior Anaconda" was dead. The wiser part of the region did not exult. They knew that though the combination might dissolve, the Standard Oil Company of Cleveland still controlled its one-fifth of the capacity of the country; that not only had Mr. Rockefeller been able to hold the twenty refineries he had bolted so summarily at the opening of 1872, but he had assimilated them so thoroughly that he was making enormous profits. . . . Now in 1873 he made, at the very lowest figure, three cents a gallon on his oil. Estimating his shipments simply at 700,000 barrels a year—and they were much more—his profits for that year were $1,050,000, and this accounts for no profits on about thirty-five per cent. of the Standard output, which was sold locally or shipped Westward. . . .

It is worth noticing that these great profits were not being used for private purposes. In 1872 the Standard Oil Company paid a dividend of thirty-seven per cent., but in 1873 they cut it to fifteen per cent. The profits were going almost solidly into the extension and solidification of the business. Mr. Rockefeller was building great barrel factories, thus cutting down to the minimum one of a refiner's heaviest expenses. He was buying tank cars that he might be independent of the vagaries of the railroads in allotting cars. He was gaining control of terminal facilities in New York. He was putting his plants into the most perfect condition, introducing every improved process which would cheapen his manufacturing by the smallest fraction of a cent. He was diligently hunting methods to get a larger percentage of profit from crude oil. There was, perhaps, ten per cent. of waste at that period in crude oil. It hurt him to see it unused, and no man had a heartier welcome from the president of the Standard Oil Company than he who would show him how to utilise any proportion of his residuum. In short, Mr. Rockefeller was strengthening his line at ever point, and to no part of it was he giving closer attention than to transportation.

5   LAYING THE FOUNDATIONS OF A TRUST

Evidence of reappearance of rebates soon after agreement of March 25 is signed—Principle thoroughly established that large shippers shall have advantages over small shippers in spite of railroads' duty as common carriers—Agreement worked out by which three roads are to have fixed percentage of eastern shipments—Oil regions robbed of their geographical advantage—The Rutter Circular—Rockefeller now secretly plans realisation of his dream of personal control of the refining of oil—Organisation of the Central Association—H. H. Rogers' defence of the plan—Rockefeller's quiet and successful canvass for alliances with refiners—The rebate his weapon—Consolidation by persuasion or force—More talk of a united effort to counteract the movement.

THROUGHOUT 1872, while the producers and refiners were working out associations and alliances to regulate the output of crude and refined oil, the freight rates over the three great oil-carrying roads were publicly supposed to be those settled by the agreement on March 25. Except by the sophisticated it was believed that the railroads were keeping their contracts. The Lake Shore and Michigan Southern and the New York Central had never kept them, as we have seen. Mr. Flagler's statement that the Standard received a rebate of twenty-five cents a barrel from April 1 to November 15, 1872, would seem to show that while with one hand Mr. Clark and Mr. Vanderbilt signed the agreement with the oil men that henceforth freights should be "on a basis of perfect equality to all shippers, producers and refiners, and that no rebates, drawbacks, or other arrangements of any character should be made or allowed that would give any party the slightest difference in rates or discriminations of any character whatever," with the other they had signed an arrangement to give a twenty-five-cent rebate to Mr. Rockefeller! They certainly had a strong incentive for ignoring their pledge. Consider what Mr. Rockefeller could offer the road—sixty car-loads of oil a day, over 4,000 barrels. . . . It permitted them to make up a solid oil train and run it out every day. By running nothing else they reduced the average time of a freight car from Cleveland to New York and return from thirty days to ten days. The investment for cars to handle their freight was reduced by this arrangement to about one-third what it would have been if several different persons were shipping the same amount every day. . . . If the Central did not concede to Mr. Rockefeller's terms it undoubtedly would lose the freight. There was the lake and the canal and there was the Erie!

Now it is not supposable that such an arrangement would go on long without leaking out in the upper oil circles. . . .

. . . before a year had passed after the end of the Oil War, all the roads were practising discrimination, . . . a few shippers were again engaged in a scramble for advantages, and . . . the big shippers were bent on re-establishing the principle supposed to have been overthrown by the Oil War that one shipper is more convenient and profitable for a road than many. . . .

This was the situation when in June, 1873, General Devereux, whom we have met on the Lake Shore road, became president of the Atlantic and Great Western. Now at this time Peter H. Watson, the president of the South Improvement Company, was president of the Erie. The two at once looked into the condition of their joint oil traffic. They found the rebate system abolished a year before again well intrenched. Nevertheless the Erie was not doing much business. The entire shipments of oil over the Erie for 1873 were but 762,000 barrels out of a total of 4,963,000. Naturally they went to work to build up a trade, and their relations being what they had been with the Standard, the company controlling a third of the country's refining capacity, they went to them to see if they could not get a percentage of their seaboard shipments from Cleveland. . . .

A contract was signed on April 17, 1874. By it the Standard agreed to ship fifty per cent. of the products of its refineries by the Erie at rates "no higher than is paid by the competitors of the Standard Oil Company from competing Western refineries to New York by all rail lines," and to give all oil patrons of the Erie system a uniform price and fair and equal facilities at the Weehawken yards. It was a very wise business deal for both parties. It made Mr. Rockefeller the favoured shipper of a second trunk line (the Central system was already his) and it gave him the control of that road's oil terminal so that he could know exactly what other oil patrons of the road were doing—one of the advantages the South Improvement contract looked out for, it will be remembered. As for the Erie, it tied up to them an important trade and again put them into a position to have something to say about the division of the oil traffic, the bulk of which outside of the Standard Oil Company the Pennsylvania was handling. . . . At this juncture Colonel Potts of the Empire Transportation Company, handling all of the Pennsylvania freight, suggested to his rivals that it would be a favourable time for the three trunk lines to pool their seaboard oil freight. In the discussions of this proposition, which, of course, involved a new schedule of rates, there being now practically none, it was suggested that henceforth freights be so adjusted that they would be equal to all refiners, on crude and refined from all points. . . .

By the first of September they had an agreement worked out by which each of the three roads was to have a fixed percentage of Eastern shipments. The rates to the seaboard were to amount to the same for all refiners wherever located. That is, to use one of the illustrations employed by Mr. Blanchard in explaining the scheme to the Hepburn Commission: "Suppose 100 barrels of refined oil to have been sent from Cleveland to New York by rail; the consignee was required to first pay freight therefor at New York upon delivery $1.90; to make this quantity of refined oil at that time, he had already paid freight on say 133½ barrels of crude oil from the pipes to Cleveland at thirty-five cents per barrel or say $46.67; he had therefore paid out from the pipes to the refinery and thence to New York by transportation only, on 100 barrels refined and the quantity of crude oil required to make it, $236.67 or $2.37 per barrel; therefore, at the end of the month we refunded the $46.67 already paid on the crude oil. So that the rate paid net was $1.90 to him and all other refiners."

In case of the refineries situated at the seaboard the cost of carrying from the Oil Regions the 133½ barrels of crude oil required to make 100 barrels of refined was made exactly the same as carrying the 100 barrels of refined made in the West and transported East. This really amounted to charging nothing for getting the crude oil to a refinery wherever it was situated. . . . While the railroad men were in conference at Long Branch, Henry Harley, the president of the Pennsylvania Transportation Company, came to them and said that he believed the scheme of equalisation could not be carried out unless some kind of an alliance was made with the pipe-lines. There had been a large increase in the number of pipes in the four or five years preceding, and a situation had arisen not unlike that in every other branch of the oil business. There was perhaps twice the pipe capacity needed for gathering all the oil produced, and as the pipes were under at least a dozen different managements, each fighting for business, the result was, of course, just what it had been on the railroads and in the markets—severe cutting of prices, rebates, special secret arrangements, confusion and loss. . . . Now up to this time the railroad had had nothing to do with pipe-line charges. It was, and still is, the custom for the buyer of the oil to pay the pipage, that is, the oil producer on running the oil into the pipe-line received a credit certificate for the oil. If he held it in the line long he paid a storage charge. When he sold the oil, the line ran it, and the buyer paid the charge for running. Now the United Pipe Lines proposed to the railroads a through rate from the wells to the seaboard as low as they currently made from the receiving points on the railway, the pipes to get twenty per cent. of this through rate. The railroads were to agree not to receive oil from buyers except at as high a rate as the pipes charged; and to allow no pipe-line outside of the alliance a through rate from the wells. The memorandum said squarely that the intent and purpose of this was to make the United Pipes the sole feeders of the railroads. It was a plan not unlike the South Improvement Company in design—to put everybody but yourself out of business, and it had the merit of stating its intent and purpose with perfect candour.

The railroad men seem not to have objected to the purpose, only to the terms of the proposed arrangement. Mr. Blanchard told the pipe committee that he regarded it as the most violent attempt on the part of the tail to wag the dog that he had ever seen, and the representatives of the other roads agreed. They saw at once, however, how much more solid their own position would be if they could be sure that no pipe-line delivering to them would cut its rate, if there could be in effect a through rate from the wells, and after some discussion they proposed to the pipe-lines to add twenty-two cents a barrel to the rail charges; that is, if the rate to the seaboard was $1.25, to collect from the shipper $1.47, and in case he could show that he had taken his oil from one of the United Pipes to give him a rebate of twenty-two cents. Mr. Blanchard said that they proposed to do this until proof was had that he associated pipe-lines were acting in good faith. Of course this arrangement did not change the pipe-lines' methods of collecting in the least. It simply forced a uniform charge, and this charge was to be, it should be noticed, regardless of distance. The charge for collecting and delivering oil was to be thirty cents a barrel whether it was carried one or ten miles—a practice which prevails to-day.

While these negotiations were going on, the Oil Regions as a whole was troubled by a vague rumour that freight rates were to be advanced. In the two years since the Oil War the region, as a whole, had adjusted itself to the tariff schedule of March 25, 1872, and was doing very well though working on a very much smaller margin of profits than ever before. The margin was sufficient, however, to keep the refineries in the valley running most of the time, and several of the large ones were increasing their plants. . . . The keen competition between the different refining points made it necessary to do business with economy, and a rumour of a raise of freight rates naturally was looked on with dread. It was not until September 12, however, that the new arrangements were made known, and this was some time earlier than was intended. The slip came about in this way. The general freight agent of the New York Central road, James H. Rutter, sent out on September 9 a private circular announcing the new arrangement, an advance of fifty cents a barrel on refined oil shipped to the seaboard, no corresponding advance for Cleveland and Pittsburg, a rebate of the cost of getting oil to the refineries and a rebate of twenty-two cents to those who patronised certain pipe-lines. . . .

At first the Oil Region was puzzled by the Rutter circular. It certainly was plausible. Was it not true that every man shared equally under it? As the days passed, the dazed mental condition into which it had thrown the oil men cleared up. The pipe-lines left out of the pool began to ask how it could be legal that the railroads should enter into an arrangement which obviously would drive them out of business. The creek refiners began to ask by what right the advantage of geographical position at the wells should be taken from them, and Cleveland be allowed to retain the advantages of her proximity to the Western market; Pittsburg her position on the Ohio River and the market it commanded; all of the cities the advantage of their proximity to great local markets and to such necessary supplies as barrels and acids. Besides, was it constitutional for the railroads thus to regulate interstate commerce? Was not the arrangement, as far as the Pennsylvania was concerned, plainly prohibited by the new constitution of the state of Pennsylvania? . . .

In this discussion of the Rutter circular Mr. Rockefeller's name scarcely appeared. It was known that he had been admitted to the conferences at which the tariff was arranged. This was taken as a matter of course. There was nothing which concerned the oil business which John Rockefeller was not on the inside of. Mr. Blanchard later stated that the "crude equivalent" scheme was suggested by certain Western refiners. The tremendous advantage Cleveland secured by the new arrangement, practically 300 miles of free transportation, seemed to prove, too, that Mr. Rockefeller had not been inactive during the conference. . . . For Mr. Rockefeller, quiet as he had been since the breaking up of the Refiners' Association in the summer of 1873, had by no means given up the idea of doing for the refining interest of the whole country what he had done for that of Cleveland through the South Improvement Company.

Mr. Rockefeller has shown repeatedly in his conquering business career remarkable ability to learn from experience. The breaking up of the Refiners' Association *may* have seemed a disaster to him. He did not allow it to be a profitless disaster. He extracted useful lessons from the experience, and, armed with this new wisdom, bent his whole mind to working out a third plan of campaign. He now knew that he could not hope to make again so rich a haul as he had made through the defunct South Improvement scheme. The experience of the past year with the refiners convinced him that it would take time to educate them to his idea of combination; but he had learned who of them were capable of this education. As for the producers, the alliance attempted with them was enough to demonstrate that they would never endure long the restraints of any association. Besides, the bulk of them still held the, to him, unpractical belief that rebates were *wrong*. Mr. Rockefeller had also re-learned in these eighteen months what he knew pretty well before, that the promise to give or take away a heavy freight traffic was enough to persuade any railroad king of the day to break the most solemn compact.

With all these reflections fresh in mind, Mr. Rockefeller again bent over a map of the refining interests of the United States. Here was the world he sighed to conquer. If we may suppose him to have begun his campaign as a great general with whom he has many traits in common—the First Napoleon—used to begin his, by studding a map with red-headed pegs marking the points he must capture, Mr. Rockefeller's chart would have shown in and around Boston perhaps three pegs, representing a crude capacity of 3,500 barrels; in and around New York fifteen pegs, a capacity of 9,790 barrels; in and around Philadelphia twelve pegs, a capacity of 2,061 barrels; in Pittsburg twenty-two pegs, a capacity of 6,090 barrels; on the creek twenty-seven pegs, a capacity of 9,231 barrels. His work was to get control of this multitude of red pegs and to fly above them the flag of what the irreverent call the "holy blue barrel."*

Some time in the summer of 1874, after it had become certain that Colonel Pott's plan for an equalisation of oil freights would be carried out, Mr. Rockefeller wrote to his former colleague in the South Improvement Company, W. G. Warden, of Philadelphia, telling him he wanted to talk over the condition of the oil business with him, and inviting him to bring Charles Lockhart, of Pittsburg, to that Mecca of American schemers, Saratoga, for a conference with him and Mr Flagler.... The four gentlemen breakfasted together and later strolled out to a pavilion. Here they discussed again, as they had nearly three years before, when they prepared the South Improvement assault, the condition of the oil business.

Mr. Rockefeller now had something besides a theory to present to the gentlemen he wished to go into his third scheme. He had the most persuasive of all arguments—an actual achievement. "Three years ago," he could tell them, "I took over the Cleveland refineries. I have managed them so that to-day I pay a profit to nobody. I do my own buying, I make my own acid and barrels, I control the New York terminals of both the Erie and Central roads, and ship such quantities that the railroads give me better rates than they do any other shipper. In 1873 I shipped over 700,000 barrels by the Central, and my profit on my capitalisation, $2,500,000, was over $1,000,000. This is the result of combination in one city. The railroads now have ar-

* The barrels of the Standard Oil Company are painted blue.

ranged a new tariff, by which they mean to put us all on an equal footing. They say they will give no rebates to anyone, but if we can join with Cleveland the strongest forces in other great shipping points, and apply to them the same tactics I have employed, we shall become the largest shipper, and can demand a rebate in return for an equal division of our freight. We proved in 1872-1873 that we could not do anything by an open association. Let us who see what a combination strictly carried out will effect unite secretly to accomplish it. Let us become the nucleus of a *private* company which gradually shall acquire control of all refineries everywhere, become the only shippers, and consequently the master of the railroads in the matter of freight rates." It was six hours before the gentlemen in conference left the pavilion, and when they came out Mr. Warden and Mr. Lockhart had agreed to transfer their refineries in Philadelphia and Pittsburg to the Standard Oil Company, of Cleveland, taking stock in exchange. They had also agreed to absorb, as rapidly as persuasion or other means could bring it about, the refineries in their neighbourhood. Their union with the Standard was to remain an absolute secret—the concerns operating under their respective names.

On October 15, 1874, Mr. Rockefeller consummated another purchase of as great importance. He bought the works of Charles Pratt and Company, of New York city. As before, the purchase was secret. The strategic importance of these purchases for one holding Mr. Rockefeller's vast ambition was enormous. It gave him as allies men who were among the most successful refiners, without doubt, in each of the three greatest refining centres of the country outside of Cleveland, where he ruled, and of the creek, where he had learned that neither he nor any member of the South Improvement Company could do business with facility. To meet these purchases the stock of the Standard Oil Company was increased, on March 10, 1875, to $3,500,000. . . .

The first intimation that the Oil Region had that Mr. Rockefeller was pushing another combination was in March of 1875, when it was announced that an organisation of refiners, called the Central Association, of which he was president, had been formed. Its main points were that if a refiner would lease to the association his plant for a term of months he would be allowed to subscribe for stock of the new company. The lease allowed the owner to do his own manufacturing, but gave Mr. Rockefeller's company "irrevocable authority" to make all purchases of crude oil and sales of refined, to decide how much each refinery should manufacture, and *to negotiate for all freight and pipe-line expenses.* . . .

Little as the Oil Regions knew of the real meaning of the Central Association, the news of its organisation raised a cry of monopoly, and the advocates of the new scheme felt called upon to defend it. The defense took the line that the conditions of the trade made such a combination of refineries necessary. Altogether the ablest explanation was that of H. H. Rogers, of Charles Pratt and Company, to a reporter of the New York Tribune:

"There are five refining points in the country," said Mr. Rogers, "Pittsburgh, Philadelphia, Cleveland, the Oil Regions and New York city. Each of these has certain local advantages which may be briefly stated as follows: Pittsburgh, cheap oil; Philadelphia, the seaboard; Cleveland, cheap barrels, and canal as well as railroad transportation; the Oil Regions, crude oil at the lowest figure; and all the products of petroleum have the best market in New York city. The supply of oil is three or four times greater than the demand. If the oil refineries were run to their full capacity, the market would be overstocked. The business is not regular, but spasmodic. When the market is brisk and oil is in demand, all the oil interests are busy and enjoy a fair share of prosperity. At other times, the whole trade is affected by the dullness. It has been estimated that not less than twenty millions of dollars are invested in the oil business. It is therefore to the interest of every man who has put a dollar in it to have the trade protected and established on a permanent footing. . . . Two years ago an attempt was made to organise an oil refiners' association, but it was subsequently abandoned. There was no cohesion of interests, and agreements were not kept. The movement at the present time is a revival of the former idea, and, it is believed, has already secured fully nine-tenths of the oil refiners in the country in its favour. I do not believe there is any intention among the oil men to 'bull' the market. The endeavour is to equalise all around and protect the capital invested. If by common consent, in good faith, the refiners agree to reduce the quantities to an allotment for each, made in view of the supply and demand, and the capacity for production, the market can be regulated with a reasonable profit for all. The price of oil to-day is fifteen cents per gallon. The proposed allotment of business would probably advance the price to twenty cents. . . . The oil producers to-day are bankrupt. There have been more failures during the last five months than in five years previously. An organisation to protect the oil capital is imperatively needed. Oil to yield a fair profit should be sold for twenty-five cents per gallon. That price would protect every interest and cover every outlay for getting out the crude petroleum, transporting by railroad, refining and the incidental charges of handling, etc. . . ."

The Oil Regions refused flatly to accept this view of the situation. The world would not buy refined at twenty-five cents, they argued. "You injured the foreign market in 1872 by putting up the price. Our only hope is in increasing consumption. The world is buying more oil to-day than ever before, because it is cheap. We must learn to accept small profits, as other industries do." . . .

"The most important feature of this contract," said a "veteran refiner," "is perhaps that part which provides that the Executive Committee of the Central Association are to have the exclusive power to arrange with the railroads for the carrying of the crude and refined oil. It is intended by this provision to enable the Executive Committee to speak for the whole trade in securing special rates of freight, whereby independent shippers of crude oil, and such refiners as refuse to join the combination, and any new refining interest that may be started, may be driven out of the trade. The whole general purpose of the combination is to reap a large margin by depressing crude and raising the price of refined oil, and the chief means employed is the system of discrimination in railroad freights to the seaboard." . . .

The announcement of the Central Association put an altogether new feature on oil transportation. If this organisation succeeded, and the refiners in it claimed nine-tenths of the capacity of the country—it gave Mr. Rockefeller "irrevocable authority" to negotiate freights. The Pennsylvania road immediately felt the pressure. The oil they had carried for big firms like those of Charles Lockhart in Pittsburg and of Warden, Frew and Company in Philadelphia was in the hands of the Standard Oil Company, and Mr. Rockefeller asked a rebate of ten per cent. on open rates. . . .

No one of the roads knew certainly what the others were doing for the Standard until October 1, 1875.

The freight agents then met to discuss again the freight pool they had formed in 1874. . . . At this meeting Mr. Blanchard found that both of the Erie's big rivals were granting the Standard a ten per cent. rebate. He also found that he was not getting fifty per cent. of the Standard's business as the contract called for—that the Standard controlled not only the Cleveland and New York works of which he knew, but large works in Pittsburg and Philadelphia.

Mr. Rockefeller was certainly now in an excellent condition to work out his plan of bringing under his own control all the refineries of the country. The Standard Oil Company owned in each of the great refining centres, New York, Pittsburg and Philadelphia, a large and aggressive plant run by the men who had built it up. . . . Not only had Mr. Rockefeller brought these powerful interests into his concern; he had secured for them a rebate of ten per cent. on a rate which should always be as low as any one of the roads gave any of his competitors. He had done away with middlemen, that is, he was "paying nobody a profit." He had undeniably a force wonderfully constructed for what he wanted to do and one made practically impregnable as things were in the oil business then, by virtue of its special transportation rate.

As soon as his new line was complete the work of acquiring all outside refineries began at each of the oil centres. . . .

Those who felt the hard times and had any hope of weathering them resisted at first. With many of them the resistance was due simply to their love for their business and their unwillingness to share its control with outsiders. The thing which a man has begun, cared for, led to a healthy life, from which he has begun to gather fruit, which he knows he can make greater and richer, he loves as he does his life. It is one of the fruits of his life. He is jealous of it—wishes the honour of it, will not divide it with another. He can suffer heavily his own mistakes, learn from them, correct them. He can fight opposition, bear all—so long as the work is his. There were refiners in 1875 who loved their business in this way. Why one should love an oil refinery the outsider may not see; but to the man who had begun with one still and had seen it grow by his own energy and intelligence to ten, who now sold 500 barrels a day where he once sold five, the refinery was the dearest spot on earth save his home. He walked with pride among its evil-smelling places, watched the processes with eagerness, experimented with joy and recounted triumphantly every improvement. To ask such a man to give up his refinery was to ask him to give up the thing which, after his family, meant most in life to him.

To Mr. Rockefeller this feeling was a weak sentiment. To place love of independent work above love of profits was as incomprehensible to him as a refusal to accept a rebate because it was *wrong!* Where persuasion failed then, it was necessary, in his judgment, that pressure be applied—simply a pressure sufficient to demonstrate to these blind or recalcitrant individuals the impossibility of their long being able to do business independently. It was a pressure varied according to locality. Usually it took the form of cutting their market. The system of "predatory competition" was no invention of the Standard Oil Company. It had prevailed in the oil business from the start. Indeed, it was one of the evils Mr. Rockefeller claimed his combination would cure, but until now it had been used spasmodically. Mr. Rockefeller never did anything spasmodically. He applied underselling for destroying his rivals' market with the same deliberation and persistency that characterised all his efforts, and in the long run he always won. There were other forms of pressure. Sometimes the independents found it impossible to get oil; again, they were obliged to wait days for cars to ship in; there seemed to be no end to the ways of making it hard for men to do business, of discouraging them until they would sell or lease, and always at the psychological moment a purchaser was at their side. . . . The history of oil refining on Oil Creek from 1875 to 1879 is almost uncanny. There were at the beginning of that period twenty-seven plants in the region, most of which were in a fair condition, considering the difficulties in the business. During 1873 the demand for refined oil had greatly increased, the exports nearly doubling over those of 1872. The average profit on refined that year in a well-managed refinery was not less than three cents a gallon. During the first half of 1874 the oil business had been depressed, but the oil refiners were looking for better times when the Rutter circular completely demoralised them by putting fifty cents extra freight charges on their shipments without an equivalent raise on competitive points. . . . conditions on the creek grew harder. All sorts of difficulties began to be strewn in their way—cars were hard to get, the markets they had built up were cut under them—a demoralising conviction was abroad in the trade that this new and mysterious combination was going to succeed; that it was doing rapidly what its members were reported to be saying daily: "We mean to secure the entire refining business of the world." Such was the state of things on

the creek when in the early fall of 1875 an energetic young refiner and oil buyer well known in the Oil Regions, J. D. Archbold, appeared in Titusville as the representative of a new company, the Acme Oil Company, a concern which everybody believed to be an offshoot of the Standard Oil Company of Cleveland, though nobody could prove it. . . . It was evident at once
that the Acme Oil Company had come into the Oil Regions for
the purpose of absorbing the independent interests as Mr. Rockefeller and his colleagues were absorbing them elsewhere. The
work was done with a promptness and despatch which do great
credit to the energy and resourcefulness of the engineer of the
enterprise. In three years, by 1878, all but two of the refineries
of Titusville had "retired from the business gloriously," as Mr.
Archbold, flushed with victory, told the counsel of the Commonwealth of Pennsylvania in 1879, when the state authorities
were trying to find what was at work in the oil interests to cause
such a general collapse. Most of the concerns were bought outright, the owners being convinced that it was impossible for
them to do an independent business, and being unwilling to try
combination. All down the creek the little refineries which for
years had faced every difficulty with stout hearts collapsed.
"Sold out," "dismantled," "shut down," is the melancholy record
of the industry during these four years. At the end practically
nothing was left in the Oil Regions but the Acme of Titusville
and the Imperial of Oil City, both of them now under Standard
management. To the oil men this sudden wiping out of the
score of plants with which they had been familiar for years
seemed a crime which nothing could justify. Their bitterness
of heart was only intensified by the sight of the idle refiners
thrown out of business by the sale of their factories. These men
had, many of them, handsome sums to invest, but what were
they to put them in? They were refiners, and they carried a
pledge in their pockets not to go into that business for a period
of ten years. Some of them tried the discouraged oil man's fatal
resource, the market, and as a rule left their money there. One
refiner who had, according to popular report, received $200,000
for his business, speculated the entire sum away in less than
a year. Others tried new enterprises, but men of forty learn new
trades with difficulty, and failure followed many of them. The
scars left in the Oil Regions by the Standard Combination of
1875-1879 are too deep and ugly for men and women of this
generation to forget them.

In Pittsburg the same thing was happening. . . . Many of the Pittsburg refiners made a valiant fight to get rates on their oil which would enable them to run independently. To save expense they tried to bring oil from the oil fields by barge; the pipe-lines in the pool refused to run oil to barges, the railroad to accept oil brought down by barge. An independent pipe-line attempted to bring it to Pittsburg, but to reach the works the pipe-line must run under a branch of the Pennsylvania railroad. It refused to permit this, and for months the oil from the line was hauled in wagons from the point where it had been held up, over the railroad track, and there repiped and carried to Pittsburg. At every point they met interference until finally one by one they gave in. . . .

At every point, indeed, making it difficult for the refiner to get his raw product was one of the favourite manœuvres of the combination. It was not only to crude oil it was applied. Factories which worked up the residuum or tar into lubricating oil and depended on Standard plants for their supply were cut off. There was one such in Cleveland—the firm of Morehouse and Freeman. Mr. Morehouse . . . was then making oils adapted to lubricating all kinds of machinery—he held patents for several brands and trade marks, and had produced that year over 25,000 barrels of different lubricants besides 120,000 boxes of axle grease. At this time he was buying his stock or residuum from one or another of the twenty-five Cleveland refiners. Then came the South Improvement Company and the concentration of the town's refining interest in Mr. Rockefeller's hands. Mr. Morehouse, according to the testimony he gave the Hepburn Commission in 1879, went to Mr. Rockefeller, after the consolidation, to arrange for supplies. He was welcomed—the Standard Oil Company had not at that time begun to deal in lubricating oils—and encouraged to build a new plant. This was done at a cost of $41,000, and a contract was made with the Standard Oil Company for a daily supply of eighty-five barrels of residuum. Some time in 1874 this supply was cut down to twelve barrels. The price was put up too, and contracts for several months were demanded so that Mr. Morehouse got no advantage from the variation in crude prices. Then the freights went up on the railroads. He paid $1.50 and two dollars for what he says he felt sure his big neighbour was paying but seventy or seventy-five cents. . . . Now it was impossible for Mr. Morehouse to supply his trade on twelve barrels of stock. He begged Mr. Rockefeller for more.

It was there in the Standard Oil works. Why could he not have it? He could pay for it. He and his partner offered to buy 5,000 barrels and store it, but Mr. Rockefeller was firm. All he could give Mr. Morehouse was twelve barrels a day. "I saw readily what that meant," said Mr. Morehouse, "that meant squeeze you out —buy your works. They have got the works and are running them; I am without anything. They paid about $15,000 for what cost me $41,000. . . ."

At every refining centre in the country this process of consolidation through persuasion, intimidation, or force, went on. As fast as a refinery was brought in line its work was assigned to it. If it was an old and poorly equipped plant it was usually dismantled or shut down. If it was badly placed, that is, if it was not economically placed in regard to a pipe-line and railroad, it was dismantled even though in excellent condition. If it was a large and well-equipped plant advantageously located it was assigned a certain quota to manufacture, and it did nothing but manufacture. The buying of crude, the making of freight rates, the selling of the output remained with Mr. Rockefeller. The contracts under which all the refineries brought into line were run were of the most detailed and rigid description, and they were executed as a rule with a secrecy which baffles description. . . .

But make his operations as thickly as he might in secrecy, the effect of Mr. Rockefeller's steady and united attack on the refining business was daily becoming more apparent. Before the end of 1876 the alarm among oil producers, the few independent refineries still in business, and even in certain railroad circles was serious. On all sides talk of a united effort to meet the consolidation was heard. . . .

6 STRENGTHENING THE
FOUNDATIONS

First Interstate Commerce Bill—The Bill pigeon-holed through efforts of
Standard's friends—Independents seek relief by proposed construction of
pipe-lines—Plans for the first Seaboard pipe-line—Scheme fails on account of mismanagement and Standard and railroad opposition—Development of the Empire Transportation Company and its proposed connection
with the refining business—Standard, Erie and Central fight the Empire
Transportation Company and its backer, The Pennsylvania Railroad—
The Pennsylvania finally quits after a bitter and costly war—Empire line
sold to the Standard—Entire pipe-line system of oil regions now in
Rockefeller's hands—New railroad pool between four roads—Rockefeller
puts into operation system of drawbacks on other people's shipments—
He proceeds rapidly with the work of absorbing rivals.

FROM THE time the Central Association announced
itself, independent refiners and the producers as a body watched
developments with suspicion. They had little to go on. They
had no means of proving what was actually the fact that the
Central Association was the Standard Oil Company working secretly to bring its competitors under control or drive them out of
business. They had no way of knowing what was actually the
fact that the Standard had contracts with the Central, Erie
and the Pennsylvania which gave them rebates on the lowest
tariff which others paid. That this must be the case, however, they were convinced, and they determined early in 1876 to
call on Congress for another investigation. A hearing was practically insured, for Congress since 1872 had given serious attention to the transportation troubles. The Windom Committee of
1874 had made a report, the sweeping recommendations of
which gave much encouragement to those who suffered from
the practices of the railroads. Among other things this committee recommended that all rates, drawbacks, etc., be published
at every point and no changes allowed in them without proper
notification. . . .

With Congress in such a temper the oil men felt that there
might be some hope of securing the regulation of interstate com-

71

merce they had asked for in 1872. The agitation resulted in the presentation in the House of Representatives, in April, of the first Interstate Commerce Bill which promised to be effective. The bill was presented by James H. Hopkins of Pittsburg. . . . In aid of his bill a House investigation was asked. It was soon evident that the Standard was an enemy of this investigation. Through the efforts of a good friend of the organisation—Congressman H. B. Payne, of Cleveland—the matter was referred to the Committee on Commerce, where a member of the house, J. N. Camden, whose refinery, the Camden Consolidated Oil Company, if it had not already gone, soon after went into the Standard Oil Alliance, appeared as adviser of the chairman! Now what Mr. Hopkins wanted was to compel the railroads to present their contracts with the Standard Oil Company. The Committee summoned the proper railroad officers, Messrs. Cassatt, Devereux and Rutter, and O. H. Payne, treasurer of the Standard Oil Company. Of the railroad men, only Mr. Cassatt appeared, and he refused to answer the questions asked or to furnish the documents demanded. Mr. Payne refused also to furnish the committee with information. . . .

Mr. Payne and Mr. Camden were active in securing the suppression of the investigations and they soon succeeded not only in doing that but in pigeon-holing for the time Mr. Hopkins's Interstate Commerce Bill.

But the oil men had not been trusting entirely to Congressional relief. From the time that they became convinced that the railroads meant to stand by the terms of the "Rutter Circular" they began to seek an independent outlet to the sea. The first project to attract attention was the Columbia Conduit Pipe Line. This line was begun by one of the picturesque characters of Western Pennsylvania, "Dr." David Hostetter, the maker of the famous Hostetter's Bitters. Dr. Hostetter's Bitters' headquarters were in Pittsburg. He had become interested in oil there, and had made investments in Butler County. In 1874 he found himself hampered in disposing of his oil and conceived the idea of piping it to Pittsburg, where he could make a connection with the Baltimore and Ohio road, which up to this time had refused to go into the oil pool. Now at that time the right of eminent domain for pipes had been granted in but eight counties of Western Pennsylvania. Allegheny County, in which Pittsburg is located, was not included in the eight, a restriction which the oil men attributed rightly, no doubt, to the influence of the Pennsylvania Railroad in the State Legislature. That road could hardly have been expected to allow the pipes to go to Pittsburg and connect with a rival road if it could help it. Dr. Hostetter succeeded in buying a right of way through the county, however, and laid his pipes within a few miles of the city to a point where he had to pass under a branch of the Pennsylvania Railroad. The spot chosen was the bed of a stream over which the railroad passed by a bridge. Dr. Hostetter claimed he had bought the bed of the run and that the railroad owned simply the right to span the run. He put down his pipes, and the railroad sent a force of armed men to the spot, tore up the pipes, fortified their position and prepared to hold the fort. The oil men came down in a body, and, seizing an opportune moment, got possession of the disputed point. The railroad had thirty of them arrested for riot, but was not able to get them committed; it did succeed, however, in preventing the relaying of the pipes and a long litigation over Dr. Hostetter's right to pass under the road ensued. Disgusted with this turn of affairs Dr. Hostetter leased the line to three young independent oil men of whom we are to hear more later. They were B. D. Benson, David McKelvy and Major Robert E. Hopkins, all of Titusville. Resourceful and determined they built tank wagons into which the oil from the pipe was run and was carted across the tracks on the public highway, turned into storage tanks and again repiped and pumped to Pittsburg. They were soon doing a good business. The fight to get the Columbia Conduit Line into Pittsburg aroused again the agitation in favour of a free pipe-line bill, and early in 1875 bills were presented in both the Senate and House of the state and bitter and long fights over them followed. . . . Although the bills were strongly supported, they were defeated, and the Columbia Conduit Line continued to "break bulk" and cart its oil over the railroad track.

Another route was arranged which for a time promised success. This was to bring crude oil by barges to Pittsburg, then to carry the refined down the Ohio River to Huntington and thence by the Richmond and Chesapeake road to Richmond. . . . Everything possible was done to make this attempt fail. An effort was even made to prevent the barges which came down the Allegheny River from unloading, and this actually succeeded for some time. There seemed to be always some hitch in each one of the channels which the independents tried, some point at which they could be so harassed that the chance of a living freight rate which they had seen was destroyed.

Some time in April, 1876, the most ambitious project of all was announced. This was a seaboard pipe-line to be run from the Oil Regions to Baltimore. Up to this time the pipe-lines had been used merely to gather the oil from the wells and carry it to the railroads. . . . If this seaboard line went through it was farewell to the railroad-Standard combination. Oil could be shipped to the seaboard by it at a cost of 16⅔ cents a barrel. . . . All of the interests, little and big, which believed that they would be injured by the success of the line, began an attack. . . .

It was not long, however, before something more serious than the farmers and their complaints got in the way of the Pennsylvania Transportation Company. This was a rumour that the company was financially embarrassed. Their certificates were refused on the market, and in November a receiver was appointed. Different members of the company were arrested for fraud, among them two or three of the best known men in the Oil Regions. The rumours proved only too true. The company had been grossly mismanaged, and the verification of the charges against it put an end to this first scheme for a seaboard pipe-line. . . .

Among those interested in the oil business who had watched the growing power of the Standard with most concern was the head of the Empire Transportation Company, Colonel Joseph D. Potts. In connection with the Pennsylvania Railroad Colonel Potts had built up this concern, founded in 1865, until it was the most perfectly developed oil transporter in the country. It operated 500 miles of pipe, owned a thousand oil-tank cars, controlled large oil yards at Communipaw, New Jersey, was in every respect indeed a model business organisation. . . . While the Empire had far outstripped all its early competitiors, there had grown up in the last year a rival concern which Colonel Potts must have watched with anxiety. This concern, known as the United Pipe Line, was really a Standard organisation, for Mr. Rockefeller, in carrying out his plan of controlling all the oil refineries of the country, had been forced gradually into the pipe-line business. . . .

The Standard Oil Combination in 1876 was a large transporter of oil, for the directors and leading stockholders owned and operated fully forty per cent. of the pipe-lines of the Oil Regions,

owned all but a very few of the tank cars on both the Central
and Erie roads, and controlled under leases two great oil terminals, those of the Erie and Central roads. It was little wonder
that Colonel Potts watched this rapid concentration of transportation and refining interests with dread. . . . [As he saw] the
independents of Pittsburg, Philadelphia, New York and the
creek, shutting down, selling out, going into bankruptcy, while
the Standard and its allies grew bigger day by day, as he saw
the Standard interest developing a system of transportation
greater than his own, he concluded to prevent, if possible, the
one shipper in the oil business. "We reached the conclusion,"
said Colonel Potts in 1888, "that there were three great divisions
in the petroleum business—the production, the carriage of it,
and the preparation of it for market. If any one party controlled
absolutely any one of those three divisions, it practically would
have a very fair show of controlling the others. We were particularly solicitous about the transportation, and we were a little
afraid that the refiners might combine in a single institution,
and some of them expressed a strong desire to associate themselves permanently with us. We therefore suggested to the Pennsylvania road that we should do what we did not wish to do—
associate ourselves. That is, our business was transportation and
nothing else; but, in order that we might reserve a nucleus of
refining capacity to our lines, we suggested we should become
interested in one or more refineries, and we became interested
in two, one in Philadelphia and one in New York. It was incidental merely to our transportation. The extreme limit was
4,000 barrels a day only."

It was in the spring of 1876 that the Empire began to interest
itself in refineries. No sooner did Mr. Rockefeller discover this
than he sought Mr. Scott and Mr. Cassatt, then the third
vice-president of the Pennsylvania, in charge of transportation.
It was not *fair!* Mr. Rockefeller urged. The Empire was a transportation company. If it went into the refining business it was
not to be expected that it would deal as generously with rivals
as with its own factories; besides, it would disturb the one shipper who, they all had agreed, was such a benefit to the railroads. . . .

When the Standard Oil Company and its allies, the Erie and
Central, found that the Pennsylvania would not or could not
drive the Empire from its position, they determined on war. . . .

Backed by the Erie and Central, Mr. Rockefeller, in the spring of 1877, finally told Mr. Cassatt that he would no longer send any of his freight over the Pennsylvania unless the Empire gave up its refineries. The Pennsylvania refused to compel the Empire to this course. According to Mr. Potts's own story, the road was partially goaded to its decision by a demand for more rebates, which came from Mr. Rockefeller at about the time he pronounced his ultimatum on the Empire. . . .

Spurred on then by resentment at the demands for new rebates, as well as by the injustice of Mr. Rockefeller's demand that the Empire give up its refineries, the Pennsylvania accepted the Standard's challenge, resolved to stand by the Empire, and henceforth to treat all its shippers alike. No sooner was its resolution announced in March, 1877, than all the freight of the Standard, amounting to fully sixty-five per cent. of the road's oil traffic, was taken away. An exciting situation, one of out-and-out war, developed, for the Empire at once entered on an energetic campaign to make good its loss by developing its own refineries, and by forming a loyal support among the independent oil men. . . . When Mr. Rockefeller saw this he summoned his backers to action. The Erie and Central began to cut rates to entice away the independents. It is a sad reflection on both the honour and the foresight of the body of oil men who had been crying so loudly for help, that as soon as the rates were cut on the Standard lines many of them began to attempt to force the Pennsylvania to follow. "They found the opportunity for immediate profits by playing one belligerent against the other too tempting to resist," says Colonel Potts. . . .

While the railroads were waging this costly war the Standard was carrying the fight into the refined market. The Empire had gone systematically to work to develop markets for the output of its own and of the independent refineries. Mr. Rockefeller's business was to prevent any such development. He was well equipped for the task by his system of "predatory competition," for in spite of the fact that Mr. Rockefeller claimed that underselling to drive a rival from a market was one of the evils he was called to cure, he did not hesitate to employ it himself. Indeed, he had long used his freedom to sell at any price he wished for the sake of driving a competitor out of the market with calculation and infinite patience. Other refiners burst into the market and undersold for a day; but when Mr. Rockefeller began to undersell, he kept it up day in and day out, week in and week out, month in and month out, until there was literally nothing left of his competitor. . . .

In spite of the growing bitterness and cost of the contest, the Empire had no thought of yielding. Mr. Potts's hope was in a firm alliance with the independent oil men, many of the strongest of whom were rallying to his side. . . . The attempt to enlist a solid body of oil men in the scheme was at once set on foot, but hardly was it under way before troubles of most serious import came upon the Pennsylvania road. A great and general strike on all its branches tied up its traffic for weeks. In Pittsburg hundreds of thousands of dollars' worth of property were destroyed by a mob of railroad employees. It is not too much to say that in these troubles the Pennsylvania lost millions of dollars. . . . Overwhelmed by the disasters, Mr. Scott and Mr. Cassatt felt that they could not afford any longer to sustain the Empire in its fight for the right to refine as well as transport oil.

While the coffers of the Pennsylvania were empty, those of the Standard were literally bursting with profits; for the Standard, the winter before this fight came on, had carried to completion for the first time the work which it had been organised to accomplish, that is, it had put up the price of refined oil, in defiance of all laws of supply and demand, and held it up for nearly six months. . . . The Standard then had a war budget big enough for any opposition, and it is not to be wondered at that the Pennsylvania, knowing this and finding its own treasury depleted, was ready to quit.

It was August when Mr. Scott and Mr. Cassatt decided to give up the fight. Peace negotiations were at once instituted, Mr. Cassatt going to Cleveland to see Messrs. Rockefeller and Flagler, and Mr. Warden, who was visiting them there. . . .

For twelve years the organisation had been doing a growing business. . . . Its operations were more extensive, its opportunities more promising, under fair play, than they had ever been before in its history. The band of men who had built it up to such healthy success were not giving it up because they had lost faith in it, or because they believed there were larger opportunities for them in some other business; they were giving it up because they were compelled to, and probably men never went out of business in this country with a deeper feeling of injustice than that of the officials of the Empire

Transportation Company on October 17, 1877, when they sent out the telegrams which put their great creation into liquidation. . . .

The first effect of the downfall of the Empire was a new railroad pool. Indeed when it became evident that the Pennsylvania would yield, the Erie, Central and the Standard had begun preparing a new adjustment, and the papers for this were ready to be signed on October 17, with those transferring the pipe-line property. Never had there been an arrangement which gathered up so completely the oil outlets, for now the Baltimore and Ohio road came into a pool for the first time. Mr. Garrett had always refused the advances of the other roads, but when he saw that the Columbia Conduit Line, his chief feeder, was sure to fall into Standard hands; when he began to suspect the Baltimore refiners were going into the combination, he realised that if he expected to keep an oil traffic he must join the other roads. The new pool, therefore, was between four roads. Sixty-three per cent. of the oil traffic was conceded to New York, and of the sixty-three per cent. going there the Pennsylvania road was to have twenty-one per cent. Thirty-seven per cent. of the traffic was to go to Philadelphia and Baltimore, and of this thirty-seven per cent. the Pennsylvania had twenty-six per cent. The Standard guaranteed the road not less than 2,000,000 barrels a year. . . . In return for this guarantee of quantity the Standard was to pay such rates as might be fixed from time to time by the four trunk lines . . . and it was to receive weekly a commission of ten per cent. on its shipments it controlled. No commission was to be allowed any other shipper unless he should guarantee and furnish such a quantity of oil that after deducting any commission allowed, the road realised from it the same amount of profits as it did from the Standard trade. . . .

Four months later Mr. Rockefeller was able to take another step of great advantage. He was able to put into operation the system of drawbacks on other people's shipments which the South Improvement Company contracts had provided for, and which up to this point he seems not to have been securely enough placed to demand. . . . Thus the Standard Oil Company, through the American Transfer Company, received, in addition to rebates on its own shipments, from twenty to thirty-five cents drawback a barrel on all crude oil which was sent over the trunk lines by other people as well as by itself.

The effect of this new concentration of power was immediate in all the refining centres of the country. . . .

As this work of absorption went on steadily, persistently, the superstitious fear of resistance to proposals to lease or sell which came from parties known or suspected to be working in harmony with the Standard Oil Company, which had been strong in 1875, grew almost insuperable. In Cleveland this was particularly true. A proposal from Mr. Rockefeller was certainly regarded popularly as little better than a command to "stand and deliver." "The coal oil business belongs to us," Mr. Rockefeller had told Mr. Morehouse. "We have facilities; we must have it. Any concern that starts in business we have sufficient money laid aside to wipe out"—and people believed him! The feeling is admirably shown in a remarkable case still quoted in Cleveland—and which belongs to the same period as the foregoing cases, 1878—a case which took the deeper hold on the public sympathy because the contestant was a woman, the widow of one of the first refiners of the town; a Mr. B——, who had begun refining in Cleveland in 1860. Mr. B——'s principal business was the manufacture of lubricating oil. Now at the start the Standard Oil Company handled only illuminating oil, and accordingly a contract was made between the two parties that Mr. B—— should sell to Mr. Rockefeller his refined oil, and that the Standard Oil Company should let the lubricating business in Cleveland alone. This was the status when in 1874 Mr. B—— died. What happened afterwards has been told in full in affidavits made in 1880, and they shall tell the story; the only change made in the documents being to transfer them for the sake of clarity from the legal third person to the first, and to condense them on account of space.

Mrs. B——'s story as told in her affidavit is as follows:

"My husband having contracted a debt not long prior to his death for the first time in his life, I, for the interest of my fatherless children, as well as myself, thought it my duty to endeavour to continue the business, and accordingly took $92,000 of the stock of the B—— Oil Company and afterwards reduced it to $72,000 or $75,000, the whole stock of the company being $100,000, and continued business from that time until November, 1878, making handsome profits out of the business during perhaps the hardest years of the time since Mr. B—— had commenced. Some time in November, 1878, the Standard Oil Company sent a man to me by the name of Peter S. Jennings, who had been engaged in the refining business and had sold out to the Standard Oil Company. I told Mr. Jennings that I would carry on no negotiations with him whatever, but that if the Standard Oil Company desired to buy my stock I must transact the business with its principal officer, Mr. Rockefeller. Mr. Jennings, as representing the Standard Oil Company, told me that the president of the company, Mr. Rockefeller, said that said company would control the refining business, and that he hoped it could be done in one or two years; but if not, it would be done, anyway, if it took ten years to do it.

"After two or three days' delay Mr. Rockefeller called upon me at my residence to talk over the negotiation with regard to the purchase of my stock. I told Mr. Rockefeller that I realised the fact that the B—— Oil Company was entirely in the power of the Standard Oil Company, and that all I could do would be to appeal to his honour as a gentleman and to his sympathy to do with me the best that he could; and I begged of him to consider his wife in my position—that I had been left with this business and with my fatherless children, and with a large indebtedness that Mr. B—— had just contracted for the first time in his life; that I felt that I could not do without the income arising from this business, and that I had taken it up and gone on and been successful, and I was left with it in the hardest years since my husband commenced the business. He said he was aware of what I had done, and that his wife could never have accomplished so much. I called his attention to the contract that my husband had made with him in relation to carbon oil, whereby the Standard Oil Company agreed not to touch the lubricating branch of the trade carried on by my husband, and reminded him that I had held to that contract rigidly, at a great loss to the B—— Oil Company, but did so because I regarded it a matter of honour to live up to it. I told him that I had become alarmed because the Standard Oil Company was getting control of all the refineries in the country, and that I feared that the said Standard Oil Company would go into the lubricating trade, and reminded him that he had sent me word that the Standard Oil Company would not interfere with that branch of the trade. He promised, with tears in his eyes, that he would stand by me in this transaction, and that I should not be wronged; and he told me that, in case the sale was made, I might retain whatever amount of the stock of the B—— Oil Company I desired, his object appearing to be only to get the controlling stock of the company. He said that while the negotiations were pending he would come and see me, and I thought that his feelings were such on the subject that I could trust him and that he would deal honourably by me.

"Seeing that I was compelled to sell out, I wanted the Standard Oil Company to make me a proposition and endeavoured to get them to do so, but they would not make a proposition. I then made a proposition that the whole stock of the B—— Oil Company with accrued dividends should be sold to said Standard Oil Company for $200,000, which was, in fact, much below what the stock ought to have been sold for, but they ridiculed the amount, and at last offered me only $79,000, not including accounts, and required that each stockholder in the B—— Oil Company should enter into a bond that within the period of ten years he or she would not directly or indirectly engage in or in any way be concerned in the refining, manufacturing, producing, piping, or dealing in petroleum or in any of its products within the county of Cuyahoga and state of Ohio, nor at any other place whatever.

"Seeing that the property had to go, I asked that I might, according to the understanding with the president of the company, retain $15,000 of my stock, but the reply to this request was; 'No outsiders can have any interest in this concern; the Standard Oil Company has "dallied" as long as it will over this matter; it must be settled up to-day or go,' and they insisted upon my signing the bond above referred to.

"The promises made by Mr. Rockefeller, president of the Standard Oil Company, were none of them fulfilled; he neither allowed me to retain any portion of my stock, nor did he in any way assist me in my negotiations for the sale of my stock; but, on the contrary, was largely instrumental in my being obliged to sell the property much below its true value, and requiring me to enter into the oppressive bond above referred to.

"After the arrangements for the sale of the refinery and of my stock were fully completed and the property had been sold by myself and the other stockholders, and after I had made arrangements for the disposition of my money, I received a note from Mr. Rockefeller, in reply to one that I had written to him threatening to make the transaction public, saying that he would give me back the business as it stood, or that I might retain stock if I wished to, but this was after the entire transaction was closed, and such arrangements had been made for my money that I could not then conveniently enter into it; and I was so indignant over the offer being made at that late day, after my request for the stock having been made at the proper time, that I threw the letter into the fire and paid no further attention to it."

. . . .

It is probably true, as Mr. Rockefeller states, that he could have reproduced Mrs. B——'s plant for $20,000; but the plant was but a small part of her assets. She owned one of the oldest lubricating oil refineries in the country, one with an enviable reputation for good work and fair dealing, and with a trade that had been paying an annual net income of from $30,000 to $40,-000. It was this income for which Mr. Rockefeller paid $79,000; this income with the old and honourable name of the B—— Oil Company, with not a few stills and tanks and agitators.

It is undoubtedly true, as Mr. Rockefeller avers, that Mrs. B—— was not obliged to sell out, but the fate of those who in this period of absorption refused to sell was before her eyes. She had seen the twenty Cleveland refineries fall into Mr. Rockefeller's hands in 1872. She had watched the steady collapse of the independents in all the refining centres. She had seen every effort to preserve an individual business thwarted. Rightly or wrongly she had come to believe that a refusal to sell meant a fight with Mr. Rockefeller, that a fight meant ultimately defeat, and she gave up her business to avoid ruin.

7   THE CRISIS OF 1878

A rise in oil—A blockade in exports—Producers do not get their share
of the profits—They secretly organise the Petroleum Producers' Union
and promise to support proposed independent pipe-lines—Another Interstate Commerce Bill defeated at Washington—"Immediate Shipment"—
Independents have trouble getting cars—Riots threatened—Appeal to
Governor Hartranft—Suits brought against United Pipe-lines, Pennsylvania Railroad and others—Investigations precipitated in other states—
The Hepburn Commission and the Ohio investigation—Evidence that the
Standard is a continuation of the South Improvement Company—Producers finally decide to proceed against Standard officials—Rockefeller
and eight of his associates indicted for conspiracy.

IT WAS clear enough by the opening of 1878 that
Mr. Rockefeller need no longer fear any serious trouble from the
refining element. To be sure there were scattered concerns still
holding out and some of them doing very well; but his latest
move had put him in a position to cut off or at least seriously to
interfere with the very raw material in which they worked. It
was hardly to be expected after the defeat of the Pennsylvania
that any railroad would be rash enough to combine with even
a strong group of refiners. As for independent pipe-lines, there
were so many ways of "discouraging" their building that it did
not seem probable that any one would ever go far. It was only a
matter of time, then, when all remaining outside refiners must
come into his fold or die. Mr. Rockefeller's path would now have
been smooth had it not been for the oil producers. But the oil
producers, naturally his enemy, he being the buyer and they
the seller, had become in the six years before Mr. Rockefeller
had made himself the only gatherer of their oil, irreconcilable
opponents of whatever he might do. The South Improvement
Company they regarded rightly enough as devised to control
the price of their product, and that scheme they wrongfully
laid entirely at Mr. Rockfeller's door. Mr. Rockefeller had been
only one of the originators of the South Improvement Company,
but the fact that he had become later practically its only sup-
porter, that he was the only one who had profited by it, and
that he had turned his Cleveland plant into a machine for

carrying out its provisions, had caused the oil country to fix on him the entire responsibility. Then the oil men's experience with Mr. Rockefeller in 1873 had been unfortunate. They charged the failure of their alliance to his duplicity. There is no doubt that Mr. Rockefeller played a shrewd and false game with the oil men in 1873, but the failure of their alliance was their own fault. They did not hold together—they failed to limit their production as they agreed, they suspected one another, and at a moment, when, if they had been as patient and wise as their great opponent they would have had the game in their own hands, and him at their feet, as he had been in 1872, for the sake of immediate returns, they abandoned some of the best features of their organisation, and allied themselves with a man they distrusted. When that alliance failed they threw on Mr. Rockefeller's shoulders a blame which they should have taken on their own. . . .

The abandoning of their alliance in 1873 had of course put an end to their measures for limiting production and for holding over-production until it could be sold at the prices they thought profitable. The drill had gone on merrily through 1873, 1874, and 1875, regardless of consumption or prices. By the end of 1874 there were over three and a half million barrels of oil in stoke, more than twice what there had ever been before. Production was well to a million barrels a month and prices that year averaged but $1.15 a barrel. For men who considered three dollars a starvation price this was indeed hard luck. Things looked better by the end of 1875, for production was falling off. By March, 1876, stocks had been so reduced that there was strong confidence that the price of crude oil must advance. By June the Oil City Derrick began to prophesy "three-dollar oil" and to advise oil men to hold crude for that price. In August three dollars was reached in the Oil City exchange. It had been nearly four years since that price had been paid for oil, and the day the point was reached (August 25) the brokers fairly went mad. . . . It seemed like the old times in the Oil Region—the good old flush times when people made a fortune one day and threw it away the next!

Of course refined oil went up steadily with crude. Refined reached 21⅜ cents in New York the day of this boom at Oil City. The day following the rise was one of the most exciting the oil exchange had ever seen. "Never before," declared the Derrick in its report, "was so much business done." . . . This went on for several days, when a new element in the situation began to force itself on the oil men's attention. One of the chief reasons on which they based their confidence in high prices for crude oil was the fact that the foreigners were short of refined oil. It was the custom then, as now, for exporters to buy their oil for the winter European trade in the late summer and early fall. When the boom began the harbour at New York was beginning to fill up with ships for cargoes. But to the consternation of the oil men intent on keeping up the boom, the exporters were refusing to buy. They were declaring the price to which refined had risen to be out of proportion to the price of crude. . . . It was early in September when the realisation came upon the Oil Regions that a new element was in the problem— a veritable blockade in exports. As the days went on they saw that this was no temporary affair. They saw that Mr. Rockefeller's combination was at last carrying out just what it had been organised to do—forcing the price it wanted for refined. Day after day refined was held at twenty-six cents. Day after day the exporters refused to buy. It was not until the end of September, in fact, that they began to yield—as it was inevitable they should do, for the game was certainly in the hands of the refiners, and Europe had to have its light. The exporters began to see too that if they held off longer they might have to pay higher prices, for it was rumoured that the Standard Combination was shutting down its factories, literally making refined scarce, while crude oil was piling up in Pennsylvania!

With the yielding of the exporter exactly what they feared occurred, the price was raised! The exporters balked again. . . . By the end of October New York harbour was full of vessels—a mute protest against the corner—and it was not until November that the exporters fully gave in and began to take all the oil they could get at prices asked, which ranged from twenty-six to thirty-five cents. And these prices were held all through the winter of 1876–77, up to February 22. They were held regardless of the price of crude, for, do their utmost, the producers could not keep their oil up to the corresponding price of refined. According to the scale of relative prices then accepted, twenty-six cents a gallon for refined meant five dollars a barrel for crude, yet there was not a month in the entire period of this hold-up that crude averaged that price. In December, when the average price of refined was 29⅜ cents, crude was but $3.78⅛ a barrel. The producers held meetings and passed resolutions, cursed the refiners and talked of building independent refineries, filled the columns of the Derrick with open letters advocating a shut-down, an alliance of their own, restrictive legislation, an oil men's railway, and what was more to the point some of them supported, with more or less fidelity, the efforts to build up counter movements noted in the last chapter: the Columbia Conduit Line, the seaboard pipe-line, and especially the alliance with the Empire Transportation Company, attempted in the spring of 1877. There seemed more hope in this last combination than in any other movement, for they had faith in Colonel Potts, and besides they were accustomed to seeing the Pennsylvania Railroad get what it wanted. The defeat of the Pennsylvania was therefore the heavier blow. Indeed, the news of the sale of the Empire pipe-lines to the Standard was like the sounding of the tocsin in the angry and baffled Oil Regions. It revived the spirit of 1872. But it was the spirit of 1872 with new dignity and a discretion such as had never been before seen in the blatant region. In every town from McKean County southwest to Butler the oil towns hastened to organise themselves into a secret society. Little by little it came out that a Producers' Union had been organised. From all that could be learned it looked very much as if the Petroleum Producers' Union had come into existence to do business. On November 21, 1877, the first meeting of the new organisation was held, "the Petroleum Parliament" or "Congress" it was called. This Congress, which met in Titusville, was composed of 172 delegates. It was claimed that it represented at least 2,000 oil producers, and not less than seventy-five millions in money. It is certain it included the representative men of the Oil Regions, those to whose daring, hard work, and energy the discovery and development of the oil fields, as they were known at that time, were entirely due. . . .

First and foremost they resolved to stand by all efforts to secure an outlet to the seaboard independent of the Standard and the allied railroads. Two enterprises were put before them at once. The first was what was known as the Equitable Petroleum Company, an organisation started by one of the most resourceful and active and independent men in the oil country, one of whom we are to hear more, Lewis Emery, Jr. This company, in which some 200 oil producers in the Bradford field had taken stock, proposed to lay a pipe-line to Buffalo and to ship their oil thence by the Erie Canal. . . . The second enterprise . . . engaged . . . General Herman Haupt, to survey a route from Brady's Bend on the Allegheny River to Baltimore, Maryland—a distance of 235 miles. To both of these projects the General Council of the Union gave promise of support.

The demand for interstate commerce legislation was renewed at once by the Union. . . . The bill . . . was introduced into the House of Representatives in May, 1878, by Lewis F. Watson, whose home was in Warren County, Pennsylvania. It was called into committee and came out as the Regan bill and as such was passed at the end of the year by the House, but only to be smothered later in the Senate. At the same time that the effort was going in Washington for relief the Legislature of Pennsylvania was being besieged again for a free pipe-line bill and an anti-discrimination bill. Both of these projects failed, and the committee having them in charge said bitterly in its report to the Union: "How well we have succeeded at Harrisburg you all know. It would be in vain for your committee to describe the efforts of the Council in this direction. It has been simply a history of failure and disgrace. If it has taught us anything, it is that our present law-makers, as a body, are ignorant, corrupt and unprincipled; that the majority of them are, directly or indirectly, under the control of the very monopolies against whose acts we have been seeking relief. . . . There has been invented by the Standard Oil Company no argument or assertion, however false or ridiculous, which has not found a man in the Pennsylvania Legislature mean enough to become its champion."

On every side indeed the producers hastened to protect themselves against the Lord of the Oil Regions, as Mr. Rockefeller, not inaptly, was called, on the completion of his pipe-line monopoly. That they were not merely alarmists in thinking that they must do something to protect their interests was demonstrated sooner than was anticipated. The demonstration was hurried by an unforeseen and difficult situation—a great outpouring of oil in a new field—the Bradford or Northern Field in McKean County, Pennsylvania. About the time that Mr. Rockefeller's lordship was realised it became certain that deposit of oil had been discovered which was going to lead soon to a production vastly in excess of the consumption, as well as in excess of the then existing facilities for gathering and storing oil. If Mr.

Rockefeller wished to keep his monopoly he must, it was evident, enter upon a campaign of expansion calling for an immense expenditure of energy and money. He must lay pipes in a hundred directions to get the output of new wells; he must build tanks holding thousands of barrels to receive the oil. And all of this must be done quickly if rivals were to be kept out of the way. There was no hesitation on the part of the United Pipe Lines. One of the greatest construction feats the country has ever seen was put through in the years 1878, 1879 and 1880 in the Bradford oil field by the Standard interests. It was a wonderful illustration of the surpassing intelligence, energy and courage with which the Standard Oil Company attacks its problems. But while it was putting through this feat it instituted a policy toward the producers which was regarded by them as tyrannical and unjustifiable. The first manœuvre in this new policy hit the producer in a very tender spot, for it concerned the price he was to receive for oil. . . .

In December, 1877, after the monopoly was completed, they refused to discharge their obligations in the customary way. On the plea that they had not sufficient tankage to carry oil in the Bradford field, they issued an order that no oil would be run in that district for any one unless it was sold for "immediate shipment"—that is, no oil would be taken to hold for storage; it would be taken for shipping only. At the same time the Standard buyer, J. A. Bostwick, decreed that henceforth no Bradford oil would be bought for immediate shipment unless it was offered at *less* than the market price. No fixed discount was set. The seller was asked what he would take; his offer was, of course, according to his necessities. Even then an answer was not always immediately given. The seller was told to come back in five or ten days and he would be told if his oil would be taken. A feature of the new order, particularly galling to the oil men, was the manner in which it was enforced. Formerly the buyer and seller had met freely in the oil exchanges and their business offices, and transactions had been carried on as among equals. Now the producers were obliged to form in line before the United Pipe Lines' offices and to enter one at a time to consult the buyer. . . . Here was the situation then: to keep oil from running on the ground the producer must sell it; but if he sold it he must take a price from two to twenty-five cents or more below the market. . . .

As soon as the situation of the Bradford field was realised both the United Pipes and the producers began a furious campaign of tank building. . . . The greater number of these belonged to the producers. According to the United Pipe Lines' statement, there was under their control in the entire Oil Regions in October 5,200,000 barrels of tankage, two-thirds of which belonged to producers, but was held by them under a lease. But oil poured from the ground faster than tanks could be built. . . . That it was a most difficult situation for everybody is evident. There was but one way to prevent loss—shut down the wells and stop the drill; but this the producers refused to consider. Of course the price of oil went down rapidly, so far did the production exceed consumption. But why, cried the producer, when oil is already so low, take advantage of our necessity and force us into competition with each other; why enforce this immediate shipment? They answered their questions themselves, and began then to make a charge against the Standard, which they continue to make to-day; that is, that it habitually meets the extraordinary expenses to which it is put by depressing the price of crude oil —"taking it out of the producer." . . .

A few months after "immediate shipment" was begun a new cause for dissatisfaction arose. More or less private tankage leased to the lines had always been in existence. It enabled a producer to carry his oil without paying storage, and, of course, it was the business of the company to empty this storage within a reasonable time after the owner demanded it. But in the spring the lines, under the same plea of under capacity, refused to carry out this duty to the tank owner; that is, they refused to give him his tankage, although he had sold his oil. Thus A owns 5,000 barrels of tankage. It is full. He sells a portion of it to Mr. Bostwick and asks the United Pipe Lines to run the oil accumulated at his wells. But the United Pipe Lines refuses on the ground that the line is full. The loss to producers incident upon these orders was terrible. All over the Bradford field men saw their oil running on the ground, though they offered to sell it at ruinous prices, and though they might have thousands of barrels of tankage leased to the United Lines. Yet they did not riot; conscious that their own reckless drilling had brought on the trouble, they cursed the Standard, and put down more wells!

But in the spring of 1878 Mr. Rockefeller and his colleagues instituted a series of manœuvres which shattered the last remnant of confidence the oil men had in the sincerity of their claim that they were doing their utmost to relieve the distressed Oil Regions, and that their measures were necessary to hold the producers in check. The pipe-lines began to refuse to load cars for the shippers who supplied the few independent refiners with oil. . . .

Now, while the railroads were refusing cars to independent shippers,—or if they gave an order for them, the United Pipe Lines were refusing to load them,—while the Standard and the railroads were doing their utmost to prevent the Equitable Line doing business, and were discouraging in every way the sea-board pipe-line—new routes which would take care of a propor-tion, at least, of the oil which they claimed they could not handle—thousands of barrels of oil were running on the ground in Bradford, and two of the independent refineries of New York shut down entirely in order that a third of their number might get oil enough to fill an order.

This interference with the outside interests, thus preventing the small degree of relief which they would have afforded, and a growing conviction that the Standard meant to keep up the "immediate shipment" order, at least until it had built the pipes and tanks needed in the Bradford field, finally aroused the region to a point where riot was imminent. . . .

The only thing which prevented a riot at this time and great destruction of property, if not of life, was the strong hand the Petroleum Producers' Union had on the country. Fearing that if violence did occur the different movements they had under way would be prejudiced, they sent a committee of twenty-five men to Harrisburg to see Governor Hartranft. They laid before him and the attorney-general of the state the grievance of the oil producers in an "appeal" reviewing the history of the industry. They demanded that the United Pipe Lines be made to per-form its duty as a public carrier, and the railroads be made to cease their discrimination against shippers both in the matter of rebates and in furnishing cars. . . . Governor Hartranft was much stirred by the story of the producers. He went himself to the Oil Regions to see the situation, and in August directed the producers to put their demands into the form of an appeal. This was done, and it was decided to bring proceedings by writ of *quo warranto* against the United Pipe Lines, and by separate bills in equity against the Pennsylvania Railroad and the other lines doing business in the state. It was September before the state authorities began their investigation of the United Pipe Lines. the hearings being held in Titusville. Many witnesses summoned failed to appear, but enough testimony was brought out in this investigation to show that the railroads had refused to furnish cars for independents when they had them empty, and that the United Pipe Lines had clearly violated its duty as a common carrier. In his report on this investigation the secretary of internal affairs, William McCandless, rendered a verdict that the charges of the oil producers had not been substantiated in any way that demanded action.

The indignation which followed this report was intense. . . . Throughout the oil country there was hardly an oil producer to be found not associated with the Standard Oil Company who did not believe that McCandless had sold himself and his office to the Standard Oil Combination for $20,000, and used the money to help in his Congressional canvass. . . .

Early in 1879 the hearing in the suits in equity brought by the commonwealth against the various transportation companies of which the producers had been complaining were begun. The witnesses subpœnaed failed at first to appear, and when on the stand they frequently refused to reply; but it soon became apparent to them that the state authorities were in earnest, and that they must "answer or go to Europe." By March, 1879, an important array of testimony had been brought out. . . . The most important witness from the railroad circles, and, indeed, the most important witness who appeared, was A. J. Cassatt. Mr. Cassatt's testimony was startling in its candour and its completeness, and substantiated in every particular what the oil men had been claiming: that the Pennsylvania Railroad had become the creature of the Standard Oil Company; that it was not only giving that company rates much lower than to any other organisation, but that it was using its facilities with a direct view of preventing any outside refiner or dealer in oil from carrying on an independent business.

The same or similar conditions, not only in oil, but in other products, which led to these suits, led to investigations in other states. Toward the end of 1878 the Chamber of Commerce of New York City demanded from the Legislature of the state an investigation of the New York railroads. This investigation was carried on from the beginning of 1879. The revelations were amazing. Before the Hepburn Commission, as it was called from the name of the chairman, was through with its work. . . . William H. Vanderbilt had been examined, and G. H. Blanchard, the freight agent of the Erie road, had given a full account of the relation of the Erie to the Standard, perhaps the most useful piece of testimony, after that of Mr. Cassatt, belonging to this period of the Standard's history.

At the same time that the Pennsylvania suits were going on, and the Hepburn Commission was doing its work, the Legislature of Ohio instituted an investigation. . . . By April, 1879, there had been brought out in these various investigations a mass of testimony sufficient in the judgment of certain of the producers to establish the truth of a charge which they had long been making, and that was that the Standard was simply a revival of the South Improvement Company. Now the verdict of the Congressional Committee had been that the South Improvement Company was a conspiracy. Therefore, said the producers, the Standard Oil Company is a conspiracy. Their hope had been, from the first, to obtain proof to establish this charge. Having this they believed they could obtain judgment from the courts against the officials of the company, and either break it up or put its members in the penitentiary. The more hotheaded of the producers believed that they now had this evidence. . . .

First—That the Standard Oil Company, like the South Improvement Company, was a secret organisaton;

Second—That both companies were composed in the main of the same parties;

Third—That it aimed, like its predecessors, at getting entire control of the refining interest;

Fourth—That it used the power the combination gave it to get rebates on its own oil shipments and drawbacks on the shipments of other people;

Fifth—That it arranged contracts which compelled the railroads to run out all competition by lowering their rates.

Sixth—That it aimed to put up the price of refined without allowing the producer a share of the profits—

Taking all these points into consideration, many of the producers, including the president of the Petroleum Producers' Union, B. B. Campbell, and certain members of his Council, came to the conclusion that as they had sufficient evidence against the members of the Standard Combination to insure conviction for criminal conspiracy, they should proceed against them. Strenuous opposition to the proceedings, as hasty and ill-advised, developed in the Council and the Legal Committee, but the majority decided that the prosecution should be instituted. Mr. Scott and Mr. Cassatt were omitted from the proposed indictment on the ground that they were already weary of the Standard, and would cease their illegal practices gladly if they could.

On the 29th day of April, 1879, the Grand Jury of the County of Clarion found an indictment against John D. Rockefeller, William Rockefeller, Jabez A. Bostwick, Daniel O'Day, William G. Warden, Charles Lockhart, Henry M. Flagler, Jacob J. Vandergrift and George W. Girty. (Girty was the cashier of the Standard Oil Company.) There were eight counts in the indictment, and charged, in brief, a conspiracy for the purpose of securing a monopoly of the business of buying and selling crude petroleum and to prevent others than themselves from buying and selling and making a legitimate profit thereby; a combination to oppress and injure those engaged in producing petroleum; a conspiracy to prevent others than themselves from engaging in the business of refining petroleum, and to secure a monopoly of that business for themselves; a combination to injure the carrying trade of the Allegheny Valley and Pennsylvania Railroad Companies by preventing them from receiving the natural petroleum traffic; to divert the traffic naturally belonging to the Pennsylvania carriers to those of other states by unlawful means; and to extort from railroad companies unreasonable rebates and commissions, and by fraudulent means and devices to control the market prices of crude and refined petroleum and acquire unlawful gains thereby. . . .

With damaging testimony piling up day by day in three states, and with an indictment for conspiracy hanging over the heads of himself and eight of his associates, matters looked gloomy for John D. Rockefeller in the spring of 1879. "The good of the oil business" certainly seemed in danger.

8   THE COMPROMISE OF 1880

The producers' suit against Rockefeller and his associates used by the Standard to protect itself—Suits against the transportation companies are delayed—Trial of Rockefeller and his associates for conspiracy postponed—All of the suits withdrawn in return for agreements of the Standard and the Pennsylvania to cease their practices against the producers—With this compromise the second Petroleum Producers' Union comes to an end—Producers themselves to blame for not standing behind their leaders—Standard again enforces orders objectionable to producers—More outbreaks in the oil regions—Rockefeller having silenced organised opposition proceeds to silence individual complaint.

No DOUBT the indictment of Mr. Rockefeller in the spring of 1879 seemed to him the work of malice and spite. By seven years of persistent effort he had worked out a well-conceived plan for controlling the oil business of the United States. Another year and he had reason to believe that the remnant of refiners who still rebelled against his intentions would either be convinced or dead and he could rule unimpeded. But here at the very threshold of empire a certain group of people—"people with a private grievance," "mossbacks naturally left in the lurch by the progress of this rapidly developing trade," his colleagues described them to the Hepburn Commission—stood in his way. "You have taken deliberate advantage of the iniquitous practices of the railroads to build up a monopoly," they told him. . . . And they indicted him with eight of his colleagues for conspiracy.

The evidence on which the oil men based this serious charge has already been analysed. At the moment they brought their suit for conspiracy what was their situation? They had several months before driven the commonwealth of Pennsylvania to bring suits against four railroads operating within its borders and against the Standard pipe-lines for infringing their duties as common carriers. Partial testimony had been taken in the case against the Pennsylvania road and in that against the United Pipe Lines. These suits, though far from finished, had given the Producers' Union the bulk of the proof on which they had secured the indictment of the Standard officials for conspiracy. Now, since the railroads and the pipe-lines were the guilty ones—that is, as it was they who had granted the illegal favours, and as they were the only ones that could surely be convicted, it seems clear that the only wise course for the producers would have been to prosecute energetically and exclusively these first suits. But . . . the producers interrupted their work by bringing their spectacular suit for conspiracy—a suit which perhaps might have been properly instituted after the others had been completed, but which, introduced now, completely changed the situation, for it gave the witnesses from whom they were most anxious to hear a loophole for escape.

For instance, the officials of the Standard pipe-lines had been instructed to appear on the 14th of May, 1879, to answer questions which earlier in the trial they had refused to answer "on advice of counsel." Now the president of the United Pipe Lines, J. J. Vandergrift, and the general manager, Daniel O'Day, were both included in the indictment for conspiracy. The evening before the interrogatory the producers' counsel received a telegram from the attorney-general of the state, announcing that the pipe-line people were complaining that the testimony which they would be called on to give on the morrow would be used against them in the conspiracy trial—as it undoubtedly would have been—and that he thought it only fair that their hearing be postponed until after that suit. . . . This, then, was the first fruit of the producers' hasty and vindictive suit. It had shut the mouths of the important Standard witnesses.

Discouraging as this discovery was, however, there was no reason why the suits against the railroads should not have been pushed through, and the testimony the officials unquestionably could be made to give, now that Mr. Cassatt had set the pace, have been obtained. But the Producers' Union had lost sight for the moment of the fact that the fundamental difficulty in the trouble was the illegal discrimination of the common carriers. The Union was so much more eager to punish Mr. Rockefeller than it was to punish the railroads, that in bringing the suit for conspiracy it was even guilty of leniency toward the officials of the Pennsylvania. . . . Naturally enough the railroads took advantage of these signs of leniency on the part of the producers, and brought all their enormous influence to bear on the state authorities to delay hearings and bring about a settlement. . . .

The conspiracy suit had been set for the August session of

the Clarion County court. When August came the Standard sought a continuance, and it was granted. The delay did not in any way discourage the producers, and when Mr. Rockefeller became convinced of this he tried conciliation. "Come, let us reason together," has always been a favourite proposition of Mr. Rockefeller. He would rather persuade than coerce, rather silence than fight. He had been making peace overtures ever since the suits began. . . .

Although . . . early efforts to get a wedge into the Producers' Union and thus secure a staying of the suits had no results, the Standard was not discouraged—it never is: there is no evidence in its history that it knows what the word means. Not being able to handle the Union as a whole, the Standard began working on individuals. . . . For several weeks the Oil Regions had known that President Campbell and Roger Sherman, the leading lawyer of the Union, were in conference with the Standard officials. It was rumoured that they were arranging a compromise, and it was suspected that the meeting now called was to consider the terms. . . .

The Standard contract, which Mr. Campbell then presented, pledged Mr. Rockefeller, and some sixteen associates, whose names were attached to the document, to the following policy:

1. They would hereafter make no opposition to an entire abrogation of the system of rebates, drawbacks and secret rates of freight in the transportation of petroleum on the railroads.

2. They withdrew their opposition to secrecy in rate making. . . .

3. They abandoned entirely the policy which they had been pursuing in the management of the United Pipe Lines—that is, they promised that there should be no discrimination whatever hereafter between their patrons; that the rates should be reasonable and not advanced except on thirty days' notice . . . that they would receive, transport, store and deliver all oil tendered to them, up to a production of 65,000 barrels a day. And if the production should exceed that amount they agreed that they would not purchase any so-called "immediate shipment" oil at a discount on the price of certificate oil.

4. They promised hereafter that when certificates had been given for oil taken into the custody of the pipe-lines, the transfer of these certificates should be considered as a delivery of the oil, and the tankage of the seller would be treated as free.

Mr. Rockefeller also agreed in making this contract to pay the Producers' Union $40,000 to cover the expense of their litigation. In return for this money and for the abandonment of secret rebates and of the pipe-line policy to which he had held so strenuously, what was he to receive? He was not to be tried for conspiracy. . . .

The contract with the Pennsylvania which was signed by Mr. Scott agreed, in consideration of the withdrawal of the suit against the road, to the following policy:

1. That it would make known to all shippers all rates of freight charged upon petroleum. . . .

2. If any rates of freight were allowed one shipper as against another, on demand that rate was to be made known.

3. There should be no longer any discrimination in the allotment and distribution of cars to shippers of petroleum.

4. Any rebate allowed to a large shipper was to be reasonable.

There were both humiliation and bitterness in the Council when the report was read—humiliation and bitterness that after two years of such strenuous fighting all that was achieved was a contract which sacrificed what everybody knew to be the fundamental principle, the principle which up to this point the producers had always insisted must be recognised in any negotiation—that the rebate system was wrong and must not be compromised with. . . .

By the morning of February 20 the Oil Regions knew of the compromise. The news was received in sullen anger. It was due to the cowardice of the state officials, the corrupting influence of corporations, the oil men said. They blamed everybody but themselves, and yet if they had done their duty the suits would never have been compromised. The simple fact is that the mass of oil men had not stood by their leaders in the hard fight they had been making. These leaders, Mr. Campbell the president, Mr. Sherman the chief counsel, and Mr. Patterson the head of the legislative committee, had given almost their entire time for two years to the work of the Union . . . without pay. No one outside of the Council of the Union knew the stress that came upon these three men. Up to the decision to institute the conspiracy suit they had worked in harmony. But when that was decided upon Mr. Patterson withdrew. He saw how fatal such a move must be, how completely it interfered with the real work of the Union, forcing common carriers to do their duty. He saw that the substantial steps gained were given up and that the work would all have to be done over again if their suit went on. Mr. Campbell believed in it, however, and Mr. Sherman, whether he believed in it or not, saw no way but to follow his chief. The nine months of disappointment and disillusion which followed were terrible for both men. They soon saw that the forces against them were too strong, that they would never in all probability be able to get the conspiracy suit tried, and that so long as it was on the docket the proper witnesses could not be secured for the suits against the railroads. Finally it came to be a question with them what out of the wreck of their plans and hopes could they save? And they saved what the compromise granted. If the oil producers they represented, a body of some 2,000 men, had stood behind them throughout 1879 as they did in 1878 the results would have been different. Their power, their means, were derived from this body, and this body for many months had been giving them feeble support. Scattered as they were over a great stretch of country, interested in nothing but their own oil farms, the producers could only be brought into an alliance by hope of overturning disastrous business conditions. They all felt that the monopoly the Standard had achieved was a menace to their interests, and they went willingly into the Union at the start, and supported it generously, but they were an impatient people, demanding quick results, and when they saw that the relief the Union promised could only come through lawsuits and legislation which it would take perhaps years to finish, they lost interest and refused money. . . .

Now, what was this loose and easily discouraged organisation opposing? A compact body of a few able, cold-blooded men— men to whom anything was right that they could get, men knowing exactly what they wanted, men who loved the game they played because of the reward at the goal, and, above all, men who knew how to hold their tongues and wait. "To Mr. Rockefeller," they say in the Oil Regions, "a day is as a year and a year as a day. He can wait, but he never gives up." Mr. Rockefeller knew the producers, knew how feeble their staying qualities in anything but the putting down of oil wells, and he may have said confidently, at the beginning of their suits against him, as it was reported he did say, that they would never be finished. They had not been finished from any lack of material. If the suits had been pushed but one result was possible, and that was the conviction of both the Standard and the railroads; they had been left unfinished because of the impatience and instability of the prosecuting body and the compactness, resolution and watchfulness of the defendants.

The withdrawal of the suits was a great victory for Mr. Rockefeller. There was no longer any doubt of his power in defensive operations. Having won a victory, he quickly went to work to make it secure. The Union had surrendered, but the men who had made the Union remained; the evidence against him was piled up in indestructible records. In time the same elements which had united to form the serious opposition just overthrown might come together, and if they should it was possible that they would not a second time make the mistake of vacillation. The press of the Oil Regions was largely independent. . . . Mr. Rockefeller now entered on a campaign of reconciliation which aimed to placate, or silence, every opposing force.

Many of the great human tragedies of the Oil Regions lie in the individual compromises which followed the public settlement of 1880; for then it was that man after man, from hopelessness, from disgust, from ambition, from love of money, gave up the fight for principle which he had waged for seven years. "The Union has surrendered," they said; "why fight on?" This man took a position with the Standard and became henceforth active in its business; that man took a salary and dropped out of sight; this one went his independent way, but with closed lips; that one shook the dust of the Oil Regions from his feet and went out to seek "God's country," asking only that he should never again hear the word "oil." The newspapers bowed to the victor. A sudden hush came over the region, the hush of defeat, of cowardice, of hopelessness. Only the "poor producer" grumbled. "You can't satisfy the producer," Mr. Rockefeller often has had occasion to remark benignantly and pitifully. . . . The Oil Regions as a whole was at heart as irreconcilable in 1880 as it had been after the South Improvement Company fight, and now it had added to its sense of outrage the humiliation of defeat. Its only immediate hope now was in the success of one of the transportation enterprises which had come into existence with the uprising of 1878 and to which it had been for two years giving what support it could. This enterprise was the seaboard pipe-line . . .

9 THE FIGHT FOR THE
SEABOARD PIPE-LINE

Project for Seaboard Pipe-line pushed by independents—Tidewater Pipe
Company formed—Oil pumped over mountains for the first time—Independent refiners ready to unite with Tidewater because it promises to
free them from railroads—The Standard face to face with a new
problem—Day of the railroads over as long distance transporters of oil—
National Transit Company formed—War on the Tidewater begun—Plan
to wreck its credit and buy it in—Rockefeller buys a third of the Tidewater's stock—The Standard and Tidewater become allies—National
Transit Company now controls all pipe-lines—Agreement entered into
with Pennsylvania Railroad to divide the business of transporting oil.

THE PROJECT for a seaboard pipe-line to be built by
the producers and to be kept independent of Standard capital
and direction had been pushed with amazing energy. Early in
the fall of 1878 General Haupt reported that his right of way
was complete from the Allegheny River to Baltimore; contracts
were let for the telegraph line and preparation begun to lay the
pipe. . . . The new idea was to lay a six-inch line from Rixford,
in the Bradford field, to Williamsport, on the Reading Railroad,
a distance of 109 miles. The Reading, not having had so far any
oil freight, was happy to enter into a contract with them to
run oil to both Philadelphia and New York until they could get
through to the seaboard themselves. In November, 1878, a
limited partnership, called the Tidewater Pipe Company, was
organised with a capital of $625,000 to carry out the scheme.
Many of the best known producers of the Oil Regions took stock
in the company, the largest stockholders being A. A. Sumner
and B. D. Benson.

The first work was to get a right of way. The company went
at the work with secrecy and despatch. . . . The Standard, intent on stopping them, and indeed on putting an end to all
future ventures of this sort, set out at once to get what was called
a "dead line" across the state. This was an exclusive right for
pipe-line purposes from the northern to the southern boundary
of Pennsylvania. As there was no free pipe-line bill in those days,

this "dead line," if it had been complete, would have been an effectual barrier to the Tidewater. Much money was spent in this sordid business, but they never succeeded in completing a line. The Tidewater, after a little delay, found a gap not far from where it wanted to cross, and soon had pushed itself through to Williamsport. With the actual laying of the pipe there was no interference which proved serious, though the railroads frequently held back shipments of supplies. . . .

By the end of May the company was ready for operation. . . . Up to that time oil had never been pumped over thirty miles, and no great elevation had been overcome. Here was a line 109 miles long, running over a mountain nearly 2,600 feet high. It was freely bet in the Oil Regions that the Tidewater would get nothing but a drizzle for its pains. However, oil men, Standard men, representatives of the Pennsylvania Railroad, newspaper men and natives gathered in numbers at the stations, and indeed all along the route, to watch the result.

The pump at station one was started by B. D. Benson, the president of the company. . . . Without a hitch the oil flowed in a full stream into the pipe and began its long journey over the mountains. It travelled about as fast as a man could walk and, as the pipe lay on the ground, the head of the stream could be located by the sound. Patrolmen followed the pipe the entire length watching for leaks. . . . When the oil reached the second station there was general rejoicing; nevertheless, the steepest incline, the summit of the Alleghanies, had yet to be overcome. The oil went up to the top of the mountain without difficulty, and on June 4, the seventh day after Mr. Benson opened the valve at Station One, oil flowed into the big receiving tank beyond Williamsport. A new era had come in the oil business. Oil could be pumped over the mountains. It was only a matter of time when the Tidewater would pump to New York.

Once at the seaboard, the Tidewater had a large and sure outlet for its oil in the group of independent refiners left at the mercy of the Standard in the fall of 1877 by the downfall of the Empire Line. . . .

The success of the Tidewater experiment brought Mr. Rockefeller face to face with a new situation. Just how serious this situation was is shown by the difference in the cost of transporting a barrel of oil to the seaboard by rail and transporting it by pipe. According to the calculation of Mr. Gowen, the president of the Reading Railroad, the cost by rail was at that time from thirty-five to forty-five cents. The open rate was from $1.25 to $1.40, and the Standard Oil Company probably paid about eighty-five cents, when the roads were not protecting it from "injury by competition." Now, according to General Haupt's calculation in 1876, oil could be carried in pipes from the Oil Regions to the seaboard for 16⅔ cents a barrel. General Haupt calculated the average difference in cost of the two systems to be twenty-three cents, enough to pay twenty-eight per cent. dividends on the cost of a line even if the railway put their freights down to cost. This little calculation is enough to show that the day of the railroads as long-distance transporters of crude oil was over; that the pipe-lines were bound to replace them. Now, Mr. Rockefeller had by ten years of effort made the roads his servant; would he be able to control the new carrier? A man of lesser intellect might not have foreseen the inevitableness of the new situation; a man of lesser courage would not have sprung to meet it. Mr. Rockefeller, however, is like all great generals: he never fails to foresee where the battle is to be fought; he never fails to get the choice of positions. He wasted no time now in deciding what should be done. He proposed not merely to control future long-distance oil transportation; he proposed to own it outright.

Hardly had the news of the success of the Tidewater's experiment reached the Standard before this truly Napoleonic decision was being carried out. Mr. Rockefeller had secured a right of way from the Bradford field to Bayonne, New Jersey, and was laying a seaboard pipe-line of his own. At the same time he set out to acquire a right of way to Philadelphia, and soon a line to that point was under construction. Even before these seaboard lines were ready, pipes had been laid from the Oil Regions to the Standard's inland refining points—Cleveland, Buffalo and Pittsburg. With the completion of this system Mr. Rockefeller would be independent of the railroads as far as the transportation of crude oil was concerned. . . .

And while Mr. Rockefeller was making this lavish expenditure of money and energy to meet the situation created by the bold development of the Tidewater, what was his attitude toward that company? . . . The Tidewater had been built to feed a few independent refineries in New York. If these refineries operated outside of him, they might disturb his system; that is, they might increase the output of refined and so lower its price. The Tidewater must not be allowed to live, then. But how could it be put out of commission? . . . There were several ways to accomplish his end; in two of them, at least, Mr. Rockefeller excelled from long practice. The first was to get out of the way the refineries which the Tidewater expected to feed, and this was undertaken at once. The refiners were approached usually by members of the Standard Oil Company as private individuals, and terms of purchase or lease so generous made to them that they could not afford to decline. . . . All but one firm yielded to the pressure. Ayres and Lombard stood by the Tidewater, but soon after their refusal to sell they were condemned as a public nuisance and obliged to move their works! The Tidewater met the situation by beginning to build refineries of its own—one at Bayonne, New Jersey, and another near Philadelphia—in the meantime storing the oil it had expected to sell. . . .

By January, 1882, the Tidewater was in such a satisfactory condition that it decided to negotiate a loan of $2,000,000 to carry out plans for enlargement. The First National Bank of New York, after a thorough examination of the business, agreed to take the bonds at ninety cents on the dollar, but trouble began as soon as the probable success of the bond issue was known. The officials of the First National Bank were called upon by stockholders of the Tidewater, men holding nearly a third of the company's stock, and assured that the company was insolvent, and that it would be unsafe for the bank to take the loan. The First National declined to be influenced by the information, on the ground that the disgruntled stockholders had sold themselves to the Standard Oil Company, and were trying to discredit the Tidewater, so that the Standard might buy it in. It had been planned to place some of these bonds in Europe, and Franklin B. Gowen was sent over for that purpose. . . . As soon as Mr. Gowen started from this side it was cabled to Europe that he was going over to place bonds which were not sound. . . . This report was spread so generally on the other side that it interfered seriously with Mr. Gowen's attempt to place the loan.

These manœuvres failing to ruin the Tidewater's credit, a more serious attack was made in the fall of 1882, by the filing of a long bill of complaint against the management of the company, followed by an appeal that a receiver be appointed and the business wound up. . . .

The Oil Regions watched it with keenest interest. . . . That the suit was backed by the Standard, one would have to be very naïve to doubt, but they were using . . . a faction of the company known as the "Taylor-Satterfield crowd." These men, controlling some $200,000 worth of Tidewater stock, had been professing themselves dissatisfied with the management of the business for some months, though always refusing to sell their holdings at an advanced price. It was generally believed in the Oil Regions that their "dissatisfaction" was fictitious, that they were in reality in league with the Standard in an attempt to create a panic in Tidewater stock, a belief which was strengthened when it was learned that a big oil company, which the gentlemen controlled, the Union, had been sold about that time to the Standard Oil Trust for something like $500,000 in its stock. . . . The Tidewater had no trouble in proving that the complaints of insolvency and mismanagement were without foundation, and Judge Pierson Church, of Meadville, before whom the case was argued, refused to appoint the receiver, intimating strongly that, in his judgment, the case was an attempt to levy a species of blackmail, in which it must not be expected that his court would co-operate. Judge Church's decision was given on January 15. Two days later a sensation came in Tidewater affairs . . . it was nothing less than a bold attempt by the Taylor party, or, as it was now known, "the Standard party," to seize the reins of government. It was a very cleverly planned coup.

The yearly meeting for the election of officers in the company was fixed for a certain Wednesday in January. By verbal agreement it had been postponed, in 1882, to some time in February, the controller, D. B. Stewart, a member of the Taylor faction, representing that he could not have his statement ready earlier. No notices were sent out to this effect, although this should have been done. Taylor and his party, taking advantage of this fact perfectly well known to them, appeared at the Tidewater offices on January 17, and although one of the Benson faction, as the majority was known from the name of the company's president, was present with sufficient proxies to vote nearly two-thirds of the stock, they overruled him and elected themselves to the control. . . .

The Benson party took immediate action, applying for an injunction restraining the new board from taking possession of the books and offices. This was granted and a date for a hearing appointed. Up to the hearing the old board did business behind barricaded doors! The case was heard in Meadville before Judge Pierson Church. . . . As it was a case to be decided on purely technical matters—the rules governing elections—no sensation was looked for, but one came immediately. It was a long affidavit from James R. Keene, even more notorious then than now— there were fewer of his kind—for deals and corners and devious stock tricks, declaring that both the Patterson case and this attemp to obtain control were dictated by the "malicious ingenuity" of the Standard for the purpose of destroying the Tidewater and getting hold of its property. . . . The Keene sensation was followed by a second, an affidavit from John D. Archbold, of the Standard Oil Company, denying that his company had any interest in the present suit, but adding that for sometime the officers of the Tidewater had been seeking an alliance with the Standard. . . .

Such was the character of the charges and countercharges in this purely technical case. The judge took little notice of them in his decision, but, after an exhaustive discussion of the points involved in the election, decided it was illegal and continued the injunction he had granted against the new board. Judge Church's decision aroused general exultation in the Oil Regions —as any failure of the Standard to get what it wanted was bound to do, and with good reason. . . .

But the Oil Regions have always been prone to jump at conclusions. They were forgetting Mr. Rockefeller's record when they concluded that he was through with the Tidewater. Because he had failed in his old South Improvement Company trick, that is, failed to create a panic among Tidewater stockholders, and so get their property at panic prices, was no reason at all to suppose he had abandoned the chase. There still remained a legitimate method of getting into the company, and, as a last resort, Mr. Rockefeller accepted it. He bought the minority stock of the concern, held by the Taylor party. Up to this time Mr. Rockefeller had appeared in Tidewater affairs as a destroyer. He now appeared in a role in which he is quite as able— as a pacifier, and his extraordinary persuasiveness was never exercised to better effect. "We own $200,000 worth of your stock," he could tell the people he had been fighting. "If you will consent to confine yourselves to a fixed percentage of our joint business, and will sustain pipage rates and the price of refined oil, we will let you alone. Let us dwell together in peace."

The Tidewater, tired of the fight, accepted. And so these men

—to whom the oil business owes one of its most remarkable developments, who, in face of the most powerful and unscrupulous opposition, had in four years built up a business worth five and one-half millions of dollars—signed contracts in October, 1883, fixing the relative amount of business they were henceforth to do as 11½ per cent. of the aggregate, the Standard having 88½ per cent. The two simply became allies. The agreement between them was the same in effect as all Mr. Rockefeller's running agreements—it limited and kept up prices. Any benefit the oil business might have reaped from natural and decent competition between the two was of course ended by the alliance. For all practical purposes the two were one. In the phrase of the region, the Tidewater had "gone over to the Standard," and there it has always remained. . . .

Once more the good of the oil business was secure, and Mr. Rockefeller at once proceeded to arrange his great house in the new order made necessary by the introduction of the seaboard pipe-line. The entire transportation department of the business had to be reorganised. When the seaboard pipe-line became a factor in the oil business, in 1879, the Standard Oil Company owned practically the entire system of oil-gathering pipe-lines —that is, the lines carrying oil from the wells to the storing or shipping points. These lines were organised under the name of the United Pipe Lines, and the organisation was magnificent in both extent and in character of service rendered. Never, indeed, has the ability of the men Mr. Rockefeller gathered into his machine shone to better advantage than in the building up and management of the pipe-line business. At the end of 1883, when the alliance was made with the Tidewater, the United Pipe Lines were taking from the wells of Pennsylvania fully a million and a half barrels of oil a month. Their pipes, of an aggregate length of 3,000 miles, connected with thousands of wells scattered all over the wide Oil Regions.

Whenever the oil men opened a new field, no matter how remote from those already developed, the United Pipe Lines immediately went there to care for the oil. . . .

Such were the returns from the pipe-line for its services that no business ever justified more fully the extraordinary outlays of money and energy which it had taken to perfect it. For each barrel of oil the United Pipe Lines gathered, they received, when it was taken from the lines, twenty cents. The service cost them perhaps two cents after installation, though in these years, when they were obliged to carry some 30,000,000 barrels, they had constantly $6,000,000 on their books on which they did not at once realise. They could afford to let this sum stand because of the storage charge. For every 1,000 barrels carried in their tanks they received $6.25 each fifteen days—$152 a year. Now, tankage did not cost over $250 per 1,000 barrels, so that the storage more than paid its cost in two years. There were often great losses by fire, but these were paid by the owners of the oil—a pro rata assessment being made. There was a deterioration in quantity and quality of oil from holding, but this again was paid by the owners in a shrinkage charge of three per cent., deducted from the quantity of oil when run. Thus on every side the pipe-line business was guarded. So long as it could keep out competition and hold up its prices, there was no better paying business in the United States than piping oil.

As we have seen, Mr. Rockefeller began to add long-distance pipe-lines to his business as soon as the Tidewater demonstrated their feasibility, and before the time the Tidewater was brought into harmony he had a complete system to the seaboard and to his inland refinery points, organised under the name of the National Transit Company. The United Pipe Lines and the National Transit Company were really one business, the former consisting of local lines and the other of trunk lines, and to make the organisation more compact the former was transferred to the latter on April 1, 1884. The paid-up capital of the concern at this date was $31,000,000. Just as Mr. Rockefeller claimed, in 1878, that he was "prepared to enter into a contract to refine all the petroleum that could be sold in the markets of the world," so now he could announce that he was prepared to gather, store and transport all the crude petroleum not only that the markets of the world demanded, but that the producers took from the ground. As things now stood the only remaining point where he could possibly be affected by competition was the railroads. A new relation to the railroads was created by the new development. Mr. Rockefeller was not only independent of them, he was their competitor, for, like them, he was a common carrier obliged to transport what was offered. His open rate to New York was forty-five cents, to Philadelphia forty, though the actual service probably did not cost over ten cents. By the alliance with the Tidewater any danger of competition from a pipe-line, which could of course afford to cut the price, was shut off. The railroads might possibly, however, lower the prices a little and still make a profit. It was very necessary that the price be kept up in order that too much encouragement should not be given to outside refiners. The only group which threatened to grow to large proportions, at this time, was in the Oil Regions, a group which was the direct out-growth of the compromise of 1880. As will be remembered, the agreement with the Pennsylvania Railroad made then stipulated that all rates should be open, and that if a rebate was given to one shipper another could have it on demand. After the compromise the Pennsylvania had undertaken again to stimulate the growth of independent refineries, and several plants had been built in Titusville and Oil City. Having removed the New York group from competition by the alliance with the Tidewater it was Mr. Rockefeller's business to make it as hard as possible for the independents in the Oil Regions to do business, and to do this he must make a contract with the Pennsylvania. . . .

A new arrangement was now necessary in order to prevent competition, and in August, 1884, a contract was signed, for "considerations mutually interchanged," by which the National Transit Company agreed to give to the Pennsylvania Railroad twenty-six per cent. of "all petroleum brought to the Atlantic seaboard by all existing carriers, whether rail or pipe, now engaged in transporting such property, or which may hereafter engage in such transportation in conjunction with the Transit Company's pipes." . . .

With the removal of danger of any competition by the Pennsylvania Railroad, the transportation department of the Standard Oil Trust seems to have been as nearly a perfect machine, both in efficiency and in its monopolistic power, as ever has been devised. It was more perfect, indeed, than the refining end of the trust, for independent refiners did exist, and since 1880 they had been showing increasing vigour, whereas there seemed now no opportunity for an independent pipe-line ever again to develop. Who, with the Tidewater's story in mind, would be bold enough to attempt to reach the sea? For the time being, then, the Standard Oil Company had things all its own way. It collected with its ally, the Tidewater, practically the entire output of a great raw product. It manufactured fully ninety per cent. of this product, and aimed to manufacture 100 per cent. It was a common carrier, and so obliged to deliver oil to rival refineries if they called for it, but these refineries paid forty or forty-five cents for a service which cost the Standard Oil Trust not over one-fourth of the sum.

Mr. Rockefeller had every reason to be satisfied with oil transportation in 1884, but there was a part of the oil business which was not so completely in his grasp. The markets of the country were still open. There the few independent refiners who had escaped strangulation were free to barter as they could. But the right to make all the oil in the world, which Mr. Rockefeller claimed, carried with it the right to sell all the oil the world consumed. The independent was therefore a poacher in the market and must be driven out.

10 . CUTTING TO KILL

Rockefeller now plans to organise oil marketing as he had already organised oil transporting and refining—Wonderfully efficient and economical system installed—Curious practices introduced—Reports of competitors' business secured from railway agents—Competitors' clerks sometimes secured as allies—In many instances full records of all oil shipped are given Standard by railway and steamship companies—This information is used by Standard to fight competitors—Competitors driven out by underselling—Evidence from all over the country—Pretended independent oil companies started by the Standard—Standard's explanation of these practices is not satisfactory—Public derives no benefit from temporary lowering of prices—Prices made abnormally high when competition is destroyed.

To KNOW every detail of the oil trade, to be able to reach at any moment its remotest point, to control even its weakest factor—this was John D. Rockefeller's ideal of doing business. It seemed to be an intellectual necessity for him to be able to direct the course of any particular gallon of oil from the moment it gushed from the earth until it went into the lamp of a housewife. There must be nothing—*nothing* in his great machine he did not know to be working right. It was to complete this ideal, to satisfy this necessity, that he undertook, late in the seventies, to organise the oil markets of the world, as he had already organised oil refining and oil transporting. Mr. Rockefeller was driven to this new task of organisation not only by his own curious intellect; he was driven to it by that thing so abhorrent to his mind—competition. If, as he claimed, the oil business belonged to him, and if, as he had announced, he was prepared to refine all the oil that men would consume, it followed as a corollary that the markets of the world belonged to him. . . .

When Mr. Rockefeller began to gather the oil markets into his hands he had a task whose field was literally the world, for already, in 1871, the year before he first appeared as an important factor in the oil trade, refined oil was going into every civilised country of the globe. Of the five and a half million barrels of crude oil produced that year, the world used five millions, over three and a half of which went to foreign lands. This was the market which had been built up in the first ten years of business by the men who had developed the oil territory and invented the processes of refining and transporting, and this was the market, still further developed, of course, that Mr. Rockefeller inherited when he succeeded in corralling the refining and transporting of oil. It was this market he proceeded to organise.

The process of organisation seems to have been natural and highly intelligent. The entire country was buying refined oil for illumination. Many refiners had their own agents out looking for markets; others sold to wholesale dealers, or jobbers, who placed trade with local dealers, usually grocers. Mr. Rockefeller's business was to replace independent agents and jobbers by his own employees. The United States was mapped out and agents appointed over these great divisions. Thus, a certain portion of the Southwest—including Kansas, Missouri, Arkansas and Texas—the Waters-Pierce Oil Company, of St. Louis, Missouri, had charge of; a portion of the South—including Kentucky, Tennessee and Mississippi—Chess, Carley and Company, of Louisville, Kentucky, had charge of. These companies in turn divided their territory into sections, and put the subdivisions in the charge of local agents. These local agents had stations where oil was received and stored, and from which they and their salesmen carried on their campaigns. This system, inaugurated in the seventies, has been developed until now the Standard Oil Company of each state has its own marketing department, whose territory is divided and watched over in the above fashion. The entire oil-buying territory of the country is thus covered by local agents reporting to division headquarters. These report in turn to the head of the state marketing department, and his reports go to the general marketing headquarters in New York.

To those who know anything of the way in which Mr. Rockefeller does business, it will go without saying that this marketing department was conducted from the start with the greatest efficiency and economy. Its aim was to make every local station as nearly perfect in its service as it could be. The buyer must receive his oil promptly, in good condition, and of the grade he desired. If a customer complained, the case received prompt attention and the cause was found and corrected. He did not only receive oil; he could have proper lamps and wicks and burners, and directions about using them.

The local stations from which the dealer is served to-day are models of their kind, and one can easily believe they have always been so. Oil, even refined, is a difficult thing to handle without much disagreeable odour and stain, but the local stations of the Standard Oil Company, like its refineries, are kept orderly and clean by a rigid system of inspection. Every two or three months an inspector goes through each station and reports to headquarters on a multitude of details—whether barrels are properly bunged, filled, stencilled, painted, glued; whether tank wagons, buckets, faucets, pipes, are leaking; whether the glue trough is clean, the ground around the tanks dry, the locks in good condition; the horses properly cared for; the weeds cut in the yard. The time the agent gets around in the morning and the time he takes for lunch are reported. The prices he pays for feed for his horses, for coal, for repairs, are noted. In fact, the condition of every local station, at any given period, can be accurately known at marketing headquarters if desired. All of this tends, of course, to the greatest economy and efficiency in the local agents.

But the Standard Oil agents were not sent into a territory back in the seventies simply to sell all the oil they could by efficient service and aggressive pushing; they were sent there to sell all the oil that was bought. "The coal-oil business belongs to us," was Mr. Rockefeller's motto, and from the beginning of his campaign in the markets his agents accepted and acted on that principle. If a dealer bought but a barrel of oil a year, it must be from Mr. Rockefeller. This ambition made it necessary that the agents have accurate knowledge of all outside transactions in oil, however small, made in their field. . . .

For many years independent refiners have declared that the details of their shipments were leaking regularly from their own employees or from clerks in freight offices. At every investigation made these declarations have been repeated and occasional proof has been offered; for instance, a Cleveland refiner, John Teagle, testified in 1888 to the Congressional Committee that one day in 1883 his bookkeeper came to him and told him that he had been approached by a brother of the secretary of the Standard Oil Company at Cleveland, who had asked him if he did not wish to make some money. The bookkeeper asked how, and after some talk he was informed that it would be by his giving information concerning the business of his firm to the Standard. The bookkeeper seems to have been a wary fellow, for he dismissed his interlocutor without arousing suspicion and then took the case to Mr. Teagle, who asked him to make some kind of an arrangement in order to find out just what information the Standard wanted. The man did this. For twenty-five dollars down and a small sum per year he was to make a transcript of Mr. Teagle's daily shipments with net price received for the same; he was to tell what the cost of manufacturing in the refinery was; the amount of gasoline and naphtha made and the net price received for them; what was done with the tar; and what percentage of different grades of oil was made; also how much oil was exported. This information was to be mailed regularly to Box 164 of the Cleveland post-office. Mr. Teagle, who at that moment was hot on the tracks of the Standard in the courts, got an affidavit from the bookkeeper. This he took with the money which the clerk had received to the secretary of the Standard Oil Company and charged him with bribery. At first the gentleman denied having any knowledge of the matter, but he finally confessed and even took back the money. Mr. Teagle then gave the whole story to the newspapers, where it of course made much noise.

Several gentlemen testified before the recent Industrial Commission to the belief that their business was under the constant espionage of the Standard Oil Company. Theodore Westgate, an oil refiner of Titusville, told the Commission that all of his shipments were watched. The inference from his testimony was that the Standard Oil Company received reports direct from the freight houses. Lewis Emery, Jr., of Bradford, a life-long contestant of the Standard, declared that he knew his business was followed now in the same way as it was in 1872 under the South Improvement Company contract. He gave one or two instances from his own business experience to justify his statements, and he added that he could give many others if necessary. Mr. Gall, of Montreal, Canada, declared that these same methods were in operation in Canada. . . . Mrs. G. C. Butts, a daughter of George Rice, an independent refiner of Marietta, Ohio, told the Ohio Senate Committee which investigated trusts in 1898 that a railroad agent of their town had notified them that he had been approached by a Standard representative who asked him for a full report of all independent shipments, to whom and where going. . . .

But while the proofs the independents have offered of their charges show that such leaks have occurred at intervals all over the country, they do not show anything like a regular system of collecting information through this channel. From the evidence one would be justified in believing that the cases were rare, occurring only when a not over-nice Standard manager got into hot competition with a rival and prevailed upon a freight agent to give him information to help in his fight. In 1903, however, the writer came into possession of a large mass of documents of unquestionable authenticity, bearing out all and more than the independents charge. They show that the Standard Oil Company receives regularly to-day, at least from the railroads and steamship lines represented in these papers, information of *all* oil shipped. A study of these papers shows beyond question that somebody having access to the books of the freight offices records regularly each oil shipment passing the office—the names of consignor and consignee, the addresses of each, and the quantity and kind of oil are given in each case. This record is made out usually on a sheet of blank paper, though occasionally the recorder has been indiscreet enough to use the railroad company's stationery. The reports are evidently intended not to be signed, though there are cases in the documents where the name of the sender has been signed and erased; in one case a printed head bearing the name of the freight agent had been used. The name had been cut out, but so carelessly that it was easy to identify him. These reports had evidently been sent to the office of the Standard Oil Company, where they had received a careful examination, and the information they contained had been classified. Wherever the shipment entered was from one of the distributing stations of the Standard Oil Company, a line was drawn through it, or it was checked off in some way. In every other case in the mass of reports there was written, opposite the name of the consignee, the name of a person *known* to be a Standard agent or salesman in the territory where the shipment had gone.

Now what is this for? Copies of letters and telegrams accompanying the reports show that as soon as a particular report had reached Standard headquarters and it was known that a carload, or even a barrel, of independent oil was on its way to a dealer, the Standard agent whose name was written after the shipment on the record had been notified. "If you can stop car going to X, authorise rebate to Z (name of dealer) of three-quarters cent per gallon," one of the telegrams reads. There is plenty of evidence to show how an agent receiving such information "stops" the oil. He *persuades* the dealer to countermand the order. George Rice, when before the House Committee on Manufactures in 1888, presented a number of telegrams as samples of his experience in having orders countermanded in Texas. Four of these were sent on the same day from different dealers in the same town, San Angelo. Mr. Rice investigated the cause, and, by letters from the various firms, learned that the Standard agent had been around "threatening the trade that if they bought of me they would not sell them any more," as he put it.

Mrs. Butts in her testimony in 1898 said that her firm had a customer in New Orleans to whom they had been selling from 500 to 1,000 barrels a month, and that the Standard representative made a contract with him to pay him $10,000 a year for five years to stop handling the independent oil and take Standard oil! . . .

In the Ohio Investigation of 1898 John Teagle, of Cleveland, being upon his oath, said that his firm had had great difficulty in getting goods accepted because the Standard agents would persuade the dealers to cancel the orders. "They would have their local man, or some other man, call upon the trade and use their influence and talk lower prices, or make a lower retail price, or something to convince them that they'd better not take our oil, and, I suppose, to buy theirs." Mr. Teagle presented the following letter, signed by a Standard representative, explaining such a countermand:

John Fowler,   Des Moines, Iowa, January 14, 1891.
    Hampton, Iowa.
Dear Sir:—Our Marshalltown manager, Mr. Ruth, has explained the circumstances regarding the purchase and subsequent countermand of a car of oil from our competitors. He desires to have us express to you our promise that we will stand all expense provided there should be any trouble growing out of the countermand of this car. We cheerfully promise to do this; we have the best legal advice which can be obtained in Iowa, bearing on the points in this case. An order can be countermanded either before or after the goods have been shipped, and, in fact, can be countermanded even

if the goods have already arrived and are at the depot. A firm is absolutely obliged to accept a countermand. The fact that the order has been signed does not make any difference. We want you to absolutely refuse, under any circumstances, to accept the car of oil. We are standing back of you in this matter, and will protect you in every way, and would kindly ask you to keep this letter strictly confidential. . . .

Yours truly,   E. P. PRATT.

Peter Shull, of the Independent Oil Company of Mansfield, Ohio, testified before the same committee to experiences similar to those of Mr. Teagle.

"If I put a man on the road to sell goods for me," said Mr. Shull, "and he takes orders to the amount of 200 to 300 barrels a week, before I am able to ship these goods possibly, the Standard Oil Company has gone there and compelled those people to countermand those orders under a threat that, if they don't countermand them, they will put the price of oil down to such a price that they cannot afford to handle the goods."

In support of his assertion Mr. Shull offered letters from firms he has been dealing with. The following citations show the character of them:

TIFFIN, OHIO, February 1, 1898.

INDEPENDENT OIL COMPANY,
    Mansfield, Ohio.

Dear Sirs:—The Standard Oil Company, after your man was here, had the cheek to come in and ask how many barrels of oil we bought and so forth, then asked us to countermand the order, saying it would be for our best; we understand they have put their oil in our next door and offer it at six cents per gallon, at retail. Shall we turn tail or show them fight? If so, will you help us out any? . . .

Yours truly,   TALBOTT AND SON.

. . . .

In case the agent cannot persuade the dealer to countermand his order, more strenuous measures are applied. The letters quoted above hint at what they will be. Many letters have been presented by witnesses under oath in various investigations showing that Standard Oil agents in all parts of the country have found it necessary for the last twenty-five years to act at times as these letters threaten. One of the most aggressive of these campaigns waged at the beginning of this war of exterminating independent dealers was by the Standard marketing agent at Louisville, Kentucky—Chess, Carley and Company. This concern claimed a large section of the South as its territory. George Rice, of Marietta, Ohio, had been in this field for eight or ten years, having many regular customers. It became Chess, Carley and Company's business to secure these customers and to prevent his getting others. Mr. Rice was handicapped to begin with by railroad discrimination. He was never able to secure the rates of his big rival on any of the Southern roads. In 1888 the Interstate Commerce Commission examined his complaints against eight different Southern and Western roads, and found that no one of them treated him with "relative justice." Railroad discriminations were not sufficient to drive him out of the Southwest, however, and a war of prices was begun. . . .

Rice carried on his fight for a market in the most aggressive way, and everywhere he met disastrous competition. In 1892 he published a large pamphlet of documents illustrating Standard methods, in which he included citations from some seventy letters from dealers in Texas, received by him between 1881 and 1889, showing the kind of competition his oil met there from the Waters-Pierce Oil Company, the Standard's Texas agents:

"I have had wonderful competition on this car. As soon as my car arrived the Waters-Pierce Oil Company, who has an agent here, slapped the price down to $1.80 per case 110."

". . . Oil was selling at this point for $2.50 per case, and as soon as your car arrived it was put down to $1.50, which it is selling at to-day."

"The Waters-Pierce Oil Company reduced their prices on Brilliant oil from $2.60 to $1.50 per case and is waging a fierce war."

"Waters-Pierce Oil Company has our state by the throat and we would like to be extricated."

"I would like to handle your oil if I could be protected against the Waters-Pierce Oil Company. I am afraid if I would buy a car of oil from you this company would put the oil way below what I pay and make me lose big money. I can handle your oil in large quantities if you would protect me against them."

"The Waters-Pierce Oil Company has cut the stuffing out of coal-oil and have been ever since I got in my last car. They put the price to the merchants at $1.80 per case."

. . . . .

"Jobbers say when they take hold of another oil they are at once boycotted by Waters-Pierce Oil Company, who not only refuse to sell them, but put oil below what they pay for it, and thus knock them out of the oil trade, unless they sell at a loss."

"If I find that I can handle your oil in Texas without being run out and losing money by this infernal corporation, the Waters-Pierce Oil Company, I want to arrange with you to handle it extensively. I received verbal notice this morning from their agent that they would make it hot for me when my oil got here."

Mr. Rice claims, in his preface to the collection of letters here quoted from, that he has hundreds of similar ones from different states in the Union, and the writer asked to examine them. The package of documents submitted in reply to this request was made up literally of hundreds of letters. They came from twelve different states, and show everywhere the same competitive method—cutting to kill. One thing very noticeable in these letters is the indignation of the dealers at the Standard methods of securing trade. They resent threats. They complain that the Standard agents "nose" about their premises, that they ask impudent questions, and that they generally make the trade disgusting and humiliating. In Mississippi, in the eighties, the indignation of the small dealers against Chess, Carley and Company was so strong that they formed associations binding themselves not to deal with them.

These same tactics have been kept up in the Southwest ever since. A letter, dated April 28, 1891, from the vice-president of the Waters-Pierce Oil Company, A. M. Finlay, to his agent at Dallas, Texas, says bluntly: "We want to make the prices at Dallas and in the neighbourhood on Brilliant and water-white oil, that will prevent Clem (an independent dealer) from doing any business." . . .

Considerable testimony of the same sort of practices was offered in the recent "hearing before the Industrial Commission," most of it general in character. The most significant special case was offered by Mr. Westgate, the treasurer of· the American Oil Works, an independent refinery of Titusville, Pennsylvania.

The American Oil Works, it seems, were in 1894 shipping oil called "Sunlight" in barrels to South Bend, Washington. This was in the territory of the Standard agents at Portland, Oregon, one of whom wrote to a South Bend dealer when he heard of the intrusion: "We will state for your information that never a drop of oil has reached South Bend of better quality than what we have always shipped into that territory. They can name it 'Sunlight,' 'Moonlight,' or 'Starlight,' it makes no difference. You can rest assured if another carload of 'Sunlight' arrives at your place, it will be sold very cheap. We do not purpose to allow another carload to come into that territory unless it comes and is put on the market at one-half its actual cost. You can convey this idea to the young man who imported the carload of 'Sunlight' oil."

When John D. Archbold, of the Standard Oil Company, had his attention called to this letter by Professor Jenks, of the Industrial Commission, Mr. Archbold characterised the letter as "a foolish statement by a foolish and unwise man" and promised to investigate it. Later he presented the commission with an explanation from the superior of the agent, who declared that the writer of the letter did not have any authority to say that oil would be sold on the basis mentioned. "The letter," he continued, "was intended to be written in a jocular manner to deny a claim that he was selling oil inferior in quality to that sold by others." It is hard for the mere outsider to catch the jocularity of the letter, and it must have been much more difficult for the dealer who received it to appreciate it.

Independent oil dealers of the present day complain bitterly of a rather novel way employed by the Standard for bringing into line dealers whose prejudices against buying from them are too strong to be overcome by the above methods. This is through what are called "bogus" oil companies. The obdurate dealer is approached by the agent of a new independent concern, call it the A B C Oil Company, for illustration. The agent seeks trade on the ground that he represents an independent concern and that he can sell at lower prices than the firm from which the dealer is buying. Gradually he works his way into the independent's trade. As a matter of fact, the new company is merely a Standard jobbing house which makes no oil, and which conceals its realy identity under a misleading name. The mass of reports from railroad freight offices quoted from in this article corroborate this claim of the independents. The A B C Oil Company is mentioned again and again as shipping oil, and in the audited reports it is always checked off in the same fashion as the known Standard companies, and none of its shipments is referred to Standard agents. Independents all over the country tell of loss of markets through underselling by these "bogus" companies. The lower price which a supposedly independent concern gives to a dealer who will not, under any condition, buy of the Standard, need not demoralise the Standard trade in the vicinity if the concession is made with caution. After the trade is secure, that is, after the genuine independent is ousted, the masquerading concern always finds itself obliged to advance prices. When the true identity of such a company becomes known its usefulness naturally is impaired, and it withdraws from the field and a new one takes its place. . . .

The general explanation of these competitive methods which the Standard officials have offered, is that they originate with "over-zealous" employees and are disapproved of promptly if brought to the attention of the heads of the house. The cases seem rather too universal for such an explanation to be entirely satisfactory. Certainly the system of collecting information concerning competitive business is not practised by the exceptional "over-zealous" employee, but is a recognised department of the Standard Oil Company's business. In the mass of documents from which the reports of oil shipments referred to above were drawn, are certain papers showing that the system is nearly enough universal to call for elaborate and expensive bookkeeping at the headquarters of each Standard marketing division. For instance, on the next page is a fragment illustrating the page of a book kept at such a headquarters.

What does this show? Simply that every day the reports received from railroad freight agents are entered in records kept for the purpose; that there is on file at the Standard Oil headquarters a detailed list of the daily shipments which each independent refiner sends out even to the initials and number on the car in which the shipment goes. From this remarkable record the same set of documents shows that at least two sets of reports are made up. One is a report of the annual volume of business being done by each particular independent refiner or wholesale jobber, the other of the business of each individual local dealer, so far as the detectives of the Standard have been able to locate it. . . .

Oil is usually sold at retail by grocers. It is with them that the local agents deal. Now the daily reports from the freight offices show the oil they receive. The competition reports from local agents also give more or less information concerning their business. A card is made out for each of them, tabulating the date on which he received oil, the name and location of the dealer he got it from, the quality, and the price he sells at. In a space left for remarks on the card there is written in red ink any general information about . . . the dealer the agent may have picked up. Often there is an explanation of why the man does not buy Standard oil—not infrequently this explanation reads: "Is opposed to monopolies." It is impossible to say from documentary evidence how long such a card catalogue has been kept by the Standard; that it has been a practice for at least twenty-five years the following quotation from a letter written in 1903 by a prominent Standard official in the Southwest to one of his agents shows: "Where competition exists," says the official, "it has been our custom to keep a record of each merchant's daily . . . purchase of bulk oil; and I know of one town at least in the Southern Texas Division where that record has been kept, whether there was competition or not, for the past fifteen years."

The inference from this system of "keeping the eyes open" is that the Standard Oil Company knows practically where every barrel shipped by every independent dealer goes; and where every barrel bought by every corner-grocer from Maine to California comes from. The documents from which the writer draws the inference do not, to be sure, cover the entire country, but they do cover in detail many different states, and enough is known of the Standard's competitive methods in states outside this territory to justify one in believing that the system of gathering information is in use everywhere. That it is a perfect system is improbable. Bribery is not as dangerous business in this country as it deserves to be—of course nothing but a bribe would induce a clerk to give up such information as these daily reports contain—but, happily, such is the force of tradition that even those who have practised it for a long time shrink from discovery. It is one of those political and business practices which are only respectable when concealed. Naturally, then, the above system of gathering information must be handled with care, and can never have the same perfection as that Mr. Rockefeller expected when he signed the South Improvement Company charter.

The moral effect of this system on employees is even a more

serious feature of the case than the injustice it works to competition. For a "consideration" railroad freight clerks give confidential information concerning freight going through their hands. It would certainly be quite as legitimate for post-office clerks to allow Mr. Rockefeller to read the private letters of his competitors, as it is that the clerks of a railroad give him data concerning their shipments. Everybody through whose hands such information passes is contaminated by the knowledge. To be a factor, though even so small a one, in such a transaction, blunts one's sense of right and fairness. The effect on the local Standard agent cannot but be demoralising. . . .

The system results every now and then, naturally enough, in flagrant cases of bribing employees of the independents themselves. Where the freight office does not yield the information, the rival's own office may, and certainly if it is legitimate to get it from one place it is from the other. It is not an unusual thing for independent refiners to discharge a man whom they have reason to believe gives confidential information to the Standard. . . .

For the general public, absorbed chiefly in the question, "How does all this affect what we are paying for oil?" the chief point of interest in the marketing contests is that, after they were over, the price of oil has always gone back with a jerk to the point where it was when the cutting began, and not infrequently it has gone higher—the public pays. . . . A table was prepared in 1892 to show the effect of competition on the price of oil in various states of the Union. The results were startling. In California, oil which sold at non-competitive points at 26½ cents a gallon, at competitive points brought 17½ cents. In Denver, Colorado, there was an "Oil War" on in the spring of 1892, and the same oil which was selling at Montrose and Garrison at twenty-five cents a gallon, in Denver sold at seven cents. This competition finally killed opposition and Denver thereafter paid twenty-five cents. The profits on this price were certainly great enough to call for competition. The same oil which was sold in Colorado in the spring of 1892 at twenty-five cents, sold in New York for exportation at 6.10 cents. Of course the freight rates to Colorado were high, the open rate was said to be nine cents a gallon, but that it cost the Standard Oil Company nine cents a gallon to get its oil there, one would have to have documentary proof to believe, and, even if it did, there was still some ten cents profit on a gallon—five dollars on a barrel. In Kansas, this time, the difference between the price at competitive and non-competitive points was seven cents; in Indiana six cents; in South Carolina four and one-half cents. . . .

Briefly put, then, the conclusion, from a careful examination of the testimony on Standard competitive methods, is this:

The marketing department of the Standard Oil Company is organised to cover the entire country, and aims to sell all the oil sold in each of its divisions. To forestall or meet competition it has organised an elaborate secret service for locating the quantity, quality, and selling price of independent shipments. Having located an order for independent oil with a dealer, it persuades him, if possible, to countermand the order. If this is impossible, it threatens "predatory competition" that is, to sell at cost or less, until the rival is worn out. If the dealer still is obstinate, it institutes an "Oil War." In late years the cutting and the "Oil Wars" are often intrusted to so-called "bogus" companies, who retire when the real independent is put out of the way. In later years the Standard has been more cautious about beginning underselling than formerly, though if a rival offered oil at a less price than it had been getting—and generally even small refineries can contrive to sell below the non-competitive prices of the Standard—it does not hesitate to consider the lower price a declaration of war and to drop its prices and keep them down until the rival is out of the way. The price then goes back to the former figure or higher. . . . At the period we have reached in this history—that is, the completion of the monopoly of the pipe-lines in 1884 and the end of competition in transporting oil—there seemed to the independents no escape from Mr. Rockefeller in the market.

The sureness and promptness with which he located their shipments seemed uncanny to them. The ruthlessness and persistency with which he cut and continued to cut their prices drove them to despair. The character of the competition Mr. Rockefeller carried on in the markets, particularly of the South and Middle West of this country, at this time, aggravated daily the feeble refining element, and bred contempt far and wide among people who saw the cutting, and perhaps profited temporarily by it, but who had neither the power nor the courage to interfere. The knowledge of it fed greatly the bitterness in the Oil Regions. Part of the stock in conversation of every dissatisfied oil producer or ruined refiner became tales of disastrous conflicts in markets. They told of crippled men selling independent oil from a hand cart, whose trade had been wiped out by a Standard cart which followed him day by day, practically giving away oil. They told of grocers driven out of business by an attempt to stand by a refiner. They told endless tales, probably all exaggerated, perhaps some of them false, yet all of them believed, because of such facts as have been rehearsed above. There came to be a popular conviction that the "Standard would do anything." It was a condition which promised endless annoyance to Mr. Rockefeller and his colleagues. It meant popular mistrust, petty hostilities, misinterpretations, contempt, abuse. There were plenty of people even willing to deny Mr. Rockefeller ability. That the Standard was in a venture was enough in those people's minds to damn it. Anything the Standard wanted was wrong, anything they contested was right. A verdict for them demonstrated the corruption of the judge and jury; against them their righteousness. Mr. Rockefeller, indeed, was each year having more reason to realise monopoly building had its trials as well as its profits.

Rockefeller's silence—Belief in the oil regions that combined opposition to him was useless—Individual opposition still conspicuous—The Standard's suit against Scofield, Shurmer and Teagle—Seeks to enforce an agreement with that firm to limit output of refined oil—Scofield, Shurmer and Teagle attempt to do business independently of the Standard and its rebates—Find their lot hard—They sue the Lake Shore and Michigan Southern Railway for discriminating against them—A famous case and one the railway loses—Another case in this war of individuals on the rebate shows the Standard still to be taking drawbacks—The case of George Rice against the receiver of the Cincinnati and Marietta Railroad.

THE apathy and inaction which naturally flow from a great defeat lay over the Oil Regions of Northwestern Pennsylvania long after the compromise with John D. Rockefeller in 1880, followed, as it was, by the combination with the Standard of the great independent seaboard pipe-line which had grown up under the oil men's encouragement and patronage. Years of war with a humiliating outcome had inspired the producers with the conviction that fighting was useless, that they were dealing with a power verging on the superhuman—a power carrying concealed weapons, fighting in the dark, and endowed with an altogether diabolic cleverness. Strange as the statement may appear, there is no disputing that by 1884 the Oil Regions as a whole looked on Mr. Rockefeller with superstitious awe. Their notion of him was very like that which the English common people had for Napoleon in the first part of the 19th century, which the peasants of Brittany have even to-day for the English—a dread power, cruel, omniscient, always ready to spring.

This attitude of mind, altogether abnormal in daring, impetuous, and self-confident men, as those of the Oil Regions were, was based on something more than the series of bold and admirably executed attacks which had made Mr. Rockefeller master of the oil business. The first reason for it was the atmosphere of mystery in which Mr. Rockefeller had succeeded in enveloping himself. He seems by nature to dislike the public eye. In his early years his home, his office, and the Baptist church were practically the only places which saw him. He did not frequent clubs, theatres, public meetings. When his manœuvres began to bring public criticism upon him, his dislike of the public eye seems to have increased. He took a residence in New York, but he was unknown there save to those who did business with him or were interested in his church and charities. His was perhaps the least familiar face in the Standard Oil Company. He never went to the Oil Regions, and the Oil Regions said he was afraid to come, which might or might not have been true. Certainly the Oil Regions never hesitated to express opinions about him calculated to make a discreet man keep his distance.

Even in Cleveland, his home for twenty-five years, Mr. Rockefeller was believed to conceal himself from his townsmen. It is certain that the operations of his great business were guarded with the most jealous care. The New York Sun sent an "experienced observer" to Cleveland in 1882 to write up the Standard concern. He speaks with amazement in his letters of the atmosphere of secrecy and mystery which he found enveloping everything connected with Mr. Rockefeller. You could not get an interview with him, the observer complained; even his home papers had ceased to go to the Standard offices to inquire about the truth of rumours which reached them from the outside. The hundreds of employees of the trust in the town were as silent as their master in all that concerned the business, and if one talked—well, he was not long an employee of Mr. Rockefeller. There was between the Standard Oil Company and the town and press of Cleveland none of the camaraderie, the mutual good-will and pride and confidence which usually characterise the relations between great businesses and their environment.

In Cleveland, as in the Oil Regions, Mr. Rockefeller's careful effort to cover up his intentions and his tracks had been at first met with jeers and blunt rebuffs, but he had finally succeeded in silencing and awing the people. It is worth noting that while all of the members of the Standard Oil Company followed Mr. Rockefeller's policy of saying nothing, there was no such popular dread of any other one of them. In the Oil Regions, for instance, there was a bitter hatred of the Standard Oil Company as an organisation, but for the most part the people liked the men who served it, and certainly had no awe of them, for these men circulated freely among their fellow-townsmen; they were active in all the pleasures and enterprises of the communites in which they lived; they were generous, able, cordial, and whatever the people said of the concern they served, they generally qualified it by expressing their personal likings for the men themselves.

A second reason for the popular dread of Mr. Rockefeller was that this man, whom nobody saw and who never talked, knew everything—even unexpected and trivial things—and those who saw the effect of this knowledge and did not see how he could obtain it, regarded him as little short of an omniscient being. There was really nothing in the least occult about Mr. Rockefeller's omniscience. He obtained part of his knowledge of other people's affairs by a most extensive and thoroughly organised system of news-gathering, such as any bright business man of wide sweep might properly employ. But he combined with this perfectly legitimate work the sordid methods of securing confidential information described in the last chapter. Certainly there is nothing of the transcendental in this kind of omniscience, and the feeling of supernaturalism which Mr. Rockefeller had inspired by 1884 has entirely evaporated since, as evidence of his methods has been circulated. The source was, however, long secret, and when again and again men who could hardly suppose their existence known to Mr. Rockefeller saw movements anticipated which they believed known only to themselves and their confidential agents, they began to dread him and to invest him with mysterious qualities. If Mr. Rockefeller had been as great psychologist as he is business manipulator he would have realised that he was awakening a terrible popular dread, and he would have foreseen that one day, with the inevitable coming to light of his methods, there would spring up about his name a crop of scorn which would choke any crop of dollars and donations which the wealth of the earth could produce.

The effect of this dread was deplorable, for it intensified the feeling, now wide-spread in the Oil Regions, that it was useless to make further effort at a combined resistance. And yet these men, who were now lying too supine in Mr. Rockefeller's steel glove even to squirm, had laid the foundation of freedom in the oil business. It has taken thirty years to demonstrate the inestimable value of the efforts which in 1884 they regarded as futile—thirty years to build even a small structure on the foundation they had laid, though that much has been done.

The situation was saved at this critical time by individuals scattered through the oil world who were resolved to test the validity of Mr. Rockefeller's claim that the coal-oil business belonged to him. "We have a right to do an independent business," they said, "and we propose to do it." They began this effort by an attack on the weak spot in Mr. Rockefeller's armour. The twelve years just passed had taught them that the realisation of Mr. Rockefeller's great purpose had been made possible by his remarkable manipulation of the railroads. It was the rebate which had made the Standard Oil Trust, the rebate, amplified, systematised, glorified into a power never equalled before or since by any business of the country. The rebate had made the trust, and the rebate, in spite of ten years of combination, Petroleum Associations, Producers' Unions, resolutions, suits in equity, suits in quo warranto, appeals to Congress, legislative investigations—the rebate still was Mr. Rockefeller's most effective weapon. If they could wrest it from his hand they could do business. They had learned something else in this period—that the whole force of public opinion and the spirit of the law were against the rebate, and that the railroads, knowing this, feared exposure of discrimination, and could be made to settle rather than have their practices made public. Therefore, said these individuals, we propose to sue for rebates and collect charges until we make it so harassing and dangerous for the railroads that they will shut down on Mr. Rockefeller.

The most interesting and certainly the most influential of these private cases was that of Scofield, Shurmer and Teagle, of Cleveland, one of the firms which, in 1876, entered into a "joint adventure" with Mr. Rockefeller for limiting the output and so holding up prices. The adventure had been most successful. The profits were enormous. . . .

After four years the Standard began to complain that their partners in the adventure were refining too much oil—the first year the books showed they had exceeded their 85,000-barrel limitation by nearly 3,000, the second year by 2,000, the third by 15,000, the fourth by 5,000. Dissatisfied, the Standard de-

128

manded that the firm pay them the entire profit upon the
excess refined; for, claimed Mr. Rockefeller, our monopoly is so
perfect that we would have sold the excess if you had not
broken the contract, consequently the profits belong to us. Scofield, Shurmer and Teagle paid half the profit on the excess,
but refused more, and they persisted in exceeding their quota;
then Mr. Rockefeller, controlling by this time the crude supply
in Cleveland through ownership of the pipe-lines, shut down
on their crude supply. If they would not obey the contract of
their own will they could not do business. The firm seems not
to have been frightened. "We are sorry that you refuse to furnish us crude oil as agreed," they wrote Mr. Rockefeller; "we do
not regard the limitation of 85,000 barrels as binding upon us,
and as we have a large number of orders for refined oil we
must fill them, and if you refuse to furnish us crude oil on
the same favourable terms as yourselves, we shall get it elsewhere as best we can and hold you responsible for its difference
in cost."

Mr. Rockefeller's reply was a prayer for an injunction against
the members of the firm, restraining them individually and
collectively from distilling at their said works at Cleveland,
Ohio, more than 85,000 barrels of crude petroleum of forty-two
gallons each in every year. . . .

Scofield, Shurmer and Teagle did not hesitate to take up the
gauntlet, and a remarkable defence they made. In their answer
they declared the so-called agreement had at all times been
"utterly void and of no effect as being by its terms in restraint
of trade and against public policy." They declared that the
Standard Oil Company had never kept the terms of the agreement, that it had intentionally withheld the benefits of the
advantages it enjoyed in freight contracts, and that it now was
pumping crude oil from the Oil Regions to Cleveland at a cost
of about twelve cents a barrel and charging them (Scofield,
Shurmer and Teagle) twenty cents. They denied that the
Standard had sustained any damage through them, but claimed
that their business had been carried on at a large profit. "There
is such a large margin between the price of crude oil and refined," declared the defendants, "that the manufacture and
sale of refined oil is attended with large profit; it is impossible
to supply the demand of the public for oil if the business and

refineries of both plaintiff and defendant are carried on and run to their full capacities, and if the business of the defendants were stopped, as prayed for by the plaintiff, it would result in a still higher price for refined oil and the establishment of more perfect monopoly in the manufacture and sale of the same by plaintiff." To establish such a monopoly, the defendants went on to declare, had been the sole object of the Standard Oil Company in making this contract with them, and similar ones with other firms, to establish a monopoly and so maintain unnaturally high prices, and certainly Scofield, Shurmer and Teagle knew whereof they swore, for they had shared in the spoils of the winter of 1876 and 1877, and at this very period, October, 1880, they were witnessing an attempt to repeat the coup. . . .

Scofield, Shurmer and Teagle were now obliged to stand on their own feet. They could refine all the oil they wished, but they must make their own freight contracts, and they found rates when you worked with Mr. Rockefeller were vastly different from rates when you competed with him. The agent of the Lake Shore Railroad, by which most of their shipments went, told them frankly that they could not have the rates of the Standard unless they gave the same volume of business. The discrimination against them was serious. For instance, in 1880, when the Standard paid sixty-five cents a barrel from Cleveland to Chicago, Scofield, Shurmer and Teagle paid eighty. From April 1 to July 1, 1881, the Standard paid fifty-five cents and their rival eighty cents; from July 1 to November 1, 1881, the rates were thirty-five and seventy cents respectively, and so it went on for three years, when the firm, despairing of any change, took the case into court. This case, fought through all the courts of Ohio, and in 1886 taken to the Supreme Court of the United States, is one of the clearest and cleanest in existence for studying all the factors in the rebate problem—the argument and pressure by which the big shipper secures and keeps his advantage, the theory and defence of the railroad in granting the discrimination, the theory on which the suffering small shipper protests, and finally the law's point of view. The first trial of the case was in the Court of Common Pleas, and the refiners won. The railroad then appealed to the District Court (the present Circuit Court), where it was argued. So "important and difficult" did the judges of the District Court find the questions involved to be, that on the plea of the railroad they sent their findings of the facts in the case to the Supreme Court of the state for decision—a privilege they had under the law in force at that time. . . .

"The manner of making shipments for plaintiffs and for the Standard Oil Company was precisely the same, and the only thing to distinguish the business of the one from the other was the aggregate yearly amounts of freight shipped," said Judge Atherton, of the Supreme Court, who gave the decision on the findings of fact, and he held in common with his predecessors that a rebate on account of volume of business only was "a discrimination in favour of capital," and contrary to a sound public policy, violation of that equality of rights guaranteed to every citizen, and a wrong to the disfavoured person. "We hold, . . ." he said, "that a discrimination in the rate of freights resting extensively on such a basis ought not to be sustained. The principle is opposed to sound public policy. It would build up and foster monopolies, add largely to the accumulated power of capital and money, and drive out all enterprise not backed by overshadowing wealth. With the doctrine, as contended for by the defendants, recognised and enforced by the courts, what will prevent the great grain interest of the Northwest, or the coal and iron interests of Pennsylvania, or any of the great commercial interests of the country bound together by the power and influence of aggregated wealth and in league with the railroads of the land, driving to the wall all private enterprises struggling for existence, and with an iron hand thrusting back all but themselves?" Judge Atherton was scathing enough in his opinion of the contract between the Lake Shore and the Standard. Look at it, he said, and see just what is shown. In consideration of the company giving to the railroad its entire freight business in oil, they transport this freight about ten cents a barrel cheaper than for any other customer. "The understanding was to keep the price *down* for the favoured customer, but *up* for all others, and the inevitable tendency and effect of this contract was to enable the Standard Oil Company to establish and maintain an overshadowing monopoly, to ruin all other operators and drive them out of business in all the region supplied by the defendant's road, its branches and connecting lines." . . .

Having lost their case in the Supreme Court of the state, the

Lake Shore now appealed to the Supreme Court of the United States, and the record was filed in November, 1886. It was never heard; the railroad evidently concluded it was useless, and finally withdrew its petition, thereby accepting the decision of the Supreme Court of Ohio restraining it from further discrimination against Scofield, Shurmer and Teagle.

This case, which was before the public constantly during the six or seven years following the breaking up of the Producers' Union, in which the Oil Regions presented no united front to Mr. Rockefeller, served to keep public attention on the ruinous effect of the rebate and to strenghen the feeling that drastic legislation must be taken if Mr. Rockefeller's exploit was to be prevented in other industries.

One other case came out in this war of individuals on the rebate system which heightened the popular indignation against the Standard. It was a case showing that the Standard Oil Company had not yet abandoned that unique feature of its railroad contracts by which a portion of the money which other people paid for their freight was handed over to them! This peculiar development of the rebate system seems to have belonged exclusively to Mr. Rockefeller. Indeed, a careful search of all the tremendous mass of materials which the various investigations of railroads produced shows no other case—so far as the writer knows—of this practice. It was the clause of the South Improvement contracts which provoked the greatest outcry. It was the feature of Mr. Cassatt's revelations in 1877 which dumfounded the public and which no one would believe until they saw the actual agreements Mr. Cassatt presented. The Oil Regions as a whole did not hesitate to say that they believed this practice was still in operation, but, naturally, proof was most difficult to secure. The demonstration came in 1885, through one of the most aggressive and violent independents which the war in oil has produced, George Rice, of Marietta, Ohio. Mr. Rice, an oil producer, had built a refinery at Marietta in 1873. He sold his oil in the state, the West, and South. Six years later his business was practically stopped by a sudden raise in rates on the Ohio roads—an advance of fully 100 per cent. being made on freights from Marietta, where there were several independent refineries, although no similar advance was made from Wheeling and Cleveland, where the

Standard refineries were located. These discriminations were fully shown in an investigation by the Ohio State Legislature in 1879. From that time on Mr. Rice was in constant difficulty about rates. He seems to have taken rebates when he could get them, but he could never get anything like what his big competitors got.

In 1883 Mr. Rice began to draw the crude supply for his refinery from his own production in the Macksburg field of Southeastern Ohio, not far from Marietta. . . . In 1883 the Standard Oil Company took their line into the field, and. . . . they immediately contracted with the road for a rate of ten cents on their own oil, instead of the fifteen cents he was getting, and a rate of thirty-five on independent oil. And in addition they asked that the extra twenty-five cents the independents paid *be turned over to them!* If this was not done the Standard would be under the painful necessity of taking away its shipments and building pipe-lines to Marietta. . . .

Now, how was this to be done "with propriety"? Simply enough. The Standard Oil Company was to be charged ten cents per barrel, less an amount equivalent to twenty-five cents per barrel upon all oil shipped by Rice. . . .

Mr. Rice, outraged as he was by the discrimination, was looking for evidence to bring suit . . . but it was not until October that he was ready to take the matter into court. On the 13th of that month he applied to Judge Baxter of the United States Circuit Court for an order that Phineas Pease, receiver of the Cleveland and Marietta Railroad, report to the court touching his freight rates and other matters complained of in the application. . . . No sooner was this order of the court . . . known than the general freight agent, Mr. Terry, hurried to Cleveland, Ohio, to meet Mr. O'Day of the Standard Oil Company, with whom he had made the contract. The upshot of that interview was that on October 29, twelve days *after* the judge had ordered the contracts produced, a check for $340, signed by J. R. Campbell, Treasurer (a Standard pipe-line official), was received from Oil City, headquarters of the Standard pipe-line, by the agent who had been collecting and dividing the freight money. This check for $340 was the amount the pipe-line had received on Mr. Rice's shipments between March 20 and April 25. The agent was instructed to send the money to the receiver, and later, by order of the court, the money was refunded to Mr. Rice. But the Standard was not out of the scrape so easily. . . .

On December 18 George K. Nash, a former governor of Ohio, was appointed master commissioner to take testimony and clear up the point doubtful in the judge's mind—to whom had the extra money paid by Rice been paid; the receiver declared that he never paid the Standard Oil Company any part of Rice's money. Mr. Nash summoned a large number of witnesses and gradually untangled the story told above. Mr. Pease spoke truly, he had never paid the Standard Oil Company any part of Mr. Rice's money. A join agent of the railroad and the pipe-line had been appointed, at a salary of eighty-five dollars a month, sixty dollars paid by Pease and twenty-five dollars by the Standard, who collected the freight on independent shipments and divided the money between the two parties. It was from this agent that it was learned that, twelve days *after* Judge Baxter ordered Receiver Pease to bring his contracts into court, the money paid on Mr. Rice's oil had been returned by the Standard Oil Company. While the investigation in regard to Mr. Rice's oil was going on, complaints came to Commissioner Nash from two other oil works at Marietta that they had been suffering a like discrimination for a much longer time. The commissioner investigated the cases and found the complaints justified. The Standard Oil Company had received $649.15 out of the money paid by one concern to the railroad for carrying its oil, and $639.75 out of the sum paid by another concern! Both of these sums were returned by the Standard.

Of course the case aroused violent comment. In 1888 it came before the Congressional Committee which was investigating trusts, and an effort was made to explain the twenty-five cents extra as a charge of the pipe-line for carrying oil to the railway. Now, the practice in vogue in the Oil Regions then and now is that the *purchaser of the oil pays the pipe-line charge*. The railroad has nothing to do with it. Even if the Standard Oil Company puts a tax on railroads for allowing them to take oil carried by its pipe-lines—thus collecting double pay—the tax would not apply in Mr. Rice's case, for the oil came to the Cincinnati and Marietta road not through Standard pipes but through Mr. Rice's own pipes. . . .

Soon after the report of the Congressional Committee was

published John D. Rockefeller himself explained the case in an interview published in the New York World for March 29, 1890: "When the arrangement was reported to the officers of the company at New York," Mr. Rockefeller told the interviewer, "it was not agreed to because our counsel pronounced it illegal in so far as it embraced oil carried by the pipe-line. Some $250 had been paid to the pipe-line under this contract on oil which the line had not transported. This was refunded. We repudiated the contract before it was passed upon by the courts and made full recompense. In a business as large as ours, conducted by so many agents, some things are likely to be done which we cannot approve. We correct them as soon as they come to our knowledge. The public hears of the wrong—it never hears of the correction." In the Digest of Evidence made by the Industrial Commission in its report published in 1900 (page 158), it is stated that the money collected was refunded *before* suit was brought. The facts show that the statement in the report of the Industrial Commission that the money was refunded *before* suit was brought is wrong, and that, while Mr. Rockefeller is technically correct in stating that the Standard repudiated the contract before it was passed on by the courts, he should have added they did not repudiate the contract until *eight months after* it was made, and did not refund the money until *twelve days after* it became certain that the contract would be produced in court. He also does not explain why the Standard Oil Company did not return the money unjustly paid to them on the shipments of the other independent oil concerns of Marietta until exposure by Commissioner Nash's investigation made it inevitable.

But it was not only manipulation of the railroads by the Standard Oil Company of which the public was complaining at this time. The policy of making it impossible for even small independent concerns to do business was attracting more and more attention. Indeed, there was going on in Buffalo, New York, simultaneously with these two cases, a most sensational trial, growing out of an indictment for the crime of conspiracy, by the Grand Jury of Erie County, New York, of three prominent members of the Standard Oil Company—H. H. Rogers, John D. Archbold and Ambrose McGregor—with two refiners with whom they were associated—H. B. Everest and C. M. Everest. The case is reported in the next chapter at some length, because of the importance it has assumed in the popular controversy which has been going on for the last twenty years over "Standard methods," it being the case on which is based the often-repeated charge that Mr. Rockefeller, to win his point, has been known to burn refineries.

12   THE BUFFALO CASE

The Standard buys three-fourths of the Vacuum Oil Works of Rochester—
Two Vacuum employees establish Buffalo Lubricating Oil Company and
take with them an experienced stillman from the Vacuum—The Buffalo
Lubricating Oil Company has an explosion and the stillman suddenly
leaves—The Buffalo Lubricating Oil Company is sued by Vacuum for
infringement of patents—Matthews sues the Everests of the Vacuum for
deliberately trying to ruin his business—Matthews wins his first civil
suit—He files a second suit for damages, and secures the indictment of
several Standard officials for criminal conspiracy—Rogers, Archbold and
McGregor acquitted—The Everests fined.

VERY SOON after Mr. Rockefeller began to "acquire" independent refineries, whose owners were loath to sell or go out of business, unpleasant stories began to be circulated in the oil world of the methods used in getting the offending plants out of the way. When freight discriminations, cutting off of crude supply, and price wars in the market failed, other means were tried, and these means included sometimes, it was whispered, the actual destruction of the plants. The only case in which this charge was made which ever came to trial was that of the Buffalo Lubricating Oil Company, Limited. For sake of clearness, a narrative of the case has been drawn from the testimony offered, no statements being admitted which were not brought out in the trials.

It seems that some time in 1879 the owners of the Vacuum Oil Works, of Rochester, New York—H. B. and C. M. Everest, father and son—sold to H. H. Rogers, J. D. Archbold and Ambrose McGregor of the Standard Oil Company, for $200,000, a three-fourths interest in that concern. . . .

The Vacuum manufactured principally lubricating oils used on harness and car wheels. It controlled several valuable patents and had been doing a prosperous business for a number of years. By the terms of the sale in 1879 the Everests remained as managers of the refinery, on a salary of $10,000 a year. They also contracted to enter into no outside oil business for ten years. The business policy of the Vacuum, including the fixing of salaries, was dictated by a board of directors made up of Messrs. Rogers, Archbold, McGregor and the two Everests. The meetings of this board were held at the office of the Standard Oil Company, in New York or in Rochester, as convenient.

So far as can be inferred from the testimony, the works were well managed, the dividends large, and the employees well treated. In 1880 the salesman of the concern, J. Scott Wilson, decided to leave the Vacuum and go into business for himself. The decision seems natural, for until 1878 Mr. Wilson had carried on an independent oil business of one kind or another. He had been a partner in a refinery and understood making oils. He had been a jobber on his own account before going with the Everests, and as such had had a considerable clientele. Wilson told one of his fellow employees, Charles B. Matthews, of his decision, and asked him to go with him. . . .

The new firm needed an experienced stillman accustomed to the Vacuum processes, and early in 1881 they asked one Albert Miller, a stillman in the Vacuum works, to join them. "If we have Miller," they told each other, "we can go to the customers of the Vacuum Oil Company and say to them: 'We have the same process and the same apparatus and the same oils as the Vacuum Oil Company, and we have their former superintendent, Mr. Miller, to manufacture the oils.'" Miller had been with the Everests for several years, having worked his way up from a labourer at two dollars a day to a position where, as stillman, he was paid by the hour, and earned from $1,200 to $1,400 a year. He and his wife had been thrifty, and had several thousand dollars in property. Miller thought there was money in the new venture, and consented to join Wilson and Matthews. The three set about carrying out their plans before they notified their employers of their intention to leave—Miller going so far as to order certain iron castings needed in the construction of their works, made after patterns owned by the Everests. He had these made at the foundry patronised by the Everests. He paid for them himself, and carried them away, presumably giving the impression that they were for his employers.

Early in March Matthews and Miller notified C. M. Everest, who was in charge, his father being in California, that they were goint to leave and establish at Buffalo an independent oil refinery. Mr. Everest, surprised out of discretion by the news, told them plainly that although he had nothing against them personally, he should do all in his power to injure the proposed concern. He asked them where they expected to get oil, and they replied that they would get it from the Atlas Refining Company, an independent concern in Buffalo, which had its own pipe-line. "You will wake up some morning and find it is in the Standard," replied Mr. Everest. . . .

About two months after the new firm began building, the elder Everest, who had been in California, returned to Rochester, and soon after had several interviews with Miller. He impressed on the man, as his son had done, that the Buffalo Lubricating Works would never succeed. He told him that the Vacuum meant to bring suit against them for infringing their patents, and would get an injunction and stop the works; that Miller would lose all the money he had put in. To save himself, Everest advised Miller to come back to the Vacuum. "But that would leave them in a pretty bad fix," Miller said. "That is exactly what I want to do," replied Everest. The fear that the new concern might be ruined through the hostility of the Vacuum, and he lose his savings, seems to have preyed on Miller's mind. . . .

In a talk with Miller a little while after this, C. M. Everest said to him: "You go back to Buffalo and construct the pipes so that they cannot make a good oil, and then, I think, if you give them a little scare. You might scare them a little, they not knowing anything about the business, and you know how to do it." On account of Miller's neglect, the first still in the new refinery was not ready to be fired until June 15—it was an ordinary still, as was the second one built—the third only was built for the Vacuum process. As soon as the still was ready it was filled with some 175 barrels of crude oil and a very hot fire—"inordinary hot" was the droll description of the fireman—built under it. Miller, who superintended the operations, swore at the fireman once or twice because the fire was not hot enough, and then disappeared. While he was gone the brickwork around the still began to crack. The safety valve finally blew off, and a yellow gas or vapour escaped in such quantities that the superintendent of a neighbouring refinery came out and warned the fireman that he was endangering property. Miller was hunted up. He had the safety valve readjusted—it was thought by certain witnesses that he had it too heavily weighted —and ordered the fires to be rebuilt, hot as before. He again disappeared. In his absence the safety valve again blew off. The run of oil was found to be a failure. It was not a pleasant augury, but oil refiners are more or less hardened to explosions and no one seems to have thought much of the accident. Nobody was injured; nothing was burned, nothing but 175 barrels of oil spoiled; that, in an oil refinery, is getting off easy.

On the 23d of June Miller made the transfer of property advised by the Everests, talked over things with Truesdale, and a week later left the Buffalo Works. . . . Miller's loss was a severe one. The men were all novices in making oil, save Wilson, and he was on the road, and they seem to have been unable to find a competent manager. The Everests soon succeeded, too, in getting Wilson out of the new firm by bringing a suit against him for damaging its business by unlawfully leaving it. The suit was withdrawn and the costs paid, when Wilson consented, in December, 1881, to leave the Buffalo Works. Wilson's loss was particularly serious, as he was a salesman of experience. . . .

The disappearance of Miller, the man on whom the firm had depended for superintending building and refining, the withdrawal of Wilson, with whom the enterprise had originated and on which it had staked its hopes of finding a ready market, and the series of suits for infringement of patents, suits which cost Matthews thousands of dollars as well as much embarrassment and delay, were troubles brought on him, so he believed, as the result of a deliberate attempt on the part of the Vacuum Oil Company to make good C. M. Everest's threat to do all in his power to ruin the Buffalo Lubricating Works, and, in the spring of 1883, he brought a civil suit against the Everests for $100,000. While Matthews was working up his case he learned that Miller had returned from California, that he had left the Everests because he claimed they had "not treated him right," and that he was idle in Rochester. . . .

When Matthews learned of Miller's return he asked him to come to Buffalo, and evidently got from him then, for the first time, the story of the pressure the Everests had brought to bear on him to leave the Buffalo Lubricating Works, the "fixing" of the still at their advice so that something would "smash," the transfer of his property, his two years of semi-idleness on $1,500 a year and a bonus of $1,000, paid for a reason which can only be surmised, and his final breaking in California, because, as he claimed, he saw no settled employment in view and no prospect of the Everests doing more for him than they were, and, as they claimed, because he believed he could get a big sum from the Standard to keep silent. To all of this Miller made deposition in July, 1884. . . .

An indictment for conspiracy of three men of such prominence as Mr. Rogers, Mr. Archbold and Mr. McGregor riveted the attention of the whole country on the coming trial. It was apparent from the first that the Standard meant to put up a big fight to have the indictment quashed. They had, indeed, set a strong machinery at work immediately to get evidence on which to bring a counter charge of conspiracy; that is, that Matthew's intention in starting the Buffalo Lubricating Works was never to do business, but to force the Standard to buy him out at a big price. They at once set a detective to work on the case, one item of his instructions reading: "We have reason to believe that the suit is brought for the purpose of forcing the Standard to purchase the works of the Buffalo Lubricating Company, and Matthews has made certain statements to that effect; would like reports of any statements or admissions by him in relation to his objects in these suits." Under the direction of this detective, a man employed in Matthews's works for some months made daily reports of what he saw and heard there, copies of which were forwarded to the Standard office in New York. A detective was also put on Miller's track. Miller was now employed in a refinery in Corry, Pennsylvania, and here he was for a long time under espionage. The chief expression obtained from him was by luring him into a saloon one Sunday afternoon and getting him half drunk. While in this condition, the saloon-keeper testified, he said the Buffalo suit was a——humbug, but there was money in it and that they (he and the persons who were drinking with him) might as well make it as anybody.

It was on May 2, 1886, that the trial began. The array of wealth and legal learning in the Buffalo court-room during the fourteen days' case set not only the town, but the country agape. . . . The Standard lawyers immediately applied for the acquittal of Mr. Rogers, Mr. Archbold and Mr. McGregor, on the ground that no fact or circumstance had been proved that connected them in the slightest degree with the charge of conspiracy to lure Miller away or to destroy the Buffalo Works. The district-attorney combated the proposition vigorously. These gentlemen, he contended, owned three-fourths of the Vacuum Works; they were always present at directors' meetings; it was a fair presumption that they knew what was done to persuade Miller to leave the Buffalo Works; they must have known the moneys paid him while he was doing little work. Mr. Rogers had certainly threatened Matthews that he would carry up the patent suits until the Buffalo Works got enough of it. Judge Haight, however, advised the jury to acquit Mr. Rogers, Mr. Archbold and Mr. McGregor. "The indictment charges a conspiracy," the judge said. "It also charges certain overt acts. . . . I have not been able to recall any evidence which shows that either of these three defendants ever knew of it, ever heard of it, or ever took any part in it at all. So far as the charge of an attempt to blow up the Buffalo Works is concerned, I have been unable to recall any evidence that has been given in which either of these three defendants ever knew of it, ever heard of it, ever advised it, or ever took any part in it whatever. . . ."

The acquittal of the three Standard gentlemen was followed by an application for the acquittal of the Everests, but the case with them was different. It had been proved conclusively that they threatened at the start to ruin the new concern, and that they had counselled Miller "to arrange the machinery so it would bust up or smash up"; there was a strong presumption that Miller, acting on this advice, had arranged for the explosion of June 15, though, as he claimed, he meant only to "give them a scare." . . . The jury was not greatly influenced by the evidence produced to show that Matthews was a blackmailer. Evidently they concluded that, granting that the Everests had cause of complaint against the men for using their processes—they certainly had no just cause in the fact of the three men setting up in business for themselves—granting that the enterprise was started for blackmailing purposes —and there was no proof offered that it was—the Everests should have taken their case into the courts—not plotted the destruction of the refinery by any such underhand methods as they employed. Whatever the jury's process of reasoning, however, it is certain that on May 16 they brought in a verdict of "guilty as charged by the indictment."[1]

[1] The eventual result of the various cases was that the Everests were fined the maximum amount of $250, but not imprisoned. They offered to settle the civil suits for $85,000, and the court ordered Matthews's Buffalo Lubricating Oil Company, now in the hands of receivers, to accept. The entire amount went to the creditors and lawyers [Editor's Summary]

This, then, in outline, is the history of the case on which are based all charges, so far as the writer knows, that the Standard Oil Company has deliberately destroyed property to get rid of rivals. The case is of importance not only as showing to what abuses the Standard policy of making it hard for a rival to do business will lead men like the Everests, but it shows to what lengths a hostile public will go in interpreting the acts of men whom it has come to believe are lawless and relentless in pursuing their own ends. The public, particularly the oil public, has always been willing to believe the worst of the Standard Oil Company. It read into the Buffalo case deliberate arson, and charged not only the Everests, but the three co-directors, with the overt acts. They refused to recognise that no evidence of the connection of Mr. Rogers, Mr. Archbold and Mr. McGregor with the overt acts was offered, but demanded that they be convicted on presumption, and when the judge refused to do this they cursed him as a traitor. To-day, in spite of the full airing this case has had in the courts and investigations, Judge Haight is still accused of selling himself to a corporation, and Mr. Rogers is accused daily in Montana of having burned a refinery in Buffalo. As a matter of fact, no refinery was burned in Buffalo, nor was it ever proved that Mr. Rogers knew anything of the attempts the Everests made to destroy Matthews's business.

13   THE STANDARD OIL
COMPANY AND POLITICS

Oil men charge Standard with intrenching itself in state and national politics—Election of Payne to Senate in Ohio in 1884 claimed to establish charge of bribery—Full investigation of Payne's election denied by United States Senate Committee on elections—Payne himself does not demand investigation—Popular feeling against Standard is aggravated—The Billingsley Bill in the Pennsylvania Legislature—A force bill directed against the Standard—Oil Men fight hard for it—The bill is defeated—Standard charged with using money against it—A growing demand for full knowledge of the Standard a result of these specific cases.

THE CASES described in the last two chapters naturally aroused intense interest in the Oil Regions. The two in Ohio demonstrated afresh the chief grievances which the oil men had against the Standard Oil Company since 1872—that they were securing rebates on their own shipments and drawbacks on those of their competitors. The Buffalo case demonstrated that when their ordinary advantages failed to get a rival out of the way they winked at methods which a jury called criminal. It was fresh proof of what the oil men had always claimed, that the Standard Oil Company was a conspiracy! At the same time that these cases were arousing their indignation anew there occurred in Ohio an affair which gave them new evidence of their old charge that the Standard was steadily intrenching itself in state and national politics in order to direct the course of legislation to suit itself. There had been many evidences of this, satisfactory enough to the initiated. There was no doubt that the investigation of 1876 and the first bill to regulate interstate commerce introduced at that time had been squelched largely through the efforts of two members of Congress, one of them directly and the other indirectly interested in the Standard—these were J. N. Camden of West Virginia, head of the Camden Consolidated Oil Company, now one of the constituent companies of the Standard Oil Trust, and H. B. Payne of Ohio, the father of the treas-

144

urer of the Standard, Oliver H. Payne. It had certainly used its influence to oppose the free pipe-line bill which the independent oil men had been fighting for since the early days of the industry. In 1878 and 1879, during the prosecution of the suits against the railroads and the Standard by the Petroleum Producers' Union, there had been incessant charge of the use of political influence to secure delay. It was a matter of constant comment in Ohio, New York and Pennsylvania that the Standard was active in all elections, and that it "stood in" with every ambitious young politician, that rarely did an able young lawyer get into office who was not retained by the Standard. . . .

But all of the examples they quoted were more or less poor in evidence. Of no one of them perhaps could they have produced satisfactory proof. Now, however, simultaneously with the three cases outlined in the last two chapters there came a case of bribery in an election which they held established their charge. The case was the familiar one of the election of H. B. Payne of Ohio to the United States Senate in January, 1884. Mr. Payne was at the time of his election the aristocrat *par excellence* of Cleveland, Ohio. He had birth and education, distinction of manner and mind. His fine old mansion still remains one of the most distinguished houses in a city of beautiful homes. He had been active in Democratic politics for many years—a member of the state Senate and a member of Congress, and he had been mentioned as the Democratic candidate for the presidency in 1880, receiving eighty-one votes on the first ballot. At the time of his election to the Senate he was a man seventy-four years old. Now Mr. Payne's son, Oliver H. Payne, was one of the thirteen original members of the South Improvement Company, and one of the rare Cleveland refiners who had a strong enough stomach to go into the Standard Oil Company when it swept up the oil trade of Cleveland in 1872, and he had gathered in his share of the spoils of that raid. Oliver Payne was proud of his father, and it was well known that he wanted to see him in the Senate of the United States, but there had been no movement to nominate him and in 1883 he seems to have made up his mind to see what he could do.

A United States Senator was to be elected in Ohio in November. In October a new State Legislature was chosen, and the Democratic members were instructed for one of two candidates for the Senate, George H. Pendleton or General Durbin Ward, both men of prominence and long service in the public life of the state. Mr. Payne's name was not mentioned in the canvass. Nevertheless, hardly had the Legislature convened when there sprang up at the Neil House in Columbus an extraordinary Payne boom. Its backers were Senator Payne's own son, Oliver H. Payne, at that time treasurer of the Standard Oil Company, and Colonel Thompson, a prominent personage in the same concern. Their lieutenants were also members of the company in one capacity or another. Large sums of money were alleged to have been circulated. There was a rumour that Oliver Payne said the election cost him $100,000. It was claimed that it could be proved that a check for $65,000 had been cashed in Cleveland by one of the men most prominent in the Payne boom, and that the whole sum had been spent in Columbus.

A perfect uproar of indignation followed the announcement of Mr. Payne's choice. All over the state the Standard Oil Company was charged with the election. . . . The scandal became one of the issues of the next campaign and was instrumental in making the next Legislature of Ohio Republican. As soon as the new Legislature convened at the opening of 1886 an investigation of the Payne case was ordered. Some fifty-five witnesses were examined, and the resulting testimony turned over to the Senate of the United States for its examination. The testimony did not prove the charge of bribery, the Ohio Legislature said, but it was of such a nature as to require the Senate's attention. The matter went to the Senate Committee on Elections, and in July, 1886, a majority reported against the further investigation asked by the state of Ohio. . . .

For three oppressive July days the Senate gave almost all of its time to a bitter debate on the report. The name of the Standard was freely used. "The Senate of the United States," said Senator Frye,[1] "when the question comes before it as this has been presented, whether or not the great Standard Oil Company, the greatest monopoly to-day in the United States of America, a power which makes itself felt in every inch of territory in this whole republic, a power which controls business, railroads, men and things, shall also control here;

[1] William P. Frye, Republican Senator from Maine, 1881-1911. [Ed.]

whether that great body has put its hands upon a legislative body and undertaken to control, has controlled, and has elected a member of the United States Senate, that Senate, I say, cannot afford to sit silent and let not its voice be heard in an inquiry as to the truth of the allegation." The majority report was adopted, however, by a vote of forty-four to seventeen. "The most unfortunate fact in the history of the Senate," said Senator Hoar.[2]

For the time the matter rested, but only for the time. The failure to investigate rather intensified the convictions that Payne's seat was bought by the Standard Oil Company. In 1887 Mr. Payne voted against the Interstate Commerce Bill. "That is why he was put in the Senate," people said bitterly. The feeling became still more intense in 1888. The question of trusts was before Congress. The Republicans had come out with an anti-trust plank in their platform; the Democrats, in response to Mr. Cleveland's message, were declaring the tariff the greatest trust-builder in existence, and calling on their opponents for reform there if they were sincere in their anti-trust attitude. In this agitation the Standard Oil Company undoubtedly exerted its influence against all trust investigation and legislation. The charge became general that they were helping the Democrats. This is why they wanted a Democratic Senate. In September, 1888, when a phase of the question was before the Senate, Mr. Hoar, with his genius for asking far-reaching questions, said one day: "Is there a Standard Oil Trust in this country or not? . . . If there be such a trust, is it represented in the Cabinet at this moment? Is it represented in the Senate? Is it represented in the councils of any important political party in the country?"

It was the first time that Mr. Payne had been sufficiently aroused to reply. "There is nothing whatever to sustain the insinuation which the honourable Senator conveys. I make the declaration now for the first time, and it will be the last time I shall ever take notice of it. The Standard Oil Company is a very remarkable and wonderful institution. It has accomplished within the last twenty years of commercial enterprise what no other company or association of modern times has accom-

[2] George F. Hoar, Republican Senator from Massachusetts, 1887-1904. [Ed.]

plished, but, Mr. President, I never had a dollar's interest in that company. I never owned a dollar of its stock; I never rendered it any service, and that company never rendered me any service. . . ."

Mr. Payne's denial was not sufficient to silence Senator Hoar. He returned to the attack. It was a "general public belief," he declared, that the Standard Oil Company was represented in the Cabinet and Senate. He called attention to the newspapers' charge to that effect, and declared that he had received many personal letters charging that the Standard was helping the Democrats. He asked for information when he asked his question; he made no charges. Mr. Whitney[3] was the member of Mr. Cleveland's Cabinet to whom Senator Hoar referred, and he promptly, in a public letter, disclaimed all connection with the Standard Oil Company. Mr. Hoar said he "cheerfully accepted" the denial. As for Mr. Payne, he was not satisfied, and when Mr. Payne in heat replied to him, Senator Hoar closed his lips forever in a burst of biting sarcasm:

"A Senator who, when the Governor of his state, when both branches of the Legislature of his state complained to us that a seat in the United States Senate had been bought, when the other Senator from the state rose and told us that that was the belief of a very large majority of the people of Ohio without distinction of party, failed to rise in his place and ask for the investigation which would have put an end to those charges if they had been unfounded, sheltering himself behind the technicalities which were found by some gentlemen on both sides of this chamber, that the investigation ought not to be made, but who could have had it by the slightest request on his own part and then remained dumb, I think should forever after hold his peace. . . . I think few men ever sat in the Senate who would refrain from demanding an investigation under such circumstances, even if it were not required by the Senate itself. . . . There were Senators who thought that the admission of that Senator, the continuance of that Senator in his seat without investigation, indicated the low-water mark of the Senate of the United States itself."

And there the Payne case rested. It was never *proved* that the Standard Oil Company had contributed a cent to his election. It was never *proved* that his seat was bought, but the fact that, in the face of such serious charges, rehearsed constantly for four years, neither Mr. Payne nor the Standard Oil

[3] William C. Whitney, Secretary of the Navy, 1885-1889. [Ed.]

Company had done aught but keep quiet, convinced a large part of the country that the suspicion under which they rested was less damaging than the truth would be. In the minds of great numbers this silence was a confession of guilt. The Payne case certainly aggravated greatly the popular feeling that the Standard Oil Company was using the legislative bodies of the country in its own interest.

This feeling was intensified in 1887 by a terrific battle between the oil producers and Standard forces in the Legislature of the state of Pennsylvania. Since the compromise of 1880 the body of the oil producers had been taking no concerted action against the Standard. But their inaction was not due to reconciliation to Standard domination. As a matter of fact they were almost as bitter in 1886 as they had been in 1878, when they formed the Union which for two years fought so good a fight. The specific complaint of the oil producers at this time was that they were being "robbed" by the National Transit Company— the big Standard pipe-line consolidation, which had secured by the series of manœuvres already outlined the monopoly of handling and transporting crude oil. If the oil producers had been making money at this time it is quite possible that they would have paid little attention to the profits of the National Transit Company. The service they got was about as perfect as any human machine could render, and they would probably have recognised this and been willing to pay high if they too had been prosperous. But the condition of the oil producer in these days was in glaring contrast to that of Mr. Rockefeller. . . . The Standard Oil Trust had from its organisation in 1882 paid dividends on its $70,000,000 capital. In spite of the extraordinary outlay for tank-building and seaboard pipe-lines made from 1881 to 1884—$30,000,000 it is computed to have been—the trust paid 10½ per cent. in 1885, ten per cent. in 1886, and Standard Oil stock stood near 200! In contrast, the oil producer, in 1886, is estimated to have lost about six per cent. on his expenditures, and oil property depreciated one-third in value.

Something was wrong. They could not charge the Standard with the price of oil. As long as over 33,000,000 barrels in stock lay on the market it could not rise. But they could and did complain of what it cost them to handle this oil, of storage and carrying charges, of the deductions for shrinkage and for loss by fire. If the Standard had not forced out every competing line, there would have been sufficient competition to have lowered these items—which at the present prices soon ate up the value of oil. And they fell to rehearsing the raids by which the various transporting companies which had fought themselves into independent positions had beeen forced into combination, their chief grievances being naturally the affair of the Tidewater. In this state of mind, and incited by the Buffalo, the Payne, and the Rice cases, it was natural enough that when suddenly, at the opening of 1887, a bill evidently intended to strike a blow at the Standard was introduced into the Legislature of Pennsylvania, the oil producers rushed pell-mell to support it. The opening sentence was enough for them. It was "An act to *punish* corporations." . . .

In April the final vote on the Billingsley Bill came. Harrisburg was alive with oil men determined that the bill should go through. The Standard was present, and if it had less of a *claque*, it had more of the "sinews of war." Indeed it was charged later by Senator Lewis Emergy that the leader of the Standard forces in the Senate received $65,000 for his services —a charge which, so far as the writer knows, has never been either proved or disproved. The bill came to a vote after a passionate wrangle. It was defeated eighteen to twenty-five. A storm of violent protest from the oil men's representatives followed the defeat, and the lobbies, the hotels, and even the streets of Harrisburg were scenes in the next hours of bitter quarrels and excited gatherings. When finally the oil men withdrew from the town it was with the understanding that they were to meet two weeks later in Oil City to organise a new protective association. The protests and resolutions passed at their final gatherings foreshadowed no intention of reviving the Billingsley Bill. Indeed, the bill itself had received scant attention from them in the violent campaign over its passage which they had carried on for three months. All their passion had been expended on the Standard. This was a question of whether the Standard Oil Company ruled the Legislature of Pennsylvania or whether the people ruled it—so declared the oil men; and when their bill was defeated they charged it was by bribery, and henceforth quoted the defeat of the Billingsley Bill along with the Payne case as proof of the corrupt power of the Standard Oil Company in politics. Their outbreak, for it was nothing else, was the culmination of their indignation and resentment at fifteen years of unfair play on the part of the Standard Oil Company, of resentment at the South Improvement Company, at forced combination of refineries and pipe-lines, at railroad rebates and drawbacks, at the immediate shipment outrages, at the Tidewater defeat. It was revolt against the incessant pressure of Mr. Rockefeller's pitiless steel grip. It was bitterness at the idea that it was he who was reaping all the profit of a business in which they were taking the chief risks, and if things went on as they were that it was he who always would. Out of their burst of passion was to grow a solid determined effort, but for the moment they were defeated, and the defeat, which really was merited, was another added to their series of just and unjust complaints against Mr. Rockefeller.

All of these bitter and spectacular struggles aroused intense public interest. The debate on the Interstate Commerce Bill was contemporaneous with them—the bill was passed in 1887, and had its effect. The feeling grew all over the country that whatever the merits of these specific cases, there was danger in the mysterious organisation by which such immense fortunes and such excessive power could be built up on one side of an industry, while another side steadily lost money and power. A new trial was coming to Mr. Rockefeller, one much more serious than any trial for overt acts, for the very nature of his great creation was to be in question. It was a hard trial, for all John D. Rockefeller asked of the world by the year 1887 was to be let alone. He had completed one of the most perfect business organisations the world has ever seen, an organisation which handled practically all of a great natural product. His factories were the most perfect and were managed with the strictest economy. He owned outright the pipe-lines which transported the crude oil. His knowledge of the consuming power of the world was accurate, and he kept his output strictly within its limit. At the same time the great marketing machinery he had put in operation carried on an aggressive campaign for new markets. In China, Africa, South America, as well as in remote parts of Europe and the United States, Standard agents carried refined oil. The Standard Oil Company had been organised to do business, and if ever a company did business it was this one. From Mr. Rockefeller himself, sitting all day in his den, hidden from everybody but the remarkable body of directors and heads of departments which he had "acquired" as he wiped up one refinery and one pipe-line after another, to the humblest clerk in the office of the most remote marketing agency, everybody worked. There was not a lazy bone in the organisation, nor an incompetent hand, nor a stupid head. It was a machine where everybody was kept on his mettle by an extraordinary system of competition, where success met immediate recognition, where opportunity was wide as the world's craving for a good light to cheer its hours of darkness. The machine was pervaded and stimulated by the consciousness of its own power and prosperity. It was a great thing to belong to an organisation which always got what it wanted, and which was making money as no business in the country had ever made it.

What more, indeed, could Mr. Rockefeller ask than to be let alone? And why not let him alone? He had the ability to keep together the wide-spread interests he had acquired—not only to keep them together, but to unify and develop them; why not let him alone? Many people even in the Oil Regions were inclined to do so, some because they feared him—rumour said Mr. Rockefeller was vindictive and never forgot opposition; others because they were canny and foresaw that they might want his help one day; still others because criticism of success is an ungracious business and arouses a suspicion that the critic may be envious or bitter. But there were a few people, as there always are, whom no cowardice, no self-interest, no fear of public opinion could keep quiet, and these people insistently urged that the Standard Oil Company was a menace to the commerce of the country. We have been and are being wronged, they repeated. We have a right to do an independent business. Interference to drive us out is conspiracy. Let Mr. Rockefeller succeed in the oil business and he will attack other industries; he will have imitators. In fifty years a handful of men will own the country.

Mr. Rockefeller handled his critics with a skill bordering on genius. He ignored them. To see them, to answer them, called attention to them. He was too busy to answer them. "We do not talk much—we saw wood." This attitude of serene indifference is supremely wise. It belittles the critic and it gives the outsider who watches the game a feeling that a serenity so high must come from an impregnable position. There is no question but many a mouth opened to testify against the Standard Oil Company has been closed by Mr. Rockefeller's policy of silence. Only the few irreconcilables withstood his sphinx-like attitude, and yearly, from the compromising of 1880, these warnings and accusations were louder and more fierce. Probably the greatest trial Mr. Rockefeller has ever had has come from the persistency with which the few malcontents kept him before the public. They interfered with two of his great principles—"hide the profits" and "say nothing." It was they who had ruined the South Improvement Company; it was they who had indicted him for conspiracy and compelled him to compromise in 1880. It was they who now, after the splendid pipe-line organisation was completed and his market machinery was in order, kept up their agitation and their cursing. Their work began to tell. The feeling grew that the Standard Oil Company, or Trust, as it was by this time generally called, must be looked into. Even those who, dazzled by Mr. Rockefeller's achievement, were inclined to overlook its ethical side and to refuse to consider to what aggregation of power and abuse it might lead, began to feel that it would be quite as well to have the matter thrashed out, to have it settled once for all, whether the thing had been so bad in its making and was so dangerous in its tendencies as the "oil-shriekers" pretended. In the House of Representatives, when the question of ordering an investigation of trusts by the Committee on Manufactures was up in 1887, the liveliest concern was shown as to whether the Standard Oil Company, "the most important case" of all, would escape. More than one member asked to be assured before consenting to the investigation that the Standard would be put on the rack. The same interest was shown in the Senate of New York State, where an investigation was ordered for February, 1888. It was certain indeed now that Mr. Rockefeller would not be allowed much longer to work in the dark. He was to be dragged into the open, much as he might deplore it, to explain what his trust really was, to prove to a suspicious and hostile public that he had a right to exist.

14   THE BREAKING UP
OF THE TRUST

Epidemic of trust investigation in 1888—Standard investigated by New York State Senate—Rockefeller's remarkable testimony—Inquiry into the nature of the mysterious Standard Oil Trust—Original Standard Oil Trust agreement revealed—Investigation of the Standard by Congress in 1888—As a result of the uncovering of the Standard Oil Trust agreement Attorney General Watson of Ohio begins an action in *quo warranto* against the Trust—Marcus A. Hanna and others try to persuade Watson not to press the suit—Watson persists—Court finally decides against Standard and Trust is forced to make an apparent dissolution.

THERE was no characteristic of Mr. Rockefeller and his great corporation which from the beginning had been more exasperating to the oil world than the secrecy with which operations were conducted. The plan of the South Improvement Company had only been revealed to those who signed an agreement to keep secret all transactions they might have with it. The purchase in 1874 and 1875 by the Standard Oil Company of Lockhart, Frew and Company of Pittsburg, of Warden, Frew and Company of Philadelphia, and of Charles Pratt and Company of New York was so thoroughly concealed that Mr. Rockefeller, five years after it occurred, dared make an affidavit that it had never occurred! Men who entered into running arrangements with Mr. Rockefeller were cautioned "not to tell their wives," and correspondence between them and the Standard Oil Company was carried on under assumed names! Whenever the subject of the relations between the various companies came up in a lawsuit or an investigation, a candid and straight-forward answer was always avoided by both Mr. Rockefeller and the men known to be associated with him in some way. For instance, in 1879, when H. H. Rogers was before the Hepburn Committee, an effort was made to find out what relation the firm of Charles Pratt and Company, of which he was a member, sustained to the Standard Oil Company. Mr. Rogers's testimony was a masterpiece of good-natured evasion, and all that the examiners could get, though they returned again and again to the inquiry, was that Charles Pratt and Company worked "in harmony" with the Standard Oil Company. . . .

In the Buffalo case, when John D. Rockefeller was on the stand, he was put through a questioning in regard to the relations of the persons concerned in the suit to the Standard Oil Trust, whose existence he admitted. Mr. Rockefeller answered all the questions his lawyers would allow, but at the end the plaintiffs had gained little or nothing, and there was a strong impression, from the attitude of his lawyers rather than from that of Mr. Rockefeller, that an effort was making to conceal the nature of the agreement or charter or whatever it was under which the companies involved were working. Naturally enough this attitude inspired resentment and aggravated the feeling that this secrecy meant evil-doing. When the epidemic of trust investigation broke out in 1888, and the Standard Oil Trust was brought up for examination, there was a general public demand to have the matter cleared up. The first investigation of importance took place in February, 1888, in New York City, and by the direction of the Senate of New York State. A list of more than a score of trusts was in the hands of the committee, and, with the limited time at their disposal, it was certain that they could not look into more than half a dozen. There seems to have been no hesitation about including the Standard Oil Trust. "This is the original trust," wrote the committee. "Its success has been the incentive to the formation of all other trusts or combinations. It is the type of a system which has spread like a disease through the commercial system of this country."

There were several things the committee wanted to know about the Standard Oil Trust, and its president was summoned for examination. (1) What was it? Was it an organisation recognised by any law of the land? Long ago men had decided that partnerships, corporations, companies, in which men united to do business, must be regulated by law and subjected to a certain amount of publicity, if the public good was to be protected. Was the Standard Oil Trust within or without the law? (2) By the testimony of its own members, in other years the Standard Combination controlled from eighty to ninety per cent. of the oil business of the country. Was this supremacy due in any measure to special privileges, such as discrimination in railroad rates? (3) Was its power used to manipulate production and prices, and to prevent men outside entering the oil business?

It was to learn these things that the commission summoned Mr. Rockefeller. Flanked by Joseph H. Choate, present Ambassador to the Court of King Edward and the most eminent lawyer of the day, and S. C. T. Dodd, a no less able if a less well-known lawyer, Mr. Rockefeller submitted himself to his questioners. . . . With an air of eager frankness he told them nothing he did not wish them to know. The committee had a desire to begin at the beginning. It evidently had heard that a short-lived organisation, called the South Improvement Company,[1] had given Mr. Rockefeller his whiphand in the oil business as far back as 1872, enabling him in three months' time to raise his daily capacity as a refiner from 1,500 to 10,000 barrels, and so they asked Mr. Rockefeller:

Q. There was such a company?
A. I have heard of such a company.
Q. Were you not in it?
A. I was not.

Another staggering bit of testimony concerned railroad rates. Asked if there had been any arrangements by which the trust or the companies controlled by it got transportation at any cheaper rates than was allowed to the general public, Mr. Rockefeller answered: "No, sir." As a matter of fact, the three great oil-carrying systems of the country—the Central, Erie and Pennsylvania—had all of them, for much of the period between 1872 and 1888, granted to Mr. Rockefeller rebates calculated to keep freight rates down for the Standard Oil Company and up for its competitors. Contracts and agreements to this effect are easily accessible to any one caring to investigate the quality of Mr. Rockefeller's "no." "No," said Mr.

[1] The South Improvement Company was sometimes incorrectly known as the "Southern" Improvement Company (See page 29). Matthew Josephson, *The Robber Barons* (New York, 1934), page 275, maintains that when investigators asked John D. Rockefeller about the famous secret agreement with the railroads, they mistakenly used the term "Southern" and the alert Rockefeller truthfully denied participation. This would explain Rockefeller's testimony, which Ida Tarbell called "staggering" in its dishonesty on this point. [Ed.]

Rockefeller, "we have had no better rates than our neighbours.". . .

The committee had a vague idea that refineries outside of the Standard Combination had had a hard time to live, and asked if the trust had sought in any way to make the operations of outsiders so unprofitable that they would either have to come in or go out of the business.

"They have not; no, sir, they have not," replied Mr. Rockefeller.

"And they have lived on good terms with their competitors?"

"They have, and have to-day very pleasant relations with those gentlemen.". . .

As pointed out in a previous chapter, there had been some kind of an agreement adopted in 1882, binding together the varied interests which controlled the oil business. But what it was, where it was kept, by what authority it lived, nobody knew. For six years it had succeeded in hiding itself. What was the understanding which had made a trust of a company? The committee asked to know. . . . Like all great things, it was simplicity itself—an agreement which anybody could understand, by which some fifty persons holding controlling interests in corporations, joint stock associations, and partnerships of different states, placed all their stock in the hands of nine trustees, receiving in return trust certificates. These nine trustees themselves owned a majority of the stock and had complete control of all the property. Mr. Rockefeller, when questioned, stated that one of the trustees was a responsible officer in almost every refinery or organisation in the trust; that the trustees, as a body, knew by reports and correspondence, and by frequent consultation in New York with active promoters of each concern, just how the business was going on. . . .

The trustees evidently ran the entire great combination under the agreement. But consider the anomaly of the situation. Thirty-nine corporations, each of them having a legal existence, obliged by the laws of the state creating it to limit its operations to certain lines and to make certain reports, had turned over their affairs to an organisation having no legal existence, independent of all authority, able to do anything it wanted anywhere; and to this point working in absolute darkness. Under their agreement, which was unrecognised by the state, a few men had united to do things which no incorporated company could do. It was a situation as puzzling as it was new. The committee in reporting on what it discovered did nothing to solve the puzzle. It simply sounded a warning:

The actual value of property in the trust control at the present time is not less than one hundred and forty-eight millions of dollars, according to the testimony of the trust's president before your committee. This sum in the hands of nine men, energetic, intelligent, and aggressive—and the trustees themselves, as has been said, own a majority of the stock of the trust which absolutely controls the one hundred and forty-eight millions of dollars—is one of the most active and possibly the most formidable moneyed power on this continent. Its influence reaches into every state and is felt in remote villages, and the products of its refineries seek a market in almost every seaport on the globe. When it is remembered that all this vast wealth is the growth of about twenty years, that this property has more than doubled in value in six years, and that with this increase the trust has made aggregate dividends during that period of over fifty millions of dollars, the people may well look with apprehension at such rapid development and centralisation of wealth wholly independent of legal control, and anxiously seek out means to modify, if not to prevent, the natural consequence of the device producing it, a device of late invention, namely, the aggregation of great corporations into partnerships with unbounded resources and a field of operations quite as extended as its resources. So much for the nature of the Standard Oil Trust. . . .

The New York Senate made its investigation of trusts in February, 1888. In March the Committee on Manufactures of the House of Representatives began a similar inquiry. This committee, like the earlier one, made the Standard its principal subject. Fully 1,000 pages of a report of 1,500 pages are devoted to Mr. Rockefeller's creation—five times the space given to the Sugar Trust, ten times that given to the Whiskey Trust. The testimony was wide in range. Indeed, from the volume alone, a pretty complete history of the Standard Oil Company up to 1888 could be written. Here are found the South Improvement Company charter and contracts in full. Here is Mr. Cassatt's testimony, taken in the case of the Commonwealth of Pennsylvania *vs.* the Pennsylvania Railroad, showing the character of the rebates the Standard Combination was able to secure from the railroads at that time. Here is a partial history of the growth of the Standard pipe-lines. Many personal histories of refiners driven out of business by the conditions brought about by railroad discriminations; full accounts of the war of the producing element on the Standard; all of the testimony in the Buffalo case, where two refiners were found guilty of conspiring to ruin an independent refining concern; the reports of the Interstate Commerce Commission in the cases of George Rice; and much interesting explanation of various matters by leading Standard Oil officials appear in the report. . . .

Full as the testimony on the Standard Oil Trust gathered by the Federal committee of 1888 is, its report touched but one point, and that was its organisation. To the committee it seemed that the agreement under which the trust operated was such as to make it exempt from the anti-trust legislation which was then contemplated by Congress. The legislation proposed was directed against "combinations to fix the price or regulate the production of merchandise or commerce." Now a mass of testimony had been presented showing that, from the starting-point of the Standard's history with the South Improvement Company, its aim has been to regulate the out-put of refined oil so as to fix the price, but this testimony, the committee saw clearly enough, did not apply to the trust which it was investigating. For—so swore the trustees—they had nothing to do with the business operations of the separate concerns. They simply held the stock of the various corporations, exercised their right as stockholders, received and distributed the dividends. Each company did its own business in its own way. The trustees were not responsible for it. There was something humorous to those familiar with the oil world, in the idea of J. D. Rockefeller, William Rockefeller, J. D. Archbold, Henry H. Rogers, Charles Pratt, H. M. Flagler, Benjamin Brewster, W. H. Tilford and O. B. Jennings, having nothing to do, as trustees of the Standard Oil Trust, but to receive and divide dividends, engrossing and interesting a task as that undoubtedly was. But, as a matter of fact, nothing else could be settled on them by anything in the testimony. For instance, in 1887 there was an alliance formed between the Oil Producers' Protective Association and the Standard for limiting the production of crude oil (a movement of which we shall hear more later). This certainly was in restraint of trade. But, on examination, the committee found the contract had been signed by the Standard Oil Company of New York. The trustees had nothing to do with it! Taking up, point by point, the conditions of which the oil producers complained, not one of them could be fixed on the trust. It had made no agreements, signed no contracts, kept no books. It had no legal existence. It was a force powerful as gravitation and as intangible. You could argue its existence from its effects, but you could never prove it. You could no more grasp it than you could an eel. Certainly the Committee on Manufactures was justified in confining its report to pointing out the fact that the Standard Oil Trust agreement was a shrewd and slippery device for evading responsibility.

And there the investigations of 1888 ended. There had been much noise over them, and for what good? So asked the discontented oil public. It simply had secured the form of an agreement which could no more be touched by legislation than human greed. It was characteristic that the oil public, intent on immediate remedies, should be discouraged. If they had applied to their cause the same patience and foresight Mr. Rockefeller did to his, they would have realised that, as a matter of fact, a respectable first step had been taken toward their real goal, a goal which has not by any means been reached— that is, a legal form of organisation for corporations doing interstate business which would enable the public to know promptly if they were securing special privileges or were restricting trade. This first step was in securing the famous trust agreement. That was now in the hands of people given to thinking about things, and something came of it, even more quickly than the philosophical observer of public events might expect, and in this wise:

In 1887 there was elected to the attorney-generalship of Ohio a lawyer, something under forty years of age, named David K. Watson. Two years later Mr. Watson was a candidate for re-election. One day, while busy with his campaign, he came out of his office in the state-house on the public square in Columbus, and, crossing the street, stopped, as he often did, at a book-shop to look over new publications. He happened there on a small yellow leatherette volume entitled "Trusts." It was written by William W. Cook, of the New York bar, and cost fifty cents. Mr. Watson bought the book and spent the evening reading it. At the end he found the Standard Oil Trust agreement. It was the first time he had ever seen it. He read it carefully and saw at once that, if it was a bona fide agreement, the Standard Oil Company of Ohio was and had been for seven years violating the laws of the state of Ohio by taking the affairs of the company from the directors and placing them in the hands of trustees, nearly all of whom were non-residents of the state. Mr. Watson knew on the instant that, if this were a bona fide agreement and he were re-elected attorney-general of Ohio, it would be his duty to bring an action against the Standard Oil Company of the state. He laid the little book away until he knew the result of the election.

A few weeks later Mr. Watson was re-elected attorney-general. He at once began a search into the authenticity of the documents in Mr. Cook's little volume. He sent for the reports of the investigations by the committees of the New York Senate and of Congress. He read the testimony word for word. But he still doubted the correctness of the document, fearing that, even if it were in the main correct, there might be some loophole by which the Standard Oil Company could escape. Now, in reading the report of the House investigations, Mr. Watson had been particularly impressed. with the clearness and directness of the questions put by one of the members of the investigating committee, Mr. Buchanan, of New Jersey. He accordingly went to Washington, inquired from a friend if Mr. Buchanan could be relied upon, and, receiving the assurance of his high character, sought an interview with him. "Was the Standard trust agreement as published in the committee's report *bona fide?*" was the inquiry. "Yes," said Mr. Buchanan. "But why do you ask?" "Because if it is," replied Mr. Watson, "I believe the Standard Oil Company of Ohio has violated the laws of the state, and on my return to Columbus I shall file an action in *quo warranto* against it in the Supreme Court of the state." . . .

"I admire your courage," said Mr. Buchanan, "but I would not do it."

On May 8, 1890, Mr. Watson filed his petition in the Supreme Court of Ohio. The petition averred that, in violation of the law of Ohio, the Standard Oil Company had entered into an agreement by which it had transferred 34,993 shares out of 35,000 to the trustees of the Standard Oil Trust, most of whom were non-residents of the state; that it was these trustees who chose the board of directors of the Standard Oil Company of Ohio, and directed its policy, and prayed that, on account of this violation of law, the company should be "adjudged to have forfeited and surrendered its corporate rights, privileges, powers and franchises, and that it be ousted and excluded therefrom, and that it be dissolved." . . .

But, while the preparation for the argument of the case was

going on, the courageous young attorney-general was beset on all sides for an explanation. *Why* had he brought the suit? What was the influence which had controlled him? Men in power took him aside to question him, incapable, evidently, of believing that an attorney-general could be produced in Ohio who would bring a suit solely because he believed it was his duty. Some suggested that some big interest, hostile to the Standard, was behind him; others said the suit was suggested by Senator Sherman, then interested in his anti-trust bill. Along with this speculation came the strong and subtle restraining pressure a great corporation is sure to exert when its ambitions are interfered with. From all sides came powerful persuasion that the suit be dropped. Mr. Watson has never made public the details of this influence in any documentary way, but the accounts he at the time gave different friends of it led to so much gossip in Ohio that in 1899 the attorney-general of the state, F. S. Monnett, made detailed charges of six deliberate attempts to bribe Mr. Watson to withdraw the suits. . . . Among Mr. Rockefeller's Ohio friends was the late Marcus A. Hanna, who was even then a strong factor in the Republican party of the state. . . . In 1897, when Mr. Hanna was a candidate for the United States Senate, an enterprising newspaper man of Ohio recalled that during 1890 it was common gossip in Ohio that Mr. Hanna had written the attorney-general a letter asking him to withdraw his suit against the Standard Oil Company. The correspondent sought Mr. Watson, who, so he avers, let him read the letter through, although he refused to allow him to copy it for publication. "No one could read it and ever forget it," said the correspondent; but to reinforce himself he sought persons who were associated with Mr. Watson at the time—yes, they remembered the letter perfectly. Certain of them said that they could never forget some of its expressions. Between them they pieced up the following portions of the letter which they declared correct and which the correspondent published in the New York World for August 11, 1897:

"I noticed some time ago that you had brought suit to take away the charter of the Standard Oil Company. I intended at the time to write you about it, but it slipped my memory. A few days ago while in New York I met a friend, John D. Rockefeller, and he called my attention to the fact that you had brought the suit, but did not ask me to influence you in any way. . . .

"I have always considered you in the line of political promotion," said Hanna, and then went on to intimate that unless the suit against the Standard was withdrawn, Watson would be the object of vengeance by the corporation and its friends forever after. As if to clinch his threat and argument, Hanna wrote: *"You have been in politics long enough to know that no man in public office owes the public anything."* . . .

The part which the terse phrase attributed to Mr. Hanna,

"NO MAN IN PUBLIC OFFICE OWES THE PUBLIC ANYTHING,"

played in the Senatorial campaign of 1897 is familiar to those who follow politics. It was kept standing for days in black-faced capitals at the head of the opposition newspapers in Ohio, and remained a potent weapon in the hands of Mr. Hanna's enemies to the time of his death.

Whatever the pressure Mr. Watson encountered, it had no effect on his purpose. He quietly went ahead, presented his brief, and, when the time came, he and Mr. Warrington argued the case. The following proposition from the brief presented by Mr. Watson and Mr. Warrington show tersely the line of their argument. . . .

Where a corporation, either directly or indirectly, submits to the domination of an agency unknown to the statute, or identifies itself with and unites in carrying out an agreement whose performance is injurious to the public, it thereby offends against the law of its creation and forfeits all rights to its franchises, and judgment of ouster should be entered against it. . . .

Joseph H. Choate appeared for the defence. The most eminent lawyer in the country, his argument must have been anxiously awaited by Mr. Watson. Curiously enough, as it seems to the non-legal mind, Mr. Choate began his plea by a *prayer for mercy*. Whatever the sins of the Standard Oil Company of Ohio, pleaded Mr. Choate, do not take away its charter. Mr. Choate then proceeded with a strong argument in which he claimed "absolute innocence and absolute merit for everything we have done within the scope of the matters brought before the court by these pleadings."

The argument did not convince the court of the innocence of the Standard in the questions at issue. The court showed, out of the mouth of the trust agreement itself, that the Standard Oil Company of Ohio was "managed in the interest of the Standard

Oil Trust—irrespective of what might be its duties to the people of the state from which it derives its corporate life." . . .

"Much has been said in favour of the objects of the Standard Oil Trust and what it has accomplished. It may be true that it has improved the quality and cheapened the cost of petroleum and its products to the consumer. But such is not one of the usual or general results of a monopoly; and it is the policy of the law to regard, not what may, but what usually happens. Experience shows that it is not wise to trust human cupidity where it has the opportunity to aggrandise itself at the expense of others. The claim of having cheapened the price to the consumer is the usual pretext on which monopolies of this kind are defended." . . .

The company was allowed to live, but it was ousted from the privilege of entering into the trust agreement, from the power of recognising the transfer of the stock, and from the power of permitting the trustees to control its affairs. It was also ordered to pay the costs of the action.

The judgment of the court was not rendered until March 2, 1892, almost two years after the filing of the petition. As soon as it was received Virgil P. Kline, the chief counsel of the Standard Oil Company of Ohio, went to New York for consultation with the trustees. Five days later he wrote to Judge Spear, the chief justice of the Ohio Supreme Court, saying: "Decisive steps will be taken at once not only to release the Standard Oil Company from any relations to the trust, but to terminate the entire trust." But there were "practical difficulties" in the task. . . . Anybody could see this would take time. The court was friendly in the matter, and Chief Justice Spear gave to Mr. Kline an informal note granting an extension. "The court is not disposed to change its order at this time," the chief justice wrote, "but, so long as those in control appear to be engaged, as now, in an honest effort to dissever the relations of the company with the trust, and liquidate and wind up the affairs of the trust, the court will not be disposed to interfere." Thus time was gained.

While Mr. Kline was securing time, the trustees were pushing a liquidation scheme. . . .

The individual holders of the trust certificates were to get in exchange a proportionate share in each of the twenty companies. "A will not get stock in one corporation and B in another; each will get his due proportion in the stocks of all," said Mr. Dodd. All of this change would make no difference with the management of affairs. Mr. Dodd assured the stockholders: "Your interests will be the same as now. The various corporations will continue to do the same business as heretofore, and your proportion of the earnings will not be changed."

The trustees went about liquidating at once, but it was not until the following November that the immense number of certificates held by them personally were exchanged. The process followed can be easily illustrated by Mr. Rockefeller's case. When the trust was ordered dissolved Mr. Rockefeller held 256,854 of the 972,500 shares of Standard Oil Trust which were out. He turned over to an attorney an assignment of this amount, with instructions to secure from each of twenty companies in the trust stock certificates for the portion belonging to him. The corporate stocks were turned over to Mr. Rockefeller, and the assignment of certificate, a properly framed and numbered document, was turned over to the liquidating trustees. This assignment of legal title, for all practical purposes, was the same thing as the trust certificate. It enabled the trustees to collect dividends from the various companies and pay them just as they had before. . . .

At the end of the first year, after the dissolution of the trust, 477,881 shares were uncancelled. . . . At the end of the fourth, 477,881. The dissolution of the trust seemed to have come to a stand-still. Mr. Dodd was right; things were going on as they did before; dividends were issued exactly as before. Nor was there any indication of an intention on the part of the liquidating trustees to change this state of things. If the monopolistic power of the Standard Oil Trust was to be broken, it was evidently not to be by any order of dissolution by the courts. Something more powerful than the courts was at work, however. The spirit of individualism was beginning to reassert itself in the oil industry—a new war for independence had been begun, was indeed well under way even before the state of Ohio made the dissolution of the trust necessary.

A MODERN WAR

FOR INDEPENDENCE

Producers' Protective Association formed—A secret independent organization intended to handle its own oil—Agreement made with Standard
to cut down production—Results of agreement not as beneficial to
producers as expected—Producers proceed to organise Producers' Oil
Company, Limited—Independent refiners agree to support movement—
Producers and Refiners' Company formed—Lewis Emery, Jr.'s, fight for
Seaboard Pipe-line—The United States Pipe Line—Standard's desperate
opposition—Independent Refiners almost worn out—They are relieved by
formation of Pure Oil Company—Pure Oil Company finally becomes head
of Independent Consolidation—Independence possible, but competition
not restored.

JOHN D. ROCKEFELLER'S one irreconcilable enemy
in the oil business has always been the oil producer. There is no
doubt that Mr. Rockefeller has sincerely deplored this. And
well he might, for he learned in his first great raid on the
industry in 1872 that the producers aroused and united made
a powerful and dangerous foe.

No doubt, if it had been practical, Mr. Rockefeller would
have begun at the start to take over oil production as he did
oil refineries and pipe-lines, and thus would have gotten his
enemy out of the way; but during the first fifteen years of his
work it was not practical. The oil fields were too vast and un-
defined. It not being practical to own the oil fields, and yet
essential that those who did own them, and of whose oil he
aspired to be the only buyer, should be kept sufficiently satisfied not to interfere with his domination or to attempt to handle
the oil for themselves, Mr. Rockefeller, whenever he had
the chance, sought to persuade the producers to do what he
would have done had he owned the oil fields—that was, to
keep the supply of crude oil short. . . .

It is quite possible that if Mr. Rockefeller had been able to
convert the majority of the producing body to this theory,
and the supply of crude oil had been kept scarce and prices
consequently high, the oil producers would have forgotten

their resentment at his early raids and would have relapsed into indifference toward his control. Material prosperity is usually benumbing in its effects. There always has been a factor in the great game playing in the Oil Regions, however, which not even Mr. Rockefeller could match. Nature has been in the oil game, and she has taken pains to prevent the only situation which would have enabled Mr. Rockefeller to reconcile the oil producers. Again and again when it seemed as if the limits of oil production were set, and when Mr. Rockefeller and his colleagues must have believed that they would soon have the industry sufficiently well in hand to pay the producers a satisfactory price for crude oil, their calculations have been upset by the discovery of a great deposit of oil which flooded the market and put down the prices. This happened so often between Mr. Rockefeller's first public appearance in the business and the time when he completed his control of transportation, refineries and markets, that the yearly production of crude oil had risen from five and a half million barrels to thirty million barrels, and instead of a half million barrels above ground in stocks there were in 1883 over thirty-five million barrels, in 1884 nearly thirty-seven million, in 1885 thirty-three and a half million. The low price for crude which these vast stocks caused, the high charges for gathering, transporting and storing, all services out of which the Standard was making big profits, the fact that the profit on refined oil steadily increased in these years—the result of the overthrow of independent refiners and pipe-lines—while the profit on crude steadily diminished, were facts which the oil producers brooded over incessantly, and the more bitterly because they felt they could do nothing to help themselves. Every enterprise looking to relief which they had undertaken had, for one reason or another, failed. They had no faith that relief was possible. The Standard would never allow any outside interest to get a foothold. It was the bitterness which this conviction caused which was at the bottom of the outburst over the Billingsley Bill described in Chapter XIII. The Billingsley Bill was defeated, as it deserved to be, but the work done was by no means lost. For the first time since 1880 the Oil Regions were aroused to concerted action. The support of the Billingsley Bill had been a spontaneous movement, a passionate, unorganised revolt against the tyranny of the Standard, but it served to bring into action men who for six long years had been saying it was no use to resist, that Mr. Rockefeller's grip was too strong to be loosened. It revived their confidence in united action and steeled them to a determination to take hold of the industry and force into it again a fair competition in handling oil.

On the very night after the defeat of the bill (April 28, 1887) the oil men who had gathered in Harrisburg to support the measure, angry and sore as they were, arranged to call an early meeting in Oil City and organise. The meeting was held. It was large, and it was followed by others. In a very short time 2,000 oil men were enrolled in a Producers' Protective Association, and thirty-six local assemblies were holding regular meetings throughout the region. . . .

Hardly had the Producers' Protective Association been organised before Mr. Rockefeller had an opportunity to try his plan for conciliation. An independent movement had been started in the summer of 1887 by certain large producers in favour of a general "shut-down," its object, of course, being to decrease the oil stocks. The president of the Producers' Association, Thomas W. Phillips, who at that time was the largest individual producer in the oil country, his production averaging not less than 6,000 barrels a day, was called into consultation with the leaders of the "shut-down" movement. Mr. Phillips promptly told the gentlemen interested that he would not join in such an undertaking unless the Standard went into it. He pointed out that the Standard owned a large proportion of the 30,000,000 barrels of oil above ground. They had bought it at low prices. If the production was shut down prices would go up and the Standard would reap largely on the oil they owned. The producers would, as usual, be standing all the loss.

The upshot of the council was that the Producers' Protective Association took hold of the shut-down movement, its representative seeking an interview with the Standard officials as to their willingness to share in the cost of reducing the production. Here was a chance for Mr. Rockefeller to apply his theory of handling the oil producers—conciliate them when possible—encourage them in limiting their production. The oil men's representatives were met half-way, and an interesting and curious plan was worked out; the producers were to agree to limit their production by 17,500 barrels a day. They were to do this by shutting down their producing wells a part or all of the time and by doing no fresh drilling for a year. If they would do this the Standard agreed to sell the association 5,000,000 barrels of oil at sixty-two cents, and let them carry it at the usual rates as long as they wanted to. Whatever advance in price came from the shut-in movement the producers were to have on their oil, and it was to be shared by them according to the amount each shut in his production. Mr. Phillips, before agreeing to this arrangement, demanded that provision be made for the workingmen who would be thrown out of employment by the shut-down, and he proposed that the association set aside for their benefit 1,000,000 barrels of the oil bought from the Standard, and that the Standard set aside another million; all the profits above sixty-two cents and the carrying charges on the 2,000,000 barrels were to go to the workingmen. A memorandum covering the above points of the agreement was drawn up, and it was accepted by the two interests represented. . . .

The shut-down went into effect the first of November, 1887. The effect on stocks and the market was immediate—stocks fell off at the rate of a million barrels a month, and prices rose by January, 1888, some twenty cents. But at the end of the year, though oil was higher and stocks considerably less, the benefits of the shut-down had not been conspicuous enough to produce that "harmonious feeling" Mr. Rockefeller so much desired; not sufficient to distract the minds of the producers from the idea they had in forming their association, and that was a co-operative enterprise for taking care of their own oil. . . .

Up to 1887, the year of the organisation of the Producers' Protective Association, Mr. Rockefeller had not taken his great combination into oil production to any extent, and wisely enough from his point of view. It was a business in which there were great risks, and as long as he could control the output by being its only buyer, why should he take them? Now, however, the situation was changing. A number of sure fields had been developed—Bradford, Ohio, West Virginia. Their value was depressed by over-production. Mr. Rockefeller had money to invest. The producers were threatening to disturb his control by a co-operative scheme. It was certain that he had not yet produced a "harmonious feeling." It was not sure he would. If he failed in that they might one day even shut off his supply of oil, as they had done in 1872, and Mr. Rockefeller, with great foresight, determined to become a producer. In 1887 he went into Ohio fields. Soon after he began quietly to buy into West Virginia. When he learned, in 1890, from Mr. Taylor and his partners, that a co-operative company of producers was on foot, he naturally enough concluded that the best way to dismember it was to buy out the largest interest in it. The Union Oil Company saw the advantage of being a member of the Standard Oil Trust, and sold. . . .

There was general consternation in producing circles, and if there had not been a number of men in the organisation who realised that the life of the independent effort was at stake, and who turned all their strength to saving it, the association would undoubtedly have gone to pieces. . . .

On January 28, 1891, the General Assembly convened at Warren, Pennsylvania. The whole miserable story of the co-operative plan which the executive board had worked out, and its destruction by the desertion of the Union Oil Company, came out. It was at once evident that, instead of disheartening the Assembly, it was going to harden their determination and spur them to action; that they would not leave Warren until they had something to work on. The session lasted three days, and before finally adjourning it had adopted a drastic plan, framed by a committee of nine, of which Mr. Quick was chairman. This plan aimed, so the resolution adopted by the Assembly stated, *to cut off the supplies of the producers' oil from the Standard Trust!* This was to be accomplished by forming a limited partnership, whose subscribers should all be trusted members of the Producers' Protective Association . . . and which should aim to take care of the crude oil from the wells of the producers who went into the movement, furnish it local transportation, and find a market for it either by building independent refineries or by alliance with those already in existence. . . .

But it is one thing to organise a company, and another to do business. Where were they to begin? Where to set foot? The only thing of which they were sure was a supply of crude oil, and in order to take care of that they began operations by putting up four iron tanks at Coraopolis, Pennsylvania, near the rich McDonald oil field. But they must have a market for it, and their first effort was to ship it abroad. At Bayonne, New

Jersey, on the border of the territory occupied by the Standard's great plant, stands an independent oil refinery, the Columbia Oil Company. The Columbia has "terminal privileges," that is, a place on the water-front from which it can ship oil—an almost impossible privilege to secure around New York harbour. The Producers' Oil Company now obtained from Hugh King, the president of the Columbia, the use of his terminal. They at once had fifty tank-cars built, and prepared to ship their crude oil, but the market was against them, stocks were increasing, prices dropping. The railroad charged a price so high for running their cars that there was no profit, and the fifty tank-cars were never used in that trade. A futile effort to use their crude oil as fuel in Pittsburg occupied their attention for a time, but it amounted to nothing. It was becoming clearer daily that they must refine their oil. The way opened to this toward the end of their first year.

In and around Oil City and Titusville there had grown up since 1881 a number of independent oil refineries. They had come into being as a direct result of the compromise made in 1880 between the producers and the Pennsylvania Railroad, a clause of which stipulated that thereafter railroad rates should be open and equal to all shippers. . . . At first things had gone very well. There were economies in refining near the point where the oil was produced, and so long as the young independents had a low rate to seaboard for their export oil they prospered. But in 1884 things began to change. In that year the Standard Pipe Line made a pooling arrangement with the Pennsylvania Railroad, by which rates from the Oil Regions were raised to fifty-two cents a barrel, an advance of seventeen cents a barrel over what they had been getting, and in return for this raise the Standard agreed to give the railroad twenty-six per cent. of all the oil shipped Eastward, or pay them for what they did not get. This advance put the independents at a great disadvantage. In September, 1888, another advance came. . . . This second advance was more than the refiners could live under, and they combined and took their case to the Interstate Commerce Commission, a hearing being given them in Titusville in May, 1889. No decision had as yet been rendered, and they in the meantime were having a more and more trying struggle for life, and their exasperation against the Standard was increasing with each week. When, therefore, the representatives of the Producers' Oil Company proposed a league with the independent refiners they were cordially welcomed. . . .

The refiners saw at once the possible future in such an arrangement, and in a short time they had gone individually into a company to be called the Producers' and Refiners' Company, with a capital of $250,000, of which the Producers' Oil Company held $160,000, and whose object was the laying of a pipe-line from the fields in which the producers were interested to the refineries at Oil City and Titusville. The new plan was carried out with the greatest secrecy and promptness. Before the Standard men in the region realised what was going on, a right of way was secured and the pipe was going down. On January 8, 1893, the first oil was run. Here, then, was the first link in a practical co-operative enterprise—independent producers and refiners of oil joined by a pipe-line of which they were the owners.

While this enterprise was being carried out in Western Pennsylvania, in the northern part of the state a still more ambitious, independent project was under way, nothing less than a double pipe-line, one for refined and the other for crude oil, from the Oil Regions to the sea. This plan had originated with Lewis Emery, Jr., one of the most implacable and intelligent opponents Mr. Rockefeller pretensions have ever met. . . .

It looked very much as if the United States Pipe Line were to be laid. Now, the strength of the Standard Oil Trust had always been due to its control of transportation. An independent pipe-line, especially to the seaboard, was considered rightly as a much more serious menace to its power than an independent refinery. The United States Pipe Line could not be allowed, and prompt and drastic measures were taken to hinder its work. There is no space here for an account of the wearisome obstructive litigation which confronted the company, for the constant interference, even by force, which followed them for months. It culminated when an attempt was made to join the pipes laid to each side of the Erie tracks near Hancock, New York, the Eastern terminal of the pipe-line. Mr. Emery, relying on the promise of the Erie's president to allow a crossing, sent his men to the railway to connect the pipes. Hardly had they arrived before there descended on them a force of seventy-five railroad men armed for war. These men took possession of the territory at the end of the pipes and intrenched themselves for attack. The pipe-line men camped near by for three months, but they never attempted to join the pipes. Mr. Emery had concluded, on investigation, that the Erie officials, like the Reading, had found that it would be unwise to disturb their relations with the Standard, and while his men were keeping attention fixed on that point he was executing a flank movement, securing a right of way from a point seventy miles back to Wilkesbarre, on the Jersey Central. This new movement was executed with such celerity that by June, 1893, the United States Pipe Line had a crude line 180 miles long connecting the Bradford oil fields with a friendly railway, and a refined line 250 miles long connecting the independent refiners of Oil City, Titusville, Warren and Bradford with the same railway.

With the completion of the refined line a question of vital importance was to be settled: Could refined oil be pumped that distance without deteriorating? The Standard had insisted loudly that it could not. When the day came to make the experiment an anxious set of men gathered at the Wilkesbarre terminal. They feared particularly that the oil would lose colour, but, to their amazement, not only was the colour kept, but it was found on experiment that the fire test was actually raised by the extra agitation the oil had undergone in the long churning through the pipes. A new advance had been made in the oil industry—the most substantial and revolutionary since the day the Tidewater demonstrated that crude oil could be pumped over the mountains. This new discovery, it is well to note, was not the work of the Standard Oil Trust, but it was accomplished in the face of their ridicule and opposition by men driven to find some way to escape from their hard dealings.

The success of the United States refined line aroused the greatest enthusiasm among the independent interests. It gave them access to the seaboard, and there was immediate talk of a closer union between them. Why should the Producers' and Refiners' Pipe Lines not be sold to the United States Line and completed to Bradford? By the spring of 1894 the project seemed certain of realisation.

The new movement was serious. Let this consolidation take place, and the producers had exactly what they had set out in 1887 to build up—a complete machine for handling the oil they produced. As the undertaking grew in solidity and completeness, the war upon it grew more systematic and determined. It took two main lines—discrediting the enterprise in the eyes of stockholders so that they would sell the stock to Standard buyers; the object being, of course, to get control of the companies; cutting the refined market until the refiners in the alliance should fail, or, becoming discouraged, sell. . . .

The efforts which the Standard made to discredit the independent companies and their leaders were accompanied by a persistent, though quiet, attempt of Standard agents to buy in all the stock in the Producers' Oil Company and the United States Pipe Lines which timid, indifferent, or financially embarrassed stockholders could be induced to give up. The movement began to be rumoured and caused no little uneasiness in independent circles. How much would the Standard get? What would they do with it? They were soon to find out.

Before the use to be made of the stock developed, however, the Standard turned against the independents the most powerful and cruel weapon it wields—its control of the markets. The refiners were to be driven from the combination. The extent to which cutting was carried on for two years, beginning with the fall of 1893, is clear from a comparison of prices. In January of 1893 crude oil was selling at 53½ cents a barrel and refined oil for export at 5.33 cents a gallon. Throughout the year the price of crude advanced until in December it was 78⅜ cents. Refined, on the contrary, fell, and it was actually eighteen points lower in December than it had been twelve months before. Throughout 1894 the Standard kept refined oil down; the average price of the year was 5.19 cents a gallon, in face of the average crude market of 83¾ cents—lower than in January, 1893, with crude at 53½ cents a barrel!

This much for the New York end of the export business. In Germany, where the export oil of the independents all went, it being handled there by one dealer, Herr Poth, whose depot was Mannheim, on the Rhine, prices were cut at every point which the independent oil reached. It was a matter of life and death to keep the foreign market they had developed, and for twenty months the independent refiners met the demand of their export agents and foreign dealers for lower prices with cut cargoes. For twenty months they lost money on every barrel they sold. . . . Had it not been for the union with pipe-lines such prices would have been impossible, but all through the struggle in the market the United States Pipe Line and the Producers' and Refiners' lines carried oil at cost or below. The pipe-lines were heavily in debt to the Reading Iron Works, but that company stood by them valiantly, extending their notes until the struggle was over and the pipe-lines able to meet them.

Such a situation could not go on forever, evidently. It had come apparently to be a question of how long the refiner had money to lose, and, as month after month the independents saw their bank accounts diminishing, and no relief in sight, the courage of a few began to ooze. Finally, late in 1894, a committee of the Western refiners . . . went to New York to consult the Standard. Is there no hope of a better market? Is there any chance for us? None whatever, they were told, except to sell. We will buy the refineries and the stock of the independent concerns, but that is all we can do. The committee came home to report. The situation was hopeless, they said, and, as for them, they should sell. As they represented three of the largest concerns in the Union, and all carried stock in the allied enterprises, their withdrawal seemed at the moment a death-blow. It was a glum and beaten body of men which listened to the report, surrender written in every line of their faces.

Now Mr. Lee and Mr. Wood, two active men of the Producers Oil Company, had been invited to the meeting of the refiners. They realised fully that if the refiners pulled out of the Union now, the independent effort would in all probability go to pieces, and before a vote to sell could be taken Mr. Lee was on his feet. In an impassioned speech he pleaded for one more effort. He pointed out the fact that the abnormal condition of the oil market could not remain, that crude oil was steadily rising, and that no monopoly could permanently hold down a manufactured product in the fact of the rising raw product. The Standard had done this for nearly two years—but it was contrary to the laws of nature that they do it for two years more. He told them that already conditions were better in Germany; that Mr. Emery had recently gone with Herr Poth, their foreign buyer, to several members of the German government, and presented to them the discrimination in prices of oil practised in the empire, oil from one and a half to three cents higher on the Elbe than on the Rhine, at points where freights were the same. He told the refiners of the interest that had been taken by the government in their case, and how they said, "Go home, gentlemen, and this shall stop," and that it had stopped. If criminal underselling can be checked in Germany, Mr. Lee argued, we can keep our market. He reminded the refiners that it was not merely a business they were establishing; it was a cause they were defending—the right of men to work in their own way without unlawful interference. The honour not only of themselves but of the Oil Regions was at stake. They were struggling for great principles. They were demonstrating that pluck, patience, and energy and brains can conquer any combination that ability and unscrupulousness can devise. "Do not give in," pleaded Mr. Lee. "Hold on, and we will go to the producers, lay your plight before them, and raise money to keep up the fight." . . .

In the next few days the leading men of the independent alliance worked with fury to call the Oil Regions into a mass-meeting. . . . All the bitterness and determination of the region poured forth against the Standard, and when a resolution was offered by David Kirk, one of the most active and forceful of the independents, to raise money to form a new company, to be called the Pure Oil Company, its immediate object being to take care of the refiners in the tight place where they were, it went through with a whoop, and in a few moments $75,000 had been subscribed. A few days later this sum was raised to $200,000.

The objects of the company, as set forth in its prospectus issued at this time, were:

To maintain and uphold the inherent right to do business, the right to transport and market the producer's own product, and his right to the just reward of his labour and capital investment. . . .

The Pure Oil Company had been organised none too soon. It was but a few months after it was well under way before a hurried meeting of the independents was called in New York. With scared faces the members learned that the German dealer, who for four years had been handling ninety per cent. of their export oil, had sold to the Standard marketing concern, the Deutsche-Amerikanische Company. Consternation was great. . . . Later they learned the truth, that Herr Poth had been informed, by what he supposed to be reliable authority, that the American independent interests had sold to the Standard. Believing that this would cut off his supply, he had turned over his concern to the Deutsche-Amerikanische. A few weeks later Herr Poth died suddenly. The story goes in independent circles that when he learned the truth he literally died of grief, believing he had perjured himself.

Herr Poth's sale left the independents in serious shape. They had cargoes of oil ready for Europe and no tankage in Europe to take it—nobody there to sell it. A meeting was at once called in Pittsburg to raise money, and in a few days Mr. Emery and Mr. Murphy went abroad, and, as quickly as such work could be done, they secured privileges in Hamburg and Rotterdam to erect tanks and establish marketing stations. The Pure Oil Company was in Europe. Once more the independents had been driven to depend on themselves, and once more they had proved sufficient to the emergency. But war was by no means over. With the establishment of the Pure Oil Company came the foreshadowing of a still closer union of the companies. At all hazards this was to be prevented. The Standard determined to play the stock of the Producers' Oil Company, Limited, and the United States Pipe Line, which it had been picking up quietly. . . .

As already noted, the Standard began to buy into that company as soon as it was under way, and by the summer of 1895 they had collected 2,613 shares. In August of that year the annual meeting of the company was held, and the agent of the Standard Oil Company who had been buying the stock, J. C. McDowell, presented himself prepared to vote. He was stopped at the door by Michael Murphy, the present president of the Pure Oil Company, and told emphatically that they considered that he was sent there by the Standard Oil Company to spy on their actions; that, legal or illegal, they would throw him out if he crossed the threshold. . . . Naturally a suit followed, but this time the independents lost. The United States Pipe Line, being a corporation, was obliged to recognise the Standard interest in the concern and eventually to allow them a director on its board.

The humiliation and disgust over this result shook the independents' interests to their foundation. There perhaps was never a period of more heart-breaking discouragement for many of the men than when they saw their dearest hopes frustrated, and a Standard representative in their councils. This defeat came, too, when they were smarting under a continued and intolerable interference by the Standard with the extension of their pipe-lines to the seaboard. That both the crude and refined lines should ultimately reach the sea had, of course, been the intention from the first. But it was not until 1895 that the company felt firm enough in its finances to push the extension. The route laid out was from Wilkesbarre to Bayonne, New Jersey, by way of Hampton Junction, on the Jersey Central Railroad. By this course two railroads were to be crossed, the Pennsylvania and the Delaware, Lackawanna and Western. Under both of them ran the pipe-lines of the Standard and the Tidewater, and the United States Pipe Line officials believed they had an equal right to go under, but they took it for granted they would be opposed, and prepared for it. Looking over the titles of the land along the Pennsylvania, Mr. Emery, the president of the company, who was personally directing the extension, found one for an acre; the owner did not know of his possession and was glad to sell it. This gave the United States people a crossing, but even then they were obliged to carry on a long litigation in the courts before they were free to use their right.

Coming to the Delaware, Lackawanna and Western, they decided to test their position by laying a pipe. It was promptly torn out. A farm over which the railroad passed was then purchased and preparations made to lay the pipe in a roadway under the tracks. As this road was some seventeen feet below the rails, any claim that there was possible danger from the oil seemed feeble. Knowing that the point was watched, Mr. Emergy tried strategy. Taking fifty men with him he went in the night to the culvert under which he meant to cross, laid his pipes four feet under ground, fastened them down with heavy timbers, piled rocks on them, anchored them with chains, established a camp on each side of the track, and prepared for war. They soon had it. First, with a body of railroad men armed with picks and bars, who invaded the camp. "I told the boys," said Mr. Emergy in describing the incident to the Industrial Commission in 1899, "to take the men by the shoulders and seat of the pants, and take them out and lay them down carefully, which they did." The next day two wrecking-cars, with 250 men, came down the road and charged the camp, but again they were routed. The matter was taken by mutual agreement into court, and while Mr. Emery was before the justice of the peace, two locomotives were run down and the camp attacked with hot water and coals!

By this time the whole countryside was aroused. The unfairness of the thing was so patent that even the railroad employees engaged in it did not hesitate to say, in excuse of their employers, that it was the Standard Oil Company which was at the bottom of the opposition! As for the inhabitants, they offered any aid they could give. The local G. A. R. sent forty-eight muskets to the scene of war. Mr. Emery bought eighteen Springfield rifles, the camp was barricaded, and for seven months the pipes were guarded while the courts were deciding the legal title to the crossing.

This interim was employed by the pipe-line people in an attempt to get a free pipe-line bill through the New Jersey Legislature. If this could be done they could go under the Delaware, Lackawanna and Western without its consent. . . . Trenton became alive with lobbyists—men well enough known to politicians. The newspapers came out boldly with the charge that the railroads and Standard were going to defeat the bill. Its friends could not believe it, nor did they until they found, the morning it was to be presented, that the Senator having it in charge had disappeared, taking with him the bill and everything concerning it. Four days later the Legislature adjourned, and the precious Senator, when next heard from, was in the far West!

Deprived of this hope, and condemned to a litigation which was certain to be made as long, as vexatious, and as costly as lawyers could make it, the chief counsel of the United States Pipe Line, Roger Sherman, advised a bold move—to bring suit against the Standard Trust under the Sherman anti-trust law. The summons was issued in July, 1897, by John Cunneen, of Buffalo. A very pretty list of wrongs it was of which the plaintiff complained: the instigation of lawsuits and the causing of injunctions without cause, and solely for the purpose of preventing the independent line from doing business; the publishing of libellous matter concerning the company and its officers in newspapers controlled by the trust; engaging bodies of men to tear up parts of pipe-line already laid; enticing away from the enterprise officers, agents and employees; chartering or purchasing any vessels carrying independent oil, solely for the purpose of interfering with the independent market; intimidating merchants by threats of underselling until they refused to buy the oil contracted for; criminal underselling solely for destroying the plaintiff's markets.

It was a serious case Mr. Sherman made out, and the evidence he collected was elaborate and detailed. But, for a sad reason, it was never to come to trial. Less than two months after the summons was issued Mr. Sherman died suddenly in New York City. The shock of his death was such that the independent companies had no heart for the suit, but allowed it to lapse.

There was nothing now but the slow course of Jersey justice for the United States Pipe Line, and for four long years it dragged itself through the courts. Twice it won, but at last, in 1899, the decisions of the lower courts were reversed and the pipe-line had to come up. Ordered out of New Jersey, the independents had to turn back to Pennsylvania. In that state there is a free pipe-line bill. Philadelphia is a shipping point. Luckily for the company, Mr. Murphy had, some time before this, and in anticipation of a defeat in New Jersey, bought on his own responsibility the land for a terminal at Marcus Hook, on the Delaware. This terminal he now sold to the company at the nominal price he had paid for it, and the United States Pipe Line was started again from Wilkesbarre to the sea. Finally, on May 2, 1901, after nine years of struggle in the face of an interference intolerable and unjust, after a quarter of a million dollars spent in litigation, in useless surveys, in laying and pulling up pipes, in loss of business, the first refined oil ever piped from the Oil Regions to the seaboard reached Philadelphia.

Mr. Emery, in telling his story of the difficulties of the United Pipe Line to the Industrial Commission in 1899, did not hesitate to attribute them to the Standard Oil Trust. John D. Archbold made a "general denial": "We have not at any time had any different relations with reference to any obstruction or effort at obstruction of their line *than would attach to any competitor in a line of business engaging against another.*" "We asked our friends on the railroad and in the New Jersey Legislature to look after our interests, of course," a Standard official told the writer in discussing this case. "That was our right." . . .

Mr. Emery, overwhelmed by the death of Roger Sherman and worn out by his six years of work and worry over the United States Pipe Line, fell ill and was obliged to resign. On every side it was fight and loss and despair, and yet these men hardened under it. Not only hardened, they expanded. Ten years after the unorganised uprising which brought them together in 1887 and forced from them the resolution to take care of their own product, what had they? A company of early 600 individual oil producers organised on a business basis, and connected by pipe-lines with some dozen individual oil re- fineries. For transporting this oil they had pipe-lines carrying both crude and refined from the Oil Regions to within fifty miles of the sea, and for markets they had those they had themselves worked up in the United States and Europe. They had something more. In spite of the continued hostility of the Standard they had the conviction that there was a fu- ture for their venture; but they saw clearly that to realise it they must get themselves into still more compact form—that their holdings must be put into the hands of trustees in a single company if they were to be free from the danger of the eventual dominance of the Standard. Now, in November, 1895, as we have seen, the independents had incorporated in New Jersey a marketing concern called the Pure Oil Company. After months of discussion it was decided to enlarge the capital of this company to $10,000,000, $2,000,000 in preferred and $8,000,000 in common stock, and put into this concern all their interests. There was opposition to the consolidation from some of the strongest interests concerned, but finally the idea pre- vailed, and in 1900 a majority of the stock of the Producers' Oil Company, the Producers' and Refiners' Company, and the United States Pipe Line was turned over to the Pure Oil Company.

The purpose of the combination was frankly stated to be the maintenance of the independence of the company. This was to be effected in the following way: the holders of 16,000 shares of stock—more than a majority—vested the voting power of these shares in fifteen persons for twenty years, and it was agreed that one-half of all shares thereafter subscribed should be transferred to those same trustees. Shares can be sold and transferred, but this transfer does not give the pur- chaser any right other than provided in the trust agreement. Any trustee may be summarily removed by three-fifths of the trustees, together with three-fifths of the shareholders in trust. It certainly looks as if the Pure Oil Company has devised an organisation which will effectually preserve its independence so long as its shareholders desire that independence. Mr. Archbold, in describing this voting trust of the Pure Oil Company to the Industrial Commission, called it "iniquitous." It is difficult to understand just how it is iniquitous, unless it is because of its success so far in keeping the Standard out of its councils. It is not a secret arrangement. It aims at no monopoly, at no restraint of trade. It claims only to be a device for protecting its obvious right to handle its own product. Of course, if we admit that the oil business belongs to the Standard, as Mr. Rockefeller claims, then the Pure Oil Company is certainly in the wrong!

As it stands to-day, the independents have a good showing for their fight. They have fully 900 stockholders, most of them producers. They handle a daily production of 8,000 barrels of crude oil; operate 1,500 miles of crude pipe-line and 400 miles of refined; are allied with some fourteen refineries, in some of which all the by-products of oil, as well as naphtha and illuminating oils, are produced; own one tank-steamer, the Penn-oil, with a capacity of 42,000 fifty-gallon barrels, and charter several others; own oil barges on the Rhine, the Elbe and the Baltic; have fully equipped stations in Europe at Hamburg, Mannheim, Riesa, Stettin and Dusseldorf, in Germany; Rotterdam and Amsterdam, Holland; London and Manchester, England; and, in the United States, New York and Philadelphia. With conservative and loyal management, there seems to be no reason that the Pure Oil Company should not become a permanent independent factor in the oil business. Such a thing is worth the best efforts of the men who have made it. Their courageous and persistent struggle no doubt seems to most of them as of purely personal and local meaning. All they asked was to get a fair share of the profits in their business. They knew they did not get it, and they believed it was because there was not fair play on the part of the railroads and the Standard Oil Company. Aroused, they each fought for the particular thing which would give them relief. They only combined because driven to. They have become a strong organisation almost solely because of the persistent opposition of the Standard Oil Trust. The Standard's efforts to break up the Producers' Protective Association by buying out the biggest producers precipitated a co-operative company for handling oil. Its efforts to drive out the independent refineries by the manipulation of the railroads drove the producers and refiners to combine. The heavy charges for handling oil by the Standard pipe-line and by the railways drove these independents to build a seaboard pipe-line for both refined and crude, and to demonstrate that refined as well as crude could be pumped to the sea in pipes. The buying out of their foreign agents forced them to develop their own market in Europe. The secret buying in of their stock, and the combined effort to force the Standard directors on them, compelled them into their present close trust organisation. It looks very much as if in trying to make way with several small scattered bodies Mr. Rockefeller had made on strong, united one.

But while the experience of the Pure Oil Company demonstrates that it is possible to-day to build up an independent oil business if men have the requisite patience and fighting quality, it by no means follows that the success of the Pure Oil Company has restored competition in the oil business or that by its success the public is getting any marked reduction in the price of oil. That the control of that price—within limits—is now and has been almost constantly since 1876 in the hands of the Standard Oil Company is demonstrated, the writer believes, by the figures and diagrams of the next chapter.

16   THE PRICE OF OIL

Earliest designs for consolidation include plans to hold up the price of oil—South Improvement Company so intends—Combination of 1872-1873 makes oil dear—Scheme fails and prices drop—The Standard's great profits in 1876-1877 through its second successful consolidation—Return of competition and lower prices—Standard's futile attempt in 1880 to repeat raid of 1876-1877—Standard is convinced that making oil too dear weakens markets and stimulates competition—Great profits of 1879-1889—Lowering of the margin on export since 1889 by reason of competition—Manipulation of domestic prices even more marked—Home consumers pay cost of Standard's fights in foreign lands—Standard's various prices for the same goods at home—High prices where there is no competition and low prices where there is competition.

IT IS quite possible that in keeping the attention fixed so long on Mr. Rockefeller's oil campaign the reader has forgotten the reason why it was undertaken. The reason was made clear enough at the start by Mr. Rockefeller himself. He and his colleagues went into their first venture, the South Improvement Company, not simply because it was a quick and effective way of putting everybody but themselves out of the refining business, but because . . . they could control the output of oil and put up its price. . . .

Four years after the failure of the first great scheme, a similar one went into effect. What was its object? J. J. Vandergrift, one of the directors of the Standard Oil Company at that time, questioned once under oath as to what they meant to do, said: "simply to hold up the price of oil—to get all we can for it." Nobody pretended anything else at the time. . . .

Now it is natural that men should struggle to keep up a profit. The refiners had become accustomed to making from twenty-five per cent. to fifty per cent., and even more, on every gallon of oil they put out. They had the same extravagant notion of what they should make as the oil producers of those early days had. No oil producer thought in the sixties that he was succeeding if his wells did not pay for themselves in six months! And as their new industry slowly but surely came under the laws of trade, increased its production, was subjected to severe competition, as they saw themselves, in order to sustain their business, forced to practise economies and to accept smaller profits, they loudly complained. There was never a set of men who found it harder to accept the limitations of economic laws than the oil producers of Pennsylvania. The oil refiners showed the same dislike of the harness, and in 1871, as we have seen, Mr. Rockefeller and a few of his friends combined to throw it off. What they proposed to do was simply to get all the refineries of the country under their control, and thereafter make only so much oil as they could sell at their own interpretation of a paying price. . . .

The success which Mr. Rockefeller had in getting the refiners of the country under his control, and the methods he took to do it, we have traced. It will be remembered that for a brief period in 1872 and 1873 he held together an association pledged to curtail the output of oil, but that in July, 1873, it went to pieces. It will be recalled that three years after, in 1875, he put a second association into operation, which in a year claimed a control of ninety per cent. of the refining power of the country, and in less than four years controlled ninety-five per cent. This large percentage Mr. Rockefeller has not been able to keep, but from 1879 to the present day there has not been a time when he has not controlled over eighty per cent. of the oil manufacturing of the country. To-day he controls about eighty-three per cent.

Now it is generally conceded that the man or men who control over seventy per cent. of a commodity control its price—within limits, very strict limits, too, such is the force of economic laws. In the case of the Standard Oil Company the control is so complete that the price of oil, both crude and refined, is actually issued from its headquarters. . . .

The first eight years of its existence had been spent in bold and relentless warfare on its competitors. Competition practically out of the way, it set all its great energies to developing what it had secured. In this period it brought into line the foreign markets and aided in increasing the exports of illuminating oil from 365,000,000 gallons in 1879 to 455,000,000 in 1888; of lubricating, from 3,000,000 to 24,000,000, and yet this great extension of the volume of business profited the consumer nothing. In this period it laid hands on the idea of the Tidewater, the long-distance pipe-lines for transporting crude oil, and so rid itself practically of the railroads, and yet this immense economy profited the public nothing. In spite of the immense development of this system and the enormous economies it brought about—a system so important that Mr. Rockefeller himself has said: "The entire oil business is dependent upon this pipe-line system. Without it every well would shut down, and every foreign market would be closed to us"—the margins never fell the fraction of a cent from 1879 to 1889, though it frequently rose. In this period, too, the by-products of oil were enormously increased. The waste, formerly as much as ten per cent. of the crude product, was reduced until practically all of the oil is worked up by the Standard people, and yet, in spite of the extension of by-products between 1879 and 1889, the margin never went below the point competition had forced it to in 1879.

The enormous profits which came to the Standard in these ten years by keeping out competition are evident if we consider for a moment the amount of business done. The exports of illuminating oil in this period were nearly 5,000,000,000 gallons; of this the Standard handled well toward ninety per cent. Consider what sums lay in the ability to hold up the price on such an amount even an eighth of a cent a gallon. Combine this control of the price of refined oil with the control over the crude product, the ability to depress the market for purchasing, an ability used most carefully, but most constantly; add to this the economies and development Mr. Rockefeller's able and energetic machine was making, and the great profits of the Standard Oil Trust between 1879 and 1889 are easily explained. In 1879, on a capital of $3,500,000, the Standard Oil Company paid $3,150,000 dividends; in 1880 it paid $1,050,000. In 1882 it capitalised itself at $70,000,000. In 1885, three years later, its net earnings were over $8,000,000; in 1886, over $15,000,000; in 1888, over $16,000,000; in 1889, nearly $15,000,000. In the meantime the net value of its holdings had increased from $72,000,000; in 1883, to over $101,000,000. While the Standard was making these great sums, the men who produced the oil saw their property depreciating, and the value of their oil actually eaten up every two years by the prices the Standard charged for gathering and storing it. . . .

With the beginning of 1889 the margin begins to fall. This is so in spite of a rising crude line. It would look as if the Standard Oil Company had suddenly had a change of heart. . . .

As a matter of fact this lowering of the margin was the direct result of competition. In 1888 a German firm, located in New York City, erected large oil plants in Rotterdam and Bremerhaven. They put up storage tanks at each place of 90,000 barrels' capacity. They also established a storage depot of 30,000 barrels at Mannheim, and took steps to extend their supply stations in Germany and Switzerland. They built tank steamers in order to ship their oil in bulk. These oil importers allied themselves with certain independent refiners, and interested themselves also in the co-operative movement which the producers of Pennsylvania were striving to get into operation at this time. The extent of the undertaking threatened serious competition. In the same year imports of Russian oil into the markets of Western Europe began for the first time to assume serious proportions. Russian oil had, from the beginning, been a possible menace to American petroleum, for the wonderful fields on the Caspian were known long before oil was "struck" in Pennsylvania. They did not begin to be exploited in a way to threaten competition until late in the eighties. . . . There was nothing in the world that gave oil consumers the benefit of the Standard's savings by economies in 1889, but the competition threatened by Russia and the American and German independent alliance. The Standard, to offset it, not only lowered its price, but it followed the German company to Rotterdam in order to put up an oil plant similar to the one which had been erected by those independents. They also purchased at this time the great oil establishments at Bremen and Hamburg which had hitherto been owned and operated by Germans. . . .

In 1892, the price of refined oil begins to fall, although crude is stationary. . . . This went on for nearly three years, until there was a margin of only three cents between crude and refined oil. . . . Now, the Standard Oil Company were not selling oil at a loss at this time out of love for the consumers, although they made enough money in 1894 on by-products and domestic oil to have done so—their net earnings were over $15,000,000 in 1894, and they reckoned an increase in net value of property of over $4,000,000—they were fighting Russian oil and the independent combination started in 1889. By 1892 this combination was in active operation. . . . At the same time certain large producers in the McDonald oil field built a pipe-line from Pittsburg to Baltimore, the Crescent Line, and began to ship crude oil to France in great quantities. It looked as if both combinations meant to do business, and the Standard set out to get them out of the way. One method they took was to prevent the refiners in the combination making any money on export oil. . . .

After two years they gave it up. It was too expensive. The Crescent Line sold to them, but the other independents were too plucky. They had lost money for two years, but they were still hanging on like grim death, and the Standard concluded to concentrate their attacks on other points of the combination rather than on this export market where it was costing them so much. . . .

Thus far the illustrations of Mr. Rockefeller's use of his power over the oil market have been drawn from export oil. It is the only market for which "official" figures can be obtained for the entire period, and it is the market usually quoted in studying the movement of prices. It is of this grade of oil that the largest percentage of product is obtained in distilling petroleum. For instance, in distilling Pennsylvania crude, fifty-two per cent. is standard-white or export oil, twenty-two per cent. water-white —the higher grade commonly used in this country—thirteen per cent. naphtha, ten per cent. tar, three per cent. loss. The runs vary with different oils, and different refiners turn out different products. The water-white oils, while they cost the same to produce, sell from two to three cents higher. The naphtha costs the same to make as export oil, but sells at a higher price, and many refiners have pet brands, for which, through some marketing trick, they get a fancy price. The Standard Oil Company has a great number of fancy brands of both illuminating and lubricating oils, for which they get large prices—although often the oil itself comes from the same barrels as the ordinary grade. Now it is from the extra price obtained from naphtha, water-white, fancy brands, and by-products that the independent refiner makes up for his loss on export oil, and the Standard Oil Trust raises its dividends to forty-eight per cent. . . .

Turn now to the price of domestic oil . . . to see if we have fared as well as the exporters. . . . It is interesting to note . . . how frequently high domestic prices are made to offset low export prices; thus, in 1889, when the Standard was holding export oil low to fight competition in Europe, it kept up domestic oil. The same thing is happening to-day. We are helping pay for the Standard's fight with Russian, Roumanian and Asiatic oils. . . . Domestic oil, indeed, has no regular price. Go back as far as anything like trustworthy documents exist, and find the most astonishing vagaries, even in the same state. For instance, in a table presented to a Congressional Committee in 1888, and complied from answers to letters sent out by George Rice, the price of 110° oil in barrels in Texas ranged from 10 to 20 cents; in Arkansas, of 150° oil in barrels, from 8 to 18; in Tennessee, the same oil, from 8 to 16; in Mississippi, the same, from 11 to 17. In the eighties, prime white oil sold in barrels, wholesale, in Arkansas, all the way from 8 to 14 cents; in Illinois, from 7½ to 10; in Mississippi, from 7¼ to 13½; in Nebraska, 7½ to 18; in South Carolina, 8 to 12½; and in Utah, 13 to 23. Freight and handling might, of course, account for one to two cents of the difference, but not more. . . .

The most elaborate investigation of oil prices ever made was that instigated by the recent Industrial Commission. In February, 1901, the commission sent out inquiries to 5,000 retail dealers, scattered from the Atlantic to the Pacific and from the Lakes to the Gulf, asking the prices of certain commodities, among them illuminating oils; 1,578 replies were received. The tables prepared offered striking examples of the variability of prices—thus:

In Colorado the wholesale price of illuminating oil (150° test) varied from 13 to 20 cents; in Delaware, 8 to 10; in Illinois, 6 to 10; in Alabama, 10.50 to 16; in Michigan, 5.50 to 12.25; in Missouri, 7.50 to 12.50; in Kentucky, 7 to 11.50; in Ohio, 5.50 to 9.75; in California, 12.50 to 20; in Utah, 20 to 22; in Maine, 8.25 to 12.75 (freight included in all these prices).

The difference between the highest and the lowest wholesale prices in the same states varies from 8 cents in Oregon (12.50 to 20.50) to 1.50 in Rhode Island (8.50 to 10). Of course, in the former case, two or even three cents of the difference may be due to freight, but hardly more. Take adjoining states, for instance. In Vermont there is a difference of 4.50 cents between the highest and lowest price of oil; in New Hampshire, only 1.75. In Delaware there is a difference of 2 cents; in Virginia, of 6. . . .

Freights and handling considered, there is, it is evident,

nothing like a settled price or profit for illuminating oil in the United States. Now, there is no one who will not admit that it is for the good of the consumer that the normal market price of any commodity should be such as will give a fair and even profit all over the country. That is, that freights and expense of handling being considered, oil should sell at the same profit in Texas as in Ohio. That such must be the case where there is free and general competition is evident. But from the beginning of its power over the market the Standard Oil Company has sold domestic oil at prices varying from less than the cost of the crude oil it took to make it up to a profit of 100 per cent. or more. Wherever there has been a loss, or merely what is called a reasonable profit of, say, ten per cent., an examination of the tables quoted above shows conclusively it has been due to competition. The competition is not, and has not been since 1879, very great. In that year the Standard Oil Company claimed ninety-five per cent. of the refining interests of the country. In 1888 they claimed about eighty per cent.; in 1898, eighty-three per cent. This five to seventeen per cent. of independent interest is too small to come into active competition, of course, at all points. So long as one interest handles eighty-three per cent. of a product it is clear that it has the trade as a whole in its hands. The competition it encounters will be local only. But it is this local competition, unquestionably, that has brought down the price of oil at various points and caused the striking variation in prices recorded in the charts of the Industrial Commission and other investigations. . . .

Every investigation made since shows that it is the touch of the competitor which brings down the price. For instance, in the cost and profit sheet from a Standard ledger referred to above, there was one station on the list at which oil was selling at a loss. On investigation the writer found it to be a point at which an independent jobber had been trying to get a market. If one examines the tables of prices in the recent report of the Industrial Commission, he finds that wherever there is a low price there is competition. Thus, at Indianapolis, the only town in the state of Indiana reporting competition, the wholesale price of oil was 5½ cents, although forty out of the fifty-three Indiana towns reporting gave from 8 cents to 10½ cents as the wholesale price per gallon. (These prices included freight. Taking Indianapolis as a centre, the local freight on oil to any point in Indiana is in no case over a cent.) In April, 1904, inquiry showed the same striking difference between prices in Indianapolis, where six independent companies are now established, and neighbouring towns to which competition has not as yet reached. . . .

And so one might go on indefinitely, showing how the introduction of an independent oil has always reduced the price. As a rule, the appearance of the oil has led to a sharp contest or "Oil War," at which, not infrequently, both sides have sold at a loss. The Standard, being able to stand a loss indefinitely, usually won out.

An interesting local "Oil War," which occurred in 1896 and 1897 in New York and Philadelphia, figured in the reports of the Industrial Commission, and illustrates very well the usual influence on Standard prices of the incoming of competition. On March 20, 1896, the Pure Oil Company put three tank-wagons into New York City. The Standard's price of water-white oil from tank-wagons that day was 9½ cents, and the Pure Oil Company followed it. In less than a week the Standard had cut to 8 cents *along the route of the Pure Oil Company wagons*. In April the price was cut to 7 cents. By December, 1896, it had fallen to 6 cents; by December, 1897, to 5.4. . . .

If competition persists the result usually has been permanently lower prices than in territory where competition has been run out or has never entered. For instance, why should oil be sold to a dealer at nearly four cents more on an average in Kansas than in Kentucky, when the freight from Whiting to Kansas is only a cent more? For no reason except that in Kentucky there has been persistent competition for twenty-five years, and in Kansas none has ever secured a solid foothold. Why should Colorado pay an average of 16.90 cents for oil per gallon and California 14.60 cents, when the freight from Whiting differs but one-tenth of one cent? For no reason except that a few years ago competition was driven from Colorado, and in California it still exists.

Indeed, any consecutive study of the Standard Oil Company's use of its power over the price of either export or domestic oil must lead to the conclusion that it has always been used to the fullest extent possible without jeopardising it; that we have always paid more for our refined oil than we would have done if there had been free competition. But why should we expect anything else? This is the chief object of combinations. Certainly the candid members of the Standard Oil Company would be the last men to argue that they give the public any more of the profits they may get by combination than they can help. One of the ablest and frankest of them, H. H. Rogers, when before the Industrial Commission in 1899, was asked how it happened that in twenty years the Standard Oil Company had never cheapened the cost of gathering and transporting oil in pipe-lines by the least fraction of a cent; that it cost the oil producer just as much now as it did twenty years ago to get his oil taken away from the wells and to transport it to New York. And Mr. Rogers answered, with delightful candour: "We are not in business for our health, but are out for the dollars."

John D. Archbold was asked at the same time if it were not true that, by virtue of its great power, the Standard Oil Company was enabled to secure prices that, on the whole, were above those under competition, and Mr. Archbold said: "Well, I hope so." . . .

For many of the world it is a matter of little moment, no doubt, whether oil sells for eight or twelve cents a gallon. It becomes a tragic matter sometimes, however, as in 1902–1903 when, in the coal famine, the poor, deprived of coal, depended on oil for heat. In January, 1903, oil was sold to dealers from tank-wagons in New York City at eleven cents a gallon. That oil cost the independent refiner, who paid full transportation charges and marketed at the cost of a cent a gallon, not over 6.4 cents. It cost the Standard Oil Company probably a cent less. That such a price could prevail under free competition is, of course, impossible. Throughout the hard winter of 1902–1903 the price of refined oil advanced. It was claimed that this was due to the advance in crude, but in every case it was considerably more than that of crude. Indeed, a careful comparative study of oil prices shows that the Standard almost always advances the refined market a good many more points than it does the crude market. . . . While this has been the rule, there are exceptions, of course, as when a rate war is on. Thus, in the spring of 1904, the severe competition in England of the Shell Transportation Company and of Russian oil caused the Standard to drop export refined considerably more than crude. But . . . domestic oil has been kept up.

As a result of the Standard's power over prices, not only does the consumer pay more for oil where competition has not reached or has been killed, but this power is used steadily and with consummate skill to make it hard for men to compete in any branch of the oil business. This history has been but a rehearsal of the operations practised by the Standard Oil Company to get rid of competition. It was to get rid of competition that the South Improvement Company was formed. It was to get rid of competition that the oil-carrying railroads were bullied or persuaded or bribed into unjust discriminations. It was to get rid of competition that the Empire Transportation Company, one of the finest transportation companies ever built up in this country, was wrested from the hands of the men who had developed it. It was to get rid of competition that war was made on the Tidewater Pipe Line, the Crescent Pipe Line, the United States Pipe Line, not to mention a number of similar smaller enterprises. It was to get rid of competition that the Standard's spy system was built up, its oil wars instituted, all its perfect methods for making it hard for rivals to do business developed.

The most curious feature perhaps of this question of the Standard Oil Company and the price of oil is that there are still people who believe that the Standard has made oil cheap! Men . . . recall that back in the late sixties and seventies they paid fifty and sixty cents a gallon for oil, which now they pay twelve and fifteen cents for. This, then, they say, is the result of the combination. Mr. Rockefeller himself pointed out this great difference in prices. "In 1861," he told the New York Senate Committee, "oil sold for sixty-four cents a gallon, and now it is six and a quarter cents." The comparision is as misleading as it was meant to be. In 1861 there was not a railway into the Oil Regions. It cost from three to ten dollars to get a barrel of oil to a shipping point. None of the appliances of transportation or storage had been devised. The process of refining was still crude, and there was great waste in the oil. Besides, the markets were undeveloped. Mr. Rockefeller should have noted that oil fell from 61½ in 1861 to 25⅝ in the year he first took hold of it, and that by his first successful manipulation it went up to 30! He should point out what the successive declines in prices since that day are due to—to the seaboard pipe-lines, to the development of by-products, to bulk instead of barrel transportation, to innumerable small economies. People who point to the differences in price, and call it combination, have never studied the price-line history in hand. They do not know the meaning of the variation of the line; that it was forced down from 1866 to 1876, when Mr. Rockefeller's first effective combination was secured by competition, and driven up in 1876 and 1877 by the stopping of competition; that it was driven down from 1877 to 1879 by the union of all sorts of competitive forces—producers, independent refiners, the developing of an independent seaboard pipe-line—to a point lower than it had ever been before. They forget that when these opposing forces were overcome, and the Standard Oil Company was at last supreme, for ten years oil never fell a point below the margin reached by competition in 1879, though frequently it rose above that margin. They forget that in 1889, when for the first time in ten years the margin between crude and refined oil began to fall, it was the competition coming from the rise of American independent interests and the development of foreign oil fields that did it.

To believe that the Standard Oil Combination, or any other similar aggregation, would lower prices except under the pressure of the competition they were trying to kill, argues an amazing gullibility. Human experience long ago taught us that if we allowed a man or a group of men autocratic powers in government or church, they used that power to oppress and defraud the public. For centuries the struggle of the nations has been to obtain stable government, with fair play to the masses. To obtain this we have hedged our kings and emperors and presidents about with a thousand constitutional restrictions. It has not been possible for us to allow even the church, inspired by religious ideals, to have the full power it has demanded in society. And yet we have here in the United States allowed men practically autocratic powers in commerce. We have allowed them special privileges in transportation, bound in no great length of time to kill their competitors, though the spirit of our laws and of the charters of the transportation lines forbade these privileges. We have allowed them to combine in great interstate aggregations, for which we have provided no form of charter or publicity, although human experience long ago decided that men united in partnerships, companies, or corporations for business purposes must have their powers defined and be subject to a reasonable inspection and publicity. As a natural result of these extraordinary powers, we see, as in the case of the Standard Oil Company, the price of a necessity of life within the control of a group of nine men, as able, as energetic, and as ruthless in business operations as any nine men the world has ever seen combined. They have exercised their power over prices with almost preternatural skill. It has been their most cruel weapon in stifling competition, a sure means of reaping usurious dividends, and, at the same time, a most persuasive argument in hoodwinking the public.

17   THE LEGITIMATE GREATNESS OF THE STANDARD OIL COMPANY

Centralisation of authority—Rockefeller and eight other trustees managing things like partners in a business—News-gathering organization for collecting all information of value to the trustees—Rockefeller gets picked men for every post and contrives to make them compete with each other—Plants wisely located—The smallest details in expense looked out for—Quick adaptability to new conditions as they arise—Economy introduced by the manufacture of supplies—Profit paid to nobody—Profitable extension of products and by-products—A general capacity for seeing big things and enough daring to lay hold of them.

WHILE there can be no doubt that the determining factor in the success of the Standard Oil Company in securing a practical monopoly of the oil industry has been the special privileges it has enjoyed since the beginning of its career, it is equally true that those privileges alone will not account for its success. Something besides illegal advantages has gone into the making of the Standard Oil Trust. Had it possessed only the qualities which the general public has always attributed to it, its overthrow would have come before this. But this huge bulk, blackened by commercial sin, has always been strong in all great business qualities—in energy, in intelligence, in dauntlessness. It has always been rich in youth as well as greed, in brains as well as unscrupulousness. If it has played its great game with contemptuous indifference to fair play, and to nice legal points of view, it has played it with consummate ability, daring and address. The silent, patient, all-seeing man who has led it in its transportation raids has led it no less successfully in what may be called its legitimate work. Nobody has appreciated more fully than he those qualities which alone make for permanent stability and growth in commercial ventures. He has insisted on these qualities, and it is because of this insistence that the Standard Oil Trust has always been something besides a fine piece of brigandage, with the fate of brigandage before it, that it has been a thing with life and future.

If one attempts to analyse what may be called the legitimate greatness of Mr. Rockefeller's creation in distinction to its illegitimate greatness, he will find at the foundation the fact that it is as perfectly centralised as the Catholic church or the Napoleonic government. As was pointed out in a former chapter, the entire business was placed in 1882 in the hands of nine trustees, of whom Mr. Rockefeller was president. These trustees have always acted exactly as if they were nine partners in a business, and the only persons concerned in it. They met daily, giving their whole time to the management and development of the concern, as the partners in a dry-goods house would. Anything in the oil world might come under their ken, from a smoking wick in Oshkosh to the competition of Russian oil in China. Everything; but nothing came unless it was necessary; for below them, and sifting things for their eyes, were committees which dealt with the various departments of the business. There was a Crude Committee which considered the subject of crude oil, the world over; a Manufacturing Committee which studied the making of refined, the utilisation of waste, the development of new products; a Marketing Committee which considered the markets. Before each of these committees was laid daily all the information to be found on earth concerning its particular field; not only were there reports made to it of what was doing in its line in the Standard Oil Trust, but information came of everything connected with such work everywhere by everybody. These committees not only knew all about their own business, they knew all about everybody else's. The Manufacturing Committee knew just what each of the feeble independent refiners still existing was doing—what its resources and advantages were; the Transportation Committee knew what rates it got; the Marketing Committee knew its market. Thus the fullest information about new developments of crude, new openings for refined, new processes of manufacture, was always at the command of the nine trustees of the trust.

How did they get this information? As the press does—by a wide-spreading system of reporters. In 1882 the Standard had correspondents in every town in the oil fields, and to-day it has them not only there but in every capital of the globe. It is a common enough thing, indeed, in European capitals to run across high-class newspaper correspondents, consuls, or business men who add to their incomes by private reporting to the Standard Oil Company. The people in their employ naturally report all they learn. There are also outsiders who report what they pick up—"occasional contributions." There is more than one man in the Oil Regions who has made his livelihood for years by picking up information for the Standard. . . .

These trustees then "know everything" about the oil business and they have used their information. Nobody ever used information more profitably. What was learned was applied, and affected the whole great structure, for by a marvellous genius in organisation Mr. Rockefeller had devised a machine with a head whose thinking was felt from the seat of power in New York City to the humblest pipe-line patrol on Oil Creek. This head controlled each one of the scattered plants with absolute precision. Take the refineries; they were individual plants, having a manager and a board of directors like any outside plant, but these plants were not free agents. According to J. J. Vandergrift's testimony in 1879, the Imperial Refinery, of which he was president, had no control of its oil after it was made. The Standard Oil Company of Cleveland took charge of it at Oil City, and arranged for transportation and for marketing. The managers of the Central Association, into which the allied refiners went in 1875 under Mr. Rockefeller's presidency, had "irrevocable authority to make all purchases of crude oil and sales of refined oil," as well as to "negotiate for all railroad and pipe-line freights and transportation expenses" for each of the refineries. . . .

One of Mr. Rockefeller's greatest achievements has been to bring men who had built up their own factories and managed them to suit themselves to work harmoniously under such limitations. As this history has shown, the first attempt to harness the refiners failed because they would not obey the rules. No doubt the chief reason why they finally consented to them was that only by so doing could they get transportation rates equally advantageous to those of the Standard Oil Company; but, having consented and finding it profitable, they were kept in line by an ingenious system of competition which must have done much to satisfy their need of individual effort and their pride in independent work. . . . Each refinery in the alliance was required to make to Mr. Rockefeller each month a detailed statement of its operations. These statements were compared and the results made known. If the Acme at Titusville had refined cheaper that month than any other member of the alliance, the fact was made known. If this cheapness continued to show, the others were sent to study the Acme methods. Whenever an improvement showed, that improvement received credit, and the others were sent to find the secret. The keenest rivalry resulted—every factory was on its mettle.

This supervision took account of the least detail. There is a story often told in the Oil Regions to illustrate the minuteness of the supervision. In commenting as usual on the monthly "competitive statements," as they are called, Mr. Rockefeller called the attention of a certain refiner to a discrepancy in his reports. It referred to *bungs*—articles worth about as much in a refinery as pins are in a household. "Last month," the comment ran, "you reported on hand 1,119 bungs. Ten thousand were sent you at the beginning of this month. You have used 9,527 this month. You report 1,012 on hand. What has become of the other five hundred and eighty?" The writer has it on high authority that the current version of this story is not true, but it reflects very well the impression the Oil Regions have of the thoroughness of Mr. Rockefeller's supervision. The Oil Regions, which were notoriously extravagant in their business methods, resented this care and called it meanness, but the Oil Regions were wrong and Mr. Rockefeller was right. Take care of the bungs and the barrels will take care of themselves, is as good a policy in a refinery as the old saw it paraphrases is in financiering.

There were other features of this revolutionary management which caused deep resentment in the oil world. Chief among them was the dismantling or abandoning of plants which the Standard had "acquired," and which it claimed were so badly placed or so equipped that it did not pay to run them. There was reason enough in many cases for dissatisfaction with the process of acquisition, but having acquired the refineries, the Standard showed its wisdom in abandoning many of them. . . . Now, one of the most melancholy sights on earth is an abandoned oil refinery; and it was the desolation of the picture, combined, as it always was in the Oil Regions, with the history of the former owners, that caused much of the outcry. It was a thing that the oil men could not get over, largely because it was a sight always before their eyes.

Bitter as this policy was for those who had suffered by the Standard's campaigns, it was, of course, the only thing for the trust to do—indeed, that was what it had been waging war on the independents for: that it might shut them down and dismantle them, that there might be less oil made and higher prices for what it made. This wisdom in locating factories has continued to characterise the Standard operations. It works only plants which pay, and it places its plants where they can be operated to the best advantage. Many fine examples of the relation of location in manufacturing to crude supply and to markets are to be seen in the Standard Oil Company plants to-day. For example, refined for foreign shipments is made at the seaboard, and the vessels which carry it are loaded at docks, as at the works at Bayonne, New Jersey. The cost of transportation from factory to ship, a large item in the old days, is eliminated entirely. The Middle West market is now supplied almost entirely from the Standard factories at Whiting, Indiana, a town built by the Standard Oil Company for refining Ohio oil. Here 25,000 barrels of oil are refined daily, and from this central point distributed to the Mississippi Valley.

All of the industries which have been grafted on to the refineries have always been run with the same exact regard to minute economies. These industries were numerous because of Mr. Rockefeller's great principle, "pay a profit to nobody." From his earliest ventures in combination he had applied this principle. . . . In 1872, when Mr. Rockefeller became master of the Cleveland oil business, the purchase of barrels was one of a refiner's heaviest expenses. In an estimate of the cost of producing a gallon of refined oil in 1873, made in the Oil City Derrick and accepted as correct by that paper, the cost of the barrel is put at four cents a gallon, which was more than the crude oil cost at that date. Even at four cents a gallon barrels were hard to get, so great was the demand. If a refiner could get his barrels back, of course there was a saving (a returned barrel was estimated to be

worth 2¾ cents), but the return could not be counted on;
empty barrels coming from Europe particularly, and con-
signed to Western shippers, were frequently seized in New
York by Eastern refiners. The need was held to justify the
deed, like thieving in famine time. Fortunes were made in
barrels, and dealers hearing of a big supply in Europe have
been known to charter a vessel and go for them, and reap
rich profits. In fact, a whole volume of commercial tragedy
and comedy hangs around the oil barrel. Now it was to the
barrel—the "holy blue barrel"—that Mr. Rockefeller gave early
attention. He determined to make it himself. One of the earliest
outside ventures of the Standard Oil Company in Cleveland
was barrel works, and Mr. Rockefeller was soon getting for
two and a half cents what his rivals paid four for. . . . In the
period since they began the manufacture of barrels their factories have introduced some small savings which in the aggregate amount to large sums. For instance, they have improved the lap of the hoop—a small thing, but one which
amounted in 1901 to something like $15,000. Some $50,000 a
year was saved by a slight increase in the size of the tankage. The Standard claims that these economies are so small
in themselves that it only pays to practise them where there is
a large aggregate business.

More important than the barrel to-day, however, is the tin can
—for it is in tin cans that all the enormous quantities of refined
sent to tropical and Oriental countries must go to prevent deterioration—and nowhere does the policy of economy which Mr.
Rockefeller has worked out show better than in one of the Standard canning works. In 1902 the writer visited the largest of the
Standard can factories, the Devoe, on the East River, Long
Island City. It has a capacity of 70,000 five-gallon cans a day,
and is probably the largest can factory in the world. At the en-
trance of the place a man was sweeping up carefully the dirt on
the floor and wheeling it away—not to be dumped in the river,
however. The dirt was to be sifted for tin filings and solder dust.
At every step something was saved. The Standard buys the tin
for its cans in Wales, because it is cheaper. It would not be
cheaper if it were not for a vagary in administering the tariff by
which the duty on tin plate is refunded if the tin is made into
receptacles to be exported. This clause was probably made for
the benefit of the Standard, it being the largest single con-

sumer of tin plate in the United States. In 1901 the Standard Oil Company imported over 60,000 tons of tin with a value of over $1,000,000. This tin comes in sheets packed in flat boxes, which are opened by throwing—it is quicker than opening by a hammer, and time is considered as valuable as tin filings. The empty boxes are sold by the hundred to the Long Island gardens for growing plants in, and the broken covers are sold for kindling. The trimmings which result from the shaping the tin sheets for a can are gathered into bundles and sold to chemical works or foundries. There is the same care taken with solder as with tin, the amount each workman uses being carefully gauged. The canning plants, like the refineries, compare their results monthly, and the laurels go to the manager who has saved the most ounces of solder, the most hours, the most footsteps. . . .

With Mr. Rockefeller's genius for detail, there went a sense of the big and vital factors in the oil business, and a daring in laying hold of them which was very like military genius. He saw strategic points like a Napoleon, and he swooped on them with the suddenness of a Napoleon. This master ability has been fully illustrated already in this work. Mr. Rockefeller's capture of the Cleveland refineries in 1872 was as dazzling an achievement as it was a hateful one. The campaign by which the Empire Transportation Company was wrested from the Pennsylvania Railroad, viewed simply as a piece of brigandage, was admirable. The man saw what was necessary to his purpose, and he never hesitated before it. His courage was steady—and his faith in his ideas unwavering. He simply knew that was the thing to do, and he went ahead with the serenity of the man who knows. . . .

From the time it completed its pipe-line monopoly the Standard has followed oil wherever found. It has had to do it to keep its hold on the business, and its courage never yet has faltered, though it has demanded some extraordinary efforts. In 1891 a great deposit of oil was tapped in the McDonald field of Southwestern Pennsylvania. The monthly production increased from 50,000 barrels in June to 1,600,000 in December. It is an actual fact that in the McDonald field the United Pipe Lines increased the daily capacity of 3,500 barrels, which they had at the beginning of July, to one of 26,000 barrels by the first of September, and by the first of

December they could handle 90,000 barrels a day. If one considers what this means one sees that it compares favourably with the great ordnance and mobilising feats of the Civil War. To accomplish it, rolling mills and boiler shops in various cities worked night and day to turn out the pipe, the pumps, the engines, the boilers which were needed. Transportation had to be arranged, crews of men obtained, a wild country prepared, sawmills to cut the quantities of timber needed built, and this vast amount of material placed and set to work.

The same audacity and effectiveness are shown by the Standard in attacking situations created by new developments in handling business. The seaboard pipe-line is a notable example. When the Standard completed its pipe-line monopoly at the end of 1877, the pipe-line was still regarded as the feeder of the railroad. Naturally the railroads were seriously opposed to its becoming anything more. In Pennsylvania particularly the laws had been so manipulated by the Pennsylvania Railroad as to prevent the pipe-line carrying oil even for short distances in competition with them. Now, for many years it had been believed that the pipe-line could carry oil long distances—many claimed to the seaboard—and as soon as the independents found that the oil-bearing roads were acting solely in the interest of the Standard they began an agitation for a seaboard line which finally terminated in the Tidewater Line, one hundred and four miles long, carrying oil from the Bradford field to Williamsport on the Reading Railroad, and it was certain that the Tidewater eventually would get to the seaboard. That the day of the railroad as a carrier of crude oil was over when the Tidewater began to pump oil was obvious both to Mr. Rockefeller and to the railroad presidents, and without hesitation he seized the idea. By 1883 the Standard was pumping oil to New York, and the railroads that had served so effectively in building up the trust were practically out of the crude business. It was this audacious and splendid stroke, practically freeing him from the railroads which had made him, which made the passage of the Interstate Commerce Bill a matter of comparatively small importance to Mr. Rockefeller. To be sure, he still needed the railroads for refined, but he could so place his refineries that this service would be greatly minimised. The legislation which the Oil Regions of Pennsylvania demanded for fifteen years in hope of securing an equal chance in transportation came too late. By the time the bill was passed the pipe had replaced the rail as the great oil carrier, and the pipes were not merely under Mr. Rockefeller's control, as the rails had been; they belonged to him. . . . Yet the seaboard pipe-line was no development of the Standard Oil Company. The idea had been conceived and the practicability demonstrated by others, but it was seized by the Standard as soon as it proved possible. This quick sense of the real value of new developments, and this alertness in seizing them, have been among the strongest elements in the Standard's success.

And every new line of action was developed to its utmost. Take the work the Standard began in 1879 on the foreign market. . . . It established stations of its own in one port after another of Europe, Asia, South America, and has built up a large oil fleet. It carried on an aggressive campaign for developing markets; it looked after hostile legislation; it studied the possible competition of native oils; it met every difficulty—prejudice, ignorance, poverty. Little by little it has done in foreign countries what it has done in the United States. To-day it even carts oil from door to door in Germany and Portugal and other countries, as it does in America, thus realising Mr. Rockefeller's vision of controlling the petroleum of America from the time it leaves the ground until it is put into the lamp of the consumer.

The same economy and alertness were applied to the matter of making oils. In laying hands on the refineries of the country, Rockefeller had acquired by 1882 about all the processes of manufacturing known, both patented and free. . . .

The real service of the Standard has been not . . . multiplication of so-called products, but in finding processes by which a poor oil like the famous Lima oil could be refined. In the case of the Lima oil the Standard claims it spent millions of dollars before it solved the problem of its usefulness. The amount of sulphur in the Lima or Ohio oil prevented its use as an illuminating oil, for the odour was intolerable, there was a disagreeable smoke, and the wick charred rapidly. The problem of deodorising it was attacked by many experimenters, and was finally practically solved by the Frasch process, which the Standard acquired after spending a large amount of money in testing its efficacy. Probably sixty per cent.

of the illuminating oil used in the United States now is manufactured from an Ohio oil base.

This multiplication of varieties is, of course, a perfectly
legitimate merchandising device, but it is not a development
of products, properly speaking. Nor indeed was it for discoveries and inventions that the Standard Oil Trust was great
in 1882, or that it is now—it is in the way it adapts and handles the discoveries and inventions it acquires. Take the matter of lubricating oils. After a long struggle it gathered to itself
the factories and the patents of lubricating oils, and it has
developed the trade amazingly; for, while in 1872 less than
a half million gallons of petroleum lubricants were going
abroad, in 1897 over 50,000,000 gallons went. . . .

Having obtained control of the lubricating oils, the Standard showed the greatest intelligence in studying the markets
and in developing the products. It makes lubricants for every
machine that works. It offers scores of cylinder oils, scores of
spindle lubricants, of valve lubricants, of gas-engine lubricants,
special brands for sewing machines, for looms, for sole leather,
for dynamos, for marine engines, for everything that runs and
works by steam power, by air, by electricity, by gas, by man, or
by beast power. . . .

Unquestionably the great strength of the Standard Trust in
1882, when it was founded as it is to-day, was the men who
formed it. However sweeping Mr. Rockefeller's commercial vision, however steady his purpose, however remarkable his in-
sight into what was essential to the realisation of his ambition,
he would have never gone far had he not drawn men into his
concern who understood what he was after and knew how to
work for it. . . . The men who in 1882 formed the Standard alliance were all from the foremost rank in the petroleum trade,
men who without question would be among those at the top
to-day if there had never been a Standard Oil Company. In
Pittsburg it was Charles Lockhart, a man interested in petroleum
before the Drake well was struck, who had begun oil operations
on Oil Creek in March, 1860, who had carried samples of crude
and refined to Europe as early as May, 1860, who had built one
of the first refineries in Pittsburg, and who was easily the largest
refiner there in 1874 when Mr. Rockefeller bought him up. In
Philadelphia, the largest refiner in 1874 was W. G. Warden of
the Atlantic Refining Company, and it was he whom Mr. Rocke-

feller wanted. In New York it was the concern of Charles Pratt and Company, one of the three largest concerns around Manhattan—the concern to which H. H. Rogers belonged. Charles Pratt had been in the oil and paint business since 1850, and he had become a refiner of petroleum at Greenpoint, Long Island, in 1867. Before Standard Oil was known outside of New York the fame of Pratt's Astral Oil had gone around the world. Mr. Pratt's concern was rated at the same daily capacity as Mr. Rockefeller's (1,500 barrels) in the spring of 1872, when the latter wiped up the Cleveland refineries and grew in a night to 10,000 barrels. Mr. Vandergrift, who united his interests with Mr. Rockefeller's in 1874 and 1875, had been a far better known man in the oil business and controlled much greater and more varied interests up to South Improvement times. When he went into the Standard he controlled the largest refinery on Oil Creek, the Imperial, of about 1,400 barrels. He was president of a large system of pipe-lines, and he was a member of one of the largest oil-producing concerns of the time—the H. L. Taylor Company. . . .

It was not only that first-rate ability was demanded at the top; it was required throughout the organisation. The very day-labourers were picked men. It was the custom to offer a little better day wages for labourers than was current and then to choose from these the most promising specimens; those men were advanced as they showed ability. To-day the very errand boys at 26 Broadway are chosen for the promise of development they show, and if they do not develop they are discharged. No dead wood is taken into the concern unless it is through the supposed necessities of family or business relations, as probably occurs to a degree in every human organisation.

The efficiency of the working force of the Standard was greatly increased when the trust was formed by the opportunity given to the employees of taking stock. They were urged to do it, and where they had no savings money was lent them on easy terms by the company. The result is that a great number of the employees of the Standard Oil Company are owners of stock which they bought at eighty, and on which for several years they have received from thirty to forty-eight per cent. dividends. It is only natural that under such circumstances the company has always a remarkably loyal and interested working force.

Mr. Rockefeller's great creation has really been strong, then, in many admirable qualities. The force of the combination has been greater because of the business habits of the independent body which has opposed it. To the Standard's caution the Oil Regions opposed recklessness; to its economy, extravagance; to its secretiveness, almost blatant frankness; to its far-sightedness, little thought of the morrow; to its close-fistedness, a spendthrift generosity; to its selfish unscrupulousness, an almost quixotic love of fair play. The Oil Regions had, besides, one fatal weakness—its passion for speculation. Now, Mr. Rockefeller never speculates. He deals only in those things which other people have proved sure!

It is when one examines the inside of the Standard Oil Trust that one sees how much reason there is for the opinion of those people who declare that Mr. Rockefeller can always sustain the monopoly of the oil business he has achieved. . . . It is not surprising that those who realise the compactness and harmony of the Standard organisation, the ability of its members, the solidity of the qualities governing its operations, are willing to forget its history. Such is the blinding quality of success! "It has achieved this," they say; "no matter what helped to rear this structure, it is here, it is admirably managed. We might as well accept it. We must do business." They are weary of contention, too—who so unwelcome as an agitator?—and they began to accept the Standard's explanation that the critics are indeed "people with a private grievance," "moss-backs left behind in the march of progress." Again and again in the history of the oil business it has looked to the outsider as if henceforth Mr. Rockefeller would have to have things his own way, for who was there to interfere with him, to dispute his position? No one, save that back in Northwestern Pennsylvania, in scrubby little oil towns, around greasy derricks, in dingy shanties, by rusty, deserted oil stills, men have always talked of the iniquity of the railroad rebate, the injustice of restraint of trade, the dangers of monopoly, the right to do an independent business; have always rehearsed with tiresome persistency the evidence by which it has been proved that the Standard Oil Company is a revival of the South Improvement Company. It has all seemed futile enough with the public listening in wonder and awe to the splendid rehearsal of figures, and the unctuous logic of the Mother of Trusts, and yet one can never tell. It was the squawking of geese that saved the Capitol.

Certain it is that many and great as are his business qualities,

John D. Rockefeller has never been allowed to enjoy the fruits of his victory in that atmosphere of leisure and adulation which the victor naturally craves. Certain it is that the incessant agitation of men with a "private grievance" has ruined some of his fairest schemes, has hauled him again and again before investigating committees, and has contributed greatly to securing a federal law authorising so fundamental and obvious a right as equal rates on common carriers. Certain it is that the incessant efforts of those who believed they had a right to do an independent business have resulted in the most important advances made in the oil business since the beginning of Mr. Rockefeller's combination, namely, the seaboard pipe-line, for transporting crude oil, due to the Tidewater Pipe Line, and later the use of the seaboard pipe-line for transporting refined oil, due to the United States Pipe Line. Certain it is, too, that all of competition which we have, with its consequent lowering of prices, is due to independent efforts.

18   CONCLUSION

Contempt proceedings begun against the Standard in Ohio in 1897 for not obeying the court's order of 1892 to dissolve the Trust—Suits begun to oust four of the Standard's constituent companies for violation of Ohio Anti-trust laws—All suits dropped because of expiration of Attorney-General Monnett's term—Standard persuaded that its only corporate refuge is New Jersey—Capital of the Standard Oil Company of New Jersey increased, and all Standard Oil business taken into new organisation—Restriction of New Jersey law small—Profits are great and Standard's control of oil business is almost absolute—Standard Oil Company essentially a realisation of the South Improvement Company's plans—The crucial question now, as always, is a transportation question—The trust question will go unsolved so long as the transportation question goes unsolved—The ethical questions involved.

FEW MEN in either the political or industrial life of this country can point to an achievement carried out in more exact accord with its first conception than John D. Rockefeller, for both in purpose and methods the Standard Oil Company is and always has been a form of the South Improvement Company, by which Mr. Rockefeller first attracted general attention in the oil industry. The original scheme has suffered many modifications. Its most offensive feature, the drawback on other people's shipments, has been cut off. Nevertheless, to-day, as at the start, the purpose of the Standard Oil Company is the purpose of the South Improvement Company—the regulation of the price of crude and refined oil by the control of the output; and the chief means for sustaining this purpose is still that of the original scheme—a control of oil transportation giving special privileges in rates.

It is now thirty-two years since Mr. Rockefeller applied the fruitful idea of the South Improvement Company to the Standard Oil Company of Ohio, a prosperous oil refinery of Cleveland, with a capital of $1,000,000 and a daily capacity for handling 1,500 barrels of crude oil. And what have we as a result? What is the Standard Oil Company to-day? First, what is its organisation? It is no longer a trust. As we have seen, the trust was obliged to liquidate in 1892. It became a "trust in liquidation," and there it remained for some five years. . . .

The only refuge offered in the United States for the Standard Oil Trust in 1898, when the possibility arose by these suits of the state of Ohio taking away the charters of four of its important constituent companies for contempt of court and violation of the anti-trust laws of the state, lay in the corporation law of the state of New Jersey, which had just been amended, and here it settled. Among the twenty companies which formed the trust was the Standard Oil Company of New Jersey, a corporation for manufacturing and marketing petroleum products. Its capital was $10,000,000. In June, 1899, this capital of $10,000,000 was increased to one of $110,000,000, and into this new organisation was dumped the entire Standard aggregation. The old trust certificates outstanding and the assignments of legal title which had succeeded them were called in, and for them were given common stock of the new Standard Oil Company. The amount of this stock which had been issued, in January, 1904, when the last report was made, was $97,448,800. Its market value at that date was $643,162,080. How it is divided is of course a matter of private concern. The number of stockholders in 1899 was about 3,500, according to Mr. Archbold's testimony to the Interstate Commerce Commission, but over one-half of the stock was owned by the directors, and probably nearly one-third was owned by Mr. Rockefeller himself.

The companies which this new Standard Oil Company has bought up with its stock are numerous and scattered. They consist of oil-producing companies like the South Penn Oil Company, the Ohio Oil Company, and the Forest Oil Company; of transporting companies like the National Transit Company, the Buckeye Pipe Line Company, the Indiana Pipe Line Company, and the Eureka Pipe Line Company; of manufacturing and marketing companies like the Atlantic Refining Company of Pennsylvania, and the Standard Oil Companies of many states—New York, Indiana, Kentucky, Ohio, Iowa; of foreign marketing concerns like the Anglo-American Company. In 1892 there were twenty of these constituent companies. There have been many added since, in whole or part, like gas companies; new producing concerns, made necessary by developments in California, Kansas and Texas; new marketing concerns for handling oil directly in Germany, Italy, Scandinavia and Portugal. What the total value of the companies owned by the present Standard Oil Company is it is impossible to say. In 1892, when the trust was on trial in Ohio, it reported the aggregate capital of its twenty companies as $102,233,700, and the appraised value was given as $121,631,312.63; that is, there was an excess of about $19,000,000.

In 1898, when Attorney-General Monnett of Ohio had the Standard Oil Company of the state on trial for contempt of court, he tried to find out from Mr. Rockefeller what the surplus of each of the various companies in the trust was at that date. Mr. Rockefeller answered: "I have not in my possession or power data showing . . . the amount of such surplus money in their hands after the payment of the last dividends." Then Mr. Rockefeller proceeded to repeat as the last he knew of the value of the holdings of the trust the list of values given six years before. . . . There is a later . . . trustworthy valuation of which the writer knows, and is found in testimony taken in 1889, in a private suit to which Mr Rockefeller was party. It is for the year 1896. This shows the "total capital and surplus" of the twenty companies to have been, on December 31 of that year, something over one hundred and forty-seven million dollars, nearly forty-nine millions of which was scheduled as "undivided profits." Of course there has been a constant increase in value since 1896.

The new Standard Oil Company is managed by a board of fourteen directors. They probably collect the dividends of the constituent companies and divide them among stockholders in exactly the same way the trustees of 1882 and the liquidating trustees of 1892 did. As for the charter under which they are operating, never since the days of the South Improvement Company has Mr. Rockefeller held privileges so in harmony with his ambition. By it he can do all kinds of mining, manufacturing, and trading business; transport goods and merchandise by land and water in any manner; buy, sell, lease, and improve lands; build houses, structures, vessels, cars, wharves, docks, and piers; lay and operate pipe-lines; erect and operate telegraph and telephone lines, and lines for conducting electricity; enter into and carry out contracts of every kind pertaining to his business; acquire, use, sell, and grant licenses under patent rights; purchase, or otherwise acquire, hold, sell, assign, and transfer shares of capital stock and bonds or other evidences of indebtedness of corporations, and exercise all the privileges of ownership, including voting upon the stocks so held; carry on its business and have offices and agencies therefor in all parts of the world, and hold, purchase, mortgage, and convey real estate and personal property outside the state of New Jersey. These privileges are, of course, subject to the laws of the state or country in which the company operates. . . . A comparison of this summary of powers with those granted by the South Improvement Company shows that in sweep of charter, at least, the Standard Oil Company of to-day has as great power as its famous progenitor.

The profits of the present Standard Oil Company are enormous. For five years the dividends have been averaging about forty-five million dollars a year, or nearly fifty per cent. on its capitalisation, a sum which capitalised at five per cent. would give $900,000,000. Of course this is not all that the combination makes in a year. It allows an annual average of 5.77 per cent. for deficit, and it carries always an ample reserve fund. When we remember that probably one-third of this immense annual revenue goes into the hands of John D. Rockefeller, that probably ninety per cent. of it goes to the few men who make up the "Standard Oil family," and that it must every year be invested, the Standard Oil Company becomes a much more serious public matter than it was in 1872, when it stamped itself as willing to enter into a conspiracy to raid the oil business—as a much more serious concern than in the years when it openly made warfare of business, and drove from the oil industry by any means it could invent all who had the hardihood to enter it. For, consider what must be done with the greater part of this $45,000,000. It must be invested. The oil business does not demand it. There is plenty of reserve for all of its ventures. It must go into other industries. Naturally, the interests sought will be allied to oil. They will be gas, and we have the Standard Oil crowd steadily acquiring the gas interests of the country. They will be railroads, for on transportation all industries depend, and, besides, railroads are one of the great consumers of oil products and must be kept in line as buyers. And we have the directors of the Standard Oil Company acting as directors on nearly all of the great railways of the country, the New York Central, New York, New Haven and Hartford, Chicago, Milwaukee and St. Paul, Union Pacific, Northern Pacific, Delaware, Lackawanna and Western, Missouri Pacific, Missouri, Kansas and Texas, Boston and Maine, and other lesser roads. They will go into copper, and we have the Amalgamated scheme. They will go into steel, and we have Mr. Rockefeller's enormous holdings in the Steel Trust. They will go into banking, and we have the National City Bank and its allied institutions in New York City and Boston, as well as a long chain running over the country. . . . The result is that the Standard Oil Company is probably in the strongest financial position of any aggregation in the world. And every year its position grows stronger, for every year there is pouring in another $45,-000,000 to be used in wiping up the property most essential to preserving and broadening its power. . . .

So much for present organisation, and now as to how far through this organisation the Standard Oil Company is able to realise the purpose for which it was organised—the control of the output, and, through that, the price, of refined oil. That is, what per cent. of the whole oil business does Mr. Rockefeller's concern control. First as to oil production. In 1898 the Standard Oil Company reported to the Industrial Commission that it produced 35.58 per cent. of Eastern crude —the production that year was about 52,000,000 barrels. . . . But while Mr. Rockefeller produces only about a third of the entire production, he controls all but about ten per cent. of it; that is, all but about ten per cent. goes immediately into his custody on coming from the wells. It passes entirely out of the hands of the producers when the Standard pipe-line takes it. The oil is in Mr. Rockefeller's hands, and he, not the producer, can decide who is to have it. The greater portion of it he takes himself, of course, for he is the chief refiner of the country. In 1898 there were about twenty-four million barrels of petroleum products made in this country. Of this amount about twenty million were made by the Standard Oil Company; fully a third of the balance was produced by the Tidewater Company, of which the Standard holds a large minority stock, and which for twenty years has had a running arrangement with the Standard. Reckoning out of the Tidewater's probable output, and we have an independent output of about 2,500,000 in twenty-four million. It is obvious that this great percentage of the business gives the

Standard the control of prices. This control can be kept in the domestic markets so long as the Standard can keep under competition as successfully as it has in the past. It can be kept in the foreign market as long as American oils can be made and sold in quantity cheaper than foreign oils. Until a decade ago the foreign market of American oils was not seriously threatened. Since 1895, however, Russia, whose annual output of petroleum had been for a number of years about equal in volume to the American output, learned to make a fairly decent product; more dangerous, she had learned to market. She first appeared in Europe in 1885. It took ten years to make her a formidable rival, but she is so to-day, and, in spite of temporary alliances and combinations, it is very doubtful whether the Standard will ever permanently control Russian oil. . . .

In the East the oil market belonged practically to the Standdard Oil Company until recently. Last year (1903), however, Sumatra imported more oil into China than America, and Russia imported nearly half as much. About 91,500,000 gallons of kerosene went into Calcutta last year, and of this only about six million gallons came from America. In Singapore representatives of Sumatra oil claim that they have two-thirds of the trade.

Combinations for offensive and defensive trade campaigns have also gone on energetically among these various companies in the last few years. One of the largest and most powerful of these aggregations now at work is in connection with an English shipping concern, the Shell Transport and Trading Company, the head of which is Sir Marcus Samuel, formerly Lord Mayor of London. This company, which formerly traded almost entirely in Russian oil, undertook a few years ago to develop the oil fields in Borneo, and they built up a large Oriental trade. They soon came into hot competition with the Royal Dutch Company, handling Sumatra oil, and a war of prices ensued which lasted nearly two years. In 1903, however, the two competitors, in connection with four other strong Sumatra and European companies, drew up an agreement in regard to markets which has put an end to their war. The "Shell" people have not only these allies, but they have a contract with Guffey Petroleum Company, the largest Texas producing concern, to handle its output, and they have gone into a German oil company, the Petroleum Produkten Aktien Gesellschaft. Having thus provided themselves with a supply they have begun developing a European trade on the same lines as their Oriental trade, and they are making serious inroads on the Standard's market.

The naphthas made from the Borneo oil have largely taken the place of American naphtha in many parts of Europe. One load of Borneo benzine even made its appearance in the American market in 1904. It is a sign of what well may happen in the future with an intelligent development of these Russian and Oriental oils—the Standard's domestic market invaded. It will be interesting to see to what further extent the American government will protect the Standard Oil Company by tariff on foreign oils if such a time does come. It has done very well already. The aggressive marketing of the "Shell" and its allies in Europe has led to a recent Oil War of great magnitude. For several months in 1904 American export oil was sold at a lower price in New York than the crude oil it takes to make it costs there. For instance, on August 13, 1904, the New York export price was 4.80 cents per gallon for Standard-white in bulk. Crude sold at the well for $1.50 a barrel of forty-two gallons, and it costs sixty cents to get it to seaboard by pipe-line; that is, forty-two gallons of crude oil costs $2.10, or five cents a gallon in New York—twenty points loss on a gallon of the raw material! But this low price for export affects the local market little or none. The tank-wagon price keeps up to ten and eleven cents in New York. Of course crude is depressed as much as possible to help carry this competition. For many months now there has been the abnormal situation of a declining crude price in face of declining stocks. The truth is the Standard Oil Company is trying to meet the competition of the low-grade Oriental and Russian oils with high-grade American oil—the crude being kept as low as possible, and the domestic market being made to pay for the foreign cutting. It seems a lack of foresight surprising in the Standard to have allowed itself to be found in such a dilemma. Certainly, for over two years the company has been making every effort to escape by getting hold of a supply of low-grade oil which would enable it to meet the competition of the foreigner. There have been more or less short-lived arrangements in Russia. An oil territory in Galicia was secured not long ago by them, and an expert refiner with a full refining plant was sent over. Various hindrances have been met in the undertaking, and the works are not yet in operation. Two years ago the Standard attempted to get hold of the rich Burma oil fields. The press of India fought them out of the country, and their weapon was the Standard Oil Company's own record for hard dealings! The Burma fields are in the hands of a monopoly of the closest sort which has never properly developed the territory, but the people and government prefer their own monopoly to one of the American type!

Altogether the most important question concerning the Standard Oil Company to-day is how far it is sustaining its power by the employment of the peculiar methods of the South Improvement Company. It should never be forgotten that Mr. Rockefeller never depended on these methods alone for securing power in the oil trade. From the beginning the Standard Oil Company has studied thoroughly everything connected with the oil business. It has known, not guessed at conditions. It has had a keen authoritative sight. It has applied itself to its tasks with indefatigable zeal. It has been as courageous as it has been cautious. Nothing has been too big to undertake, as nothing has been too small to neglect. These facts have been repeatedly pointed out in this narrative. But these are the American industrial qualities. They are common enough in all sorts of business. They have made our railroads, built up our great department stores, opened our mines. The Standard Oil Company has no monopoly in business ability. It is the thing for which American men are distinguished to-day in the world.

These qualities alone would have made a great business, and unquestionably it would have been along the line of combination, for when Mr. Rockefeller undertook to work out the good of the oil business the tendency to combination was marked throughout the industry, but it would not have been the combination whose history we have traced. To the help of these qualities Mr. Rockefeller proposed to bring the peculiar aids of the South Improvement Company. He secured an alliance with the railroads to drive out rivals. For fifteen years he received rebates of varying amounts on at least the greater part of his shipments, and for at least a portion of that time he collected drawbacks of the oil other people shipped; at the same time he worked with the railroads to prevent other people getting oil to manufacture, or if they got it he worked with the railroads to prevent the shipment of the product. If it reached a dealer, he did his utmost to bully or wheedle him to countermand his order. If he failed in that, he undersold until the dealer, losing on his purchase, was glad enough to buy thereafter of Mr. Rockefeller. How much of this system remains in force to-day? The spying on independent shipments, the effort to have orders countermanded, the predatory competition prevailing, are well enough known. . . . As for the rebates and drawbacks, if they do not exist in the forms practised up to 1887, as the Standard officials have repeatedly declared, it is not saying that the Standard enjoys no special transportation privileges. As has been pointed out, it controls the great pipe-line handling all but perhaps ten per cent. of the oil produced in the Eastern fields. This system is fully 35,000 miles long. It goes to the wells of every producer, gathers his oil into its storage tanks, and from there transports it to Philadelphia, Baltimore, New York, Chicago, Buffalo, Cleveland, or any other refining point where it is needed. This pipe-line is a common carrier by virtue of its use of the right of eminent domain, and, as a common carrier, is theoretically obliged to carry and deliver the oil of all comers, but in practice this does not always work. It has happened more than once in the history of the Standard pipes that they have refused to gather or deliver oil. Pipes have been taken up from wells belonging to individuals running or working with independent refiners. Oil has been refused delivery at points practical for independent refiners. For many years the supply of oil has been so great that the Standard could not refuse oil to the independent refiner on the ground of scarcity. However, a shortage in Pennsylvania oil occurred in 1903. A very interesting situation arose as a result. There are in Ohio and Pennsylvania several independent refiners who, for a number of years, have depended on the Standard lines (the National Transit Company) for their supply of crude. In the fall of 1903 these refiners were informed that thereafter the Standard could furnish them with only fifty per cent. of their refining capacity. It was a serious matter to the independents, who had their own markets, and some of whom were increasing their plants. . . . The independent refiners decided to compromise, and an agreement terminable by either party at short notice was made between them and the Standard, by which the members of the former were each to have eighty per cent. of their capacity of crude oil, and were to give to the Standard all of their export oil to market. As a matter of fact, the Standard's ability to cut off crude supplies from the outside refiners is much greater than in the days before the Interstate Commerce Bill, when it depended on its alliance with the railroads to prevent its rival getting oil. It goes without saying that this is an absurd power to allow in the hands of any manufacturer of a great necessity of life. It is exactly as if one corporation aiming at manufacturing all the flour of the country owned all but ten per cent. of the entire railroad system collecting and transporting wheat. They could, of course, in time of shortage, prevent any would-be competitor from getting grain to grind, and they could and would make it difficult and expensive at all times for him to get it.

It is not only in the power of the Standard to cut off outsiders from it, it is able to keep up transportation prices. Mr. Rockefeller owns the pipe system—a common carrier—and the refineries of the Standard Oil Company pay in the final accounting cost for transporting their oil, while outsiders pay just what they paid twenty-five years ago. There are lawyers who believe that if this condition were tested in the courts, the National Transit Company would be obliged to give the same rates to others as the Standard refineries ultimately pay. It would be interesting to see the attempt made.

Not only are outside refiners at just as great disadvantage in securing crude supply to-day as before the Interstate Commerce Commission was formed; they still suffer severe iscrimination on the railroads in marketing their product. . . .

There is no independent refiner or jobber who tries to ship oil freight that does not meet incessant discouragement and discrimination. Not only are rates made to favour the Standard refining points and to protect their markets, but switching charges and dock charges are multiplied. Loading and unloading facilities are refused, payment of freights on small quantities are demanded in advance, a score of different ways are found to make hard the way of the outsider. "If I get a barrel of oil out of Buffalo," an independent dealer told the writer not long ago, "I have to *sneak* it out. There are no public docks; the railroads control most of them, and they won't let me out if they can help it. If I want to ship a carload they won't take it if they can help it. They are all afraid of offending the Standard Oil Company."

This may be a rather sweeping statement, but there is too much truth in it. There is no doubt that to-day, as before the Interstate Commerce Commission, a community of interests exists between railroads and the Standard Oil Company sufficiently strong for the latter to get any help it wants in making it hard for rivals to do business. The Standard owns stock in most of the great systems. It is represented on the board of directors of nearly all the great systems, and it has an immense freight not only in oil products, but in timber, iron, acids, and all of the necessities of its factories. It is allied with many other industries, iron, steel, and copper, and can swing freight away from a road which does not oblige it. It has great influence in the money market and can help or hinder a road in securing money. It has great influence in the stock market and can depress or inflate a stock if it sets about it. Little wonder that the railroads, being what they are, are afraid to "disturb their relations with the Standard Oil Company," or that they keep alive a system of discriminations the same in effect as those which existed before 1887.

Of course such cases as those cited above are fit for the Interstate Commerce Commission, but the oil men as a body have no faith in the effectiveness of an appeal to the Commission, and in this feeling they do not reflect on the Commission, but rather on the ignorance and timidity of the Congress which, after creating a body which the people demanded, made it helpless. The case on which the Oil Regions rests its reason for its opinion has already been referred to in the chapter on the co-operative independent movement which finally resulted in the Pure Oil Company. The case first came before the Commission in 1888. . . . The hearing took place in Titusville in May, 1889 . . . and in December, 1892, it gave its decision. . . . It ordered that the railroads make the rates the same on oil in both tanks and barrels, and that they furnish shippers tanks whenever reasonable notice was given. As the amounts wrongfully collected by the railroads from the refiners could not be ascertained from the evidence already taken, the Commission decided to hold another hearing and fix the amounts. This was not done until May, 1894, five years after the first hearing. Reparation was ordered to at least eleven different firms, some of the sums amounting to several thousand dollars; the entire award ordered amounted to nearly $100,000.

In case the railroads failed to adjust the claims the refiners were ordered to proceed to enforce them in the courts. The Commission found at this hearing that none of their orders of 1892 had been followed by the roads and they were all repeated. As was to be expected, the roads refused to recognise the claims allowed by the Commission, and the case was taken by the refiners into court. It has been heard three times. Twice they have won, but each time an appeal of the roads has forced them to appear again. The case was last heard at Philadelphia in February, 1904, in the United States Circuit Court of Appeals. No decision had been rendered at this writing. . . .

See the helplessness of the Commission. It takes full testimony in 1889, digests it carefully, gives its orders in 1892, and they are not obeyed. More hearings follow, and in 1895 the orders are repeated and reparation is allowed to the injured refiners. From that time to this the case passes from court to court, the railroad seeking to escape the Commission's orders. The Interstate Commerce Commission was instituted to facilitate justice in this matter of transportation, and yet here we have still unsettled a case on which they gave their judgment twelve years ago. The lawyer who took the first appeal to the Commission . . . has been continually engaged in the case for sixteen years!

In spite of the Interstate Commerce Commission, the crucial question is still a transportation question. Until the people of the United States have solved the question of free and equal transportation it is idle to suppose that they will not have a trust question. So long as it is possible for a company to own the exclusive carrier on which a great natural product depends for transportation, and to use this carrier to limit a competitor's supply or to cut off that supply entirely if the rival is offensive, and always to make him pay a higher rate than it costs the owner, it is ignorance and folly to talk about constitutional amendments limiting trusts. So long as the great manufacturing centres of a monopolistic trust can get better rates than the centres of independent effort, it is idle to talk about laws making it a crime to undersell for the purpose of driving a competitor from a market. You must get into markets before you can compete. So long as railroads can be persuaded to interfere with independent pipe-lines, to refuse oil freight, to refuse loading facilities, lest they disturb their relations with the Standard Oil Company, it is idle to talk about investigations or anti-trust legislation or application of the Sherman law. So long as the Standard Oil Company can control transportation as it does to-day, it will remain master of the oil industry, and the people of the United States will pay for their indifference and folly in regard to transportation a good sound tax on oil, and they will yearly see an increasing concentration of natural resources and transportation systems in the Standard Oil crowd.

If all the country had suffered from these raids on competition, had been the limiting of the business opportunity of a few hundred men and a constant higher price for refined oil, the case would be serious enough, but there is a more serious side to it. The ethical cost of all this is the deep concern. We are a commercial people. We cannot boast of our arts, our crafts, our cultivation; our boast is in the wealth we produce. As a consequence business success is sanctified, and, practically, any methods which achieve it are justified by a larger and larger class. All sorts of subterfuges and sophistries and slurring over of facts are employed to explain aggregations of capital whose determining factor has been like that of the Standard Oil Company, special privileges obtained by persistent secret effort in opposition to the spirit of the law, the efforts of legislators, and the most outspoken public opinion. How often does one hear it argued, the Standard Oil Company is simply an inevitable result of economic conditions; that is, given the practices of the oil-bearing railroads in 1872 and the elements of speculation and the over-refining in the oil business, there was nothing for Mr. Rockefeller to do but secure special privileges if he wished to save his business.

Now in 1872 Mr. Rockefeller owned a successful refinery in Cleveland. He had the advantage of water transportation a part of the year, access to two great trunk lines the year around. Under such able management as he could give it his concern was bound to go on, given the demand for refined oil. It was bound to draw other firms to it. When he went into the South Improvement Company it was not to save his own business, but to destroy others. When he worked so persistently to secure rebates after the breaking up of the South Improvement Company, it was in the face of an industry united against them. It was not to save his business that he compelled the Empire Transportation Company to go out of the oil business in 1877. Nothing but grave mismanagement could have destroyed his business at that moment; it was to get every refinery in the country but his own out of the way. It was not the necessity to save his business which compelled Mr. Rockefeller to make war on the Tidewater. He and the Tidewater could both have lived. It was to prevent prices of transportation and of refined oil going down under competition. What necessity was there for Mr. Rockefeller trying to prevent the United States Pipe Line doing business?—only the greed of power and money. Every great campaign against rival interests which the Standard Oil Company has carried on has been inaugurated, not to save its life, but to build up and sustain a monopoly in the oil industry. These are not mere affirmations of a hostile critic; they are facts proved by documents and figures.

Certain defenders go further and say that if some such combination had not been formed the oil industry would have failed for lack of brains and capital. Such a statement is puerile. Here was an industry for whose output the whole world was crying. Petroleum came at the moment when the value and necessity of a new, cheap light was recognised everywhere. Before Mr. Rockefeller had ventured outside of Cleveland kerosene was going in quantities to every civilised country. Nothing could stop it, nothing check it, but the discovery of some cheaper light or the putting up of its price. The real "good of the oil business" in 1872 lay in making oil cheaper. It would flow all over the world on its own merit if cheap enough.

The claim that only by some such aggregation as Mr. Rockefeller formed could enough capital have been obtained to develop the business falls utterly in face of fact. Look at the enormous amounts of capital, large amount of it speculative, to be sure, which the oil men claim went into their business in the first ten years. It was estimated that Philadelphia alone put over $168,000,000 into the development of the Oil Regions, and New York $134,000,000, in their first decade of the business. . . . Indeed, there has always been plenty of money for oil investment. It did not require Mr. Rockefeller's capital to develop the Bradford oil fields, build the first sea-board pipe-line, open West Virginia, Texas, or Kansas. The oil business would no more have suffered for lack of capital without the Standard combination than the iron or wheat or railroad or cotton business. The claim is idle, given the wealth and energy of the country in the forty-five years since the discovery of oil.

Equally well does both the history and the present condition of the oil business show that it has not needed any such aggregation to give us cheap oil. The margin between crude and refined was made low by competition. It has rarely been as low as it would have been had there been free competition. For five years even the small independent refineries outside of the Pure Oil Company have been able to make a profit on the prices set by the Standard, and this in spite of the higher transportation they have paid on both crude and refined, and the wall of seclusion the railroads build around domestic markets.

Very often people who admit the facts, who are willing to see that Mr. Rockefeller has employed force and fraud to secure his ends, justify him by declaring, "It's business." That is, "it's business" has to come to be a legitimate excuse for hard dealing, sly tricks, special privileges. It is a common enough thing to hear men arguing that the ordinary laws of morality do not apply in business. Now, if the Standard Oil Company were the only concern in the country guilty of the practices which have given it monopolistic power, this story never would have been written. Were it alone in these methods, public scorn would long ago have made short work of the Standard Oil Company. But it is simply the most conspicuous type of what can be done by these practices. The methods it employs with such acumen, persistency, and secrecy are employed by all sorts of business men, from corner grocers up to bankers. If exposed, they are excused on the ground that this is business. If the point is pushed, frequently the defender of the practice falls back on the Christian doctrine of charity, and points that we are erring mortals and must allow for each other's weaknesses!—an excuse, which, if carried to its legitimate conclusion, would leave our business men weeping on one another's shoulders over human frailty, while they picked one another's pockets.

One of the most depressing features of the ethical side of the matter is that instead of such methods arousing contempt they are more or less openly admired. And this is logical. Canonise "business success," and men who make a success like that of the Standard Oil Trust become national heroes! The history of its organisation is studied as a practical lesson in money-making. It is the most startling feature of the case to one who would like to feel that it is possible to be a commercial people and yet a race of gentlemen. . . .

The effects on the very men who fight these methods on the ground that they are ethically wrong are deplorable. Brought into competition with the trust, badgered, foiled, spied upon, they come to feel as if anything is fair when the Standard is the opponent. The bitterness against the Standard Oil Company in many parts of Pennsylvania and Ohio is such that a verdict from a jury on the merits of the evidence is almost impossible! A case in point occurred a few years ago in the Bradford field. An oil producer was discovered stealing oil from the National Transit Company. He had tapped the main line and for at least two years had run a small but steady stream of Standard oil into his private tank. Finally the thieving pipe was discovered, and the owner of it, after acknowledging his guilt, was brought to trial. The jury gave a verdict of Not guilty! They seemed to feel that though the guilt was acknowledged, there probably was a Standard trick concealed somewhere. Anyway it was the Standard Oil Company and it deserved to be stolen from! The writer has frequently heard men, whose own business was conducted with scrupulous fairness, say in cases of similar stealing that they would never condemn a man who stole from the Standard! Of course such a state of feeling undermines the whole moral nature of a community.

The blackmailing cases of which the Standard Oil Company complain are a natural result of its own practices. Men going into an independent refining business have for years been accustomed to say: "well, if they won't let us alone, we'll make them pay a good price." The Standard complains that such men build simply to sell out. There may be cases of this. Probably there are, though the writer has no absolute proof of any such. Certainly there is no satisfactory proof that the refinery in the famous Buffalo case was built to sell, though that it was offered for sale when the opposition of the Everests, the managers of the Standard concern, had become so serious as later to be stamped as criminal by judge and jury, there is no doubt. Certainly nothing was shown to have been done or said by Mr. Matthews, the owner of the concern which the Standard was fighting, which might not have been expected from a man who had met the kind of opposition he had from the time he went into business.

The truth is, blackmail and every other business vice is the natural result of the peculiar business practices of the Standard. If business is to be treated as warfare and not as a peaceful pursuit, as they have persisted in treating it, they cannot expect the men they are fighting to lie down and die without a struggle. If they get special privileges they must expect their competitors to struggle to get them. If they will find it more profitable to buy out a refinery than to let it live, they must expect the owner to get an extortionate price if he can. And when they complain of these practices and call them blackmail, they show thin sporting blood. They must not expect to monopolise hard dealings, if they do oil.

These are considerations of the ethical effect of such business practices on those outside and in competition. As for those within the organisation there is one obvious effect worth noting. The Standard men as a body have nothing to do with public affairs, except as it is necessary to manipulate them for the "good of the oil business." The notion that the business man must not appear in politics and religion save as a "stand-patter"—not even as a thinking, aggressive force—is demoralising, intellectually and morally. Ever since 1872 the organisation has appeared in politics only to oppose legislation obviously for the public good. At that time the oil industry was young, only twelve years old, and it was suffering from too rapid growth, from speculation, from rapacity of railroads, but it was struggling manfully with all these questions. The question of railroad discriminations and extortions was one of the "live questions" of the country. The oil men as a mass were allied against it. The theory that the railroad was a public servant bound by the spirit of its charter to treat all shippers alike, that fair play demanded open equal rates to all, was generally held in the oil country at the time Mr. Rockeller and his friends sprung the South Improvement Company. One has only to read the oil journals at the time of the Oil War of

1872 to see how seriously all phases of the transportation question were considered. The country was a unit against the rebate system. Agreements were signed with the railroads that all rates henceforth should be equal. The signatures were not on before Mr. Rockefeller had a rebate, and gradually others got them until the Standard had won the advantages it expected the South Improvement Company to give it. From that time to this Mr. Rockefeller has had to fight the best sentiment of the oil country and of the country at large as to what is for the public good. He and his colleagues kept a strong alliance in Washington fighting the Interstate Commerce Bill from the time the first one was introduced in 1876 until the final passage in 1887. Every measure looking to the freedom and equalisation of transportation has met his opposition, as have bills for giving greater publicity to the operations of corporations. In many of the great state Legislatures one of the first persons to be pointed out to a visitor is the Standard Oil lobbyist. Now, no one can dispute the right of the Standard Oil Company to express its opinions on proposed legislation. It has the same right to do this as all the rest of the world. It is only the character of its opposition which is open to criticism, the fact that it is always fighting measures which equalise privileges and which make it more necessary for men to start fair and play fair in doing business.

Of course the effect of directly practising many of their methods is obvious. For example, take the whole system of keeping track of independent business. There are practices required which corrupt every man who has a hand in them. One of the most deplorable things about it is that most of the work is done by youngsters. The freight clerk who reports the independent oil shipments for a fee of five or ten dollars a month is probably a young man, learning his first lessons in corporate morality. If he happens to sit in Mr. Rockefeller's church on Sundays, through what sort of a haze will he receive the teachings? There is something alarming to those who believe that commerce should be a peaceful pursuit, and who believe that the moral law holds good throughout the entire range of human relations, in knowing that so large a body of young men in this country are consciously or unconsciously growing up with the idea that business is war and that morals have nothing to do with its practice.

And what are we going to do about it? for it is *our* business. We, the people of the United States, and nobody else, must cure whatever is wrong in the industrial situation, typified by this narrative of the growth of the Standard Oil Company. That our first task is to secure free and equal transportation privileges by rail, pipe and waterway is evident. It is not an easy matter. It is one which may require operations which will seem severe; but the whole system of discrimination has been nothing but violence, and those who have profited by it cannot complain if the curing of the evils they have wrought bring hardship in turn on them. At all events, until the transportation matter is settled, and settled right, the monopolistic trust will be with us, a leech on our pockets, a barrier to our free efforts.

As for the ethical side, there is no cure but in an increasing scorn of unfair play—an increasing sense that a thing won by breaking the rules of the game is not worth the winning. When the business man who fights to secure special privileges, to crowd his competitor off the track by other than fair competitive methods, receives the same summary disdainful ostracism by his fellows that the doctor or lawyer who is "unprofessional," the athelete who abuses the rules, receives, we shall have gone a long way toward making commerce a fit pursuit for our young men.

NINETEENTH AND TWENTIETH CENTURY
AMERICAN HISTORY IN NORTON PAPERBACK

Sarah Stage *Female Complaints: **Lydia Pinkham** and the Business of Women's Medicine* N038

Dorothy Sterling, Ed. *We Are Your Sisters: Black Women in the Nineteenth Century* 30252

Ida M. Tarbell *History of the Standard Oil Company* (David Chalmers, Ed.) N496

Tom E. Terrill and Jerrold Hirsch, Eds. *Such As Us: Southern Voices of the Thirties* N927

George Brown Tindall *The Disruption of the Solid South* N663

Richard W. Van Alstyne *The Rising American Empire* N750

Ronald G. Walters *The Antislavery Appeal: American Abolitionism After 1830* 95444

Thomas L. Webber *Deep Like the Rivers: Education in the Slave Quarter Community, 1831–1865* N998

Joel Williamson *After Slavery: The Negro in South Carolina During Reconstruction, 1861–1877* N759